In Defen ___.
Liberal Education

Philosophy and Controversies

Anthony O'Hear

UNIVERSITY OF
BUCKINGHAM
PRESS

UNIVERSITY OF BUCKINGHAM PRESS,
AN IMPRINT OF LEGEND TIMES GROUP LTD
51 Gower Street
London WC1E 6HJ
United Kingdom
www.unibuckinghampress.com

This collection first published by University of Buckingham Press in 2023

© Anthony O'Hear, 2023

The right of the author to be identified as the author of this work has been asserted in accordance with the Copyright, Designs and Patents Act 1988 British Library Cataloguing in Publication Data available.

ISBN: 978-1-91564-343-8

For Zac, Freddie and Jonah; Wilf and Phoebe; and Margot: Hope

La foi que j'aime le mieux, dit Dieu, c'est l'espérance.

Ce qui m'étonne, dit Dieu, c'est l'espérance.
Et je n'en reviens pas.
Cette petite espérance qui n'a l'air de rien du tout.
Cette petite fille espérance.
Immortelle.

(Charles Péguy, from 'Le Porche du
Mystère de la Deuxième Vertu'.)

CONTENTS

Introduction   3

1.   Liberal Education; Where Could, and Where   17
    Should It Be?

2.   Classics and Not Hog-Wash   67

3.   Philosophy and Educational Policy: 95
    Rousseau and Dewey

4.   Reason, Virtue and Character: 122
    Reflections on Moral Development

5.   Family and State in Education: What Role   152
    for Parents' Rights

6.   Educational Myths   180
    Vygotsky's Constructionism   180
    Bloom's 'Taxonomy'   191
    Hattie's Visible Learning   196
    Identity Politics   207
    Decolonising the Curriculum   212
    Creativity   223
    Independent Learning   233

7.   'D'où parles-tu?' Reflections on Power, Truth   239
    and the Open Society

8.   My Truth   249

Epilogue: Early Days of the Department of   260
Education at the University of Buckingham:
A Personal View

Acknowledgements   278

Index   279

In Defence of
Liberal Education

Introduction

Edmund Burke famously described society as a contract between those who are living, those who are dead, and those who are yet to be born. We may quibble with the use of the term 'contract' here. After all, you and I cannot make a contract with people who are no longer alive, nor they with us. Neither can we deal with those who are not yet with us. So perhaps 'covenant' would be better, suggesting something that exists, has sway over us, and of which we are a part, without any explicit agreement on the part of those tied into the covenant.

The Burkean covenant is one prime way in which human beings differ from animals, for it is through being born into an already existing culture which is built on past human behaviour and experience, that we begin to live as human beings. As we grow up, we ingest its practices and meanings so as to enter the human world. Through culture we thus build on animal instinct, which does exist in us; but human culture, verbal, literary, artistic, institutional, practical and so on, allows us to draw on the experience of past generations in a way which has no parallel in the animal kingdom. Biology allows only genes to be handed down from parents to children, and, according to the current orthodoxy, one's genes cannot be affected by what happens in one's lifetime. They are unalterable during a creature's lifetime. What parents transmit to their children biologically are genes with the same nature as the parent inherited at conception. So, against the ideas of Darwin's rival Lamarck, Darwinians will admit of no genetic transmission of lived experience through the generations, which is where cultural influence through human generations goes way beyond anything biological.

Education, formal and informal, plays an essential role in our own essential acculturation while young, and then in the way we, as adults, pass our own acculturation on to our children and to those who come after us. This process of cultural transmission has gone on throughout human history, ever since the first humans emerged from their apian or simian origins, and acquired what we would now see as their humanity. For most of that history everyone was, in a sense, home schooled, or at least schooled in their village or settlement, just by living there and being inducted into the customs and legends of the tribe. Much or most of this tribal education was informal.

But, for better or worse, and on the whole for better, we live in a society with bodies of written learning and highly developed systemised skills, scientific, artistic, and cultural, all recorded in writing or other forms which exist objectively outside the bodies and minds of individual human beings, and which do not require fallible memories to be handed down. These bodies of exosomatic learning, in libraries, books, pictures and the like, articulate traditions stemming from the activity of the dead of centuries ago, who are thus able to impart to people long after them (us, in other words) those aspects of their knowledge and experience which are recorded in written and artistic form. This is the realm of formal education, because unless these bodies of past knowledge and experience are passed on formally, young people will not encounter them in a way they can learn from them. They will have to learn how to read them, how to understand the languages in which they are written, how to interpret the visual forms in which they are encapsulated, how to apply the symbols in which musical and scientific ideas are recorded, and so on. I leave aside here the question as to whether this formal education has to happen in a school or whether it could be done in the home, for now what is called home-schooling is still formal schooling in the sense that it will involve the systematic passing on of handed down skills and content, involving explicit teaching and in most cases book-learning too.

What I am driving at here was nicely expressed by Newton, who described himself and his fellow scientists from the seventeenth century as dwarves standing on the shoulders of giants. Even in saying this, the author of *Philosophiae Naturalis Principia Mathematica* (written in ancient Latin, of course) was echoing the 12th century Bishop of Chartres, John of Salisbury, who said the same thing. John may have been sincere in what he said – despite his part in the building of Chartres Cathedral and in his contributions to scholastic philosophy, he still called himself Johannes Parvus (John the Little). Implicit in Newton's adoption of the image, however, was the thought that, dwarf though he may have been, from his vantage point on the giant's shoulders, he could see further than the giant. Actually we should not object to Newton's arrogance, if that is what it is. The Burkean educational covenant implies that we are all part of a process, educationally, scientifically, artistically, passing on what we inherit, but at the same time developing what we have been given by our forebears, reflecting on it and changing it. To echo T.S. Eliot, we know more than our forebears, and part of what we know is them.

A beautiful articulation of the idea of the Burkean covenant, and one which gives it some substance, is to be found in Wagner's opera *Die Meistersinger von Nürnberg*. Set in medieval Nuremberg, the guild of the town's mastersingers have a tradition of which they are rightly proud, but they are also jealous and protective, hostile to newcomers. An aristocratic newcomer, Walther von Stolzing, does arrive with his own beautiful original song, seeking admission. But, being young and aristocratic, he is arrogant and impatient, and his song, as he originally sang it, lacks structure, sinew, and developmental potential. It breaks the guild's rules of composition and he is sent packing by Sixtus Beckmesser, the guild's pedantic guardian of canonical musical form. However, one of the mastersingers, the cobbler Hans Sachs, does see the beauty of Walther's song (which fittingly is about spring); so he coaches Walther into bringing it into a form acceptable to the mastersingers. Thus Walther, having conformed to the tradition and improved his song, in the end wins the acceptance of the guild, with the exception of the resentful Beckmesser, who is unable to see the need for constant renewal of even the most venerable tradition. In admitting Walther and his song, the mastersinger's tradition is enlivened and refreshed by the necessary injection of a new voice and a new aesthetic, but one still emerging from the honourable and life-giving tradition.

More prosaically, we can find much the same idea expressed 'Tradition and the Individual Talent', T.S. Eliot's masterful essay from 1919, which everyone involved in education should ponder, though few these days do. Like Hans Sachs, Eliot demonstrates that immersion in a tradition of learning is not a barrier to creativity but its necessary condition. An obvious corollary is that the teacher of a form of learning should not be a Beckmesserian pedant, stifling freshness and sensitive only to the formal rules of the tradition. A good teacher is a Hans Sachs, imbued with the necessary letter to be sure, but equally with the spirit behind the letter. He or she is thus able in a generous spirit to mould youthful enthusiasm, so that it becomes a living part of the community of admired voices the newcomer both yearns to enter and, doubtless, also to surpass. Although it should not need saying, the good teacher will not be one so obsessed with targets and constrained by 'learning objectives' laid down in advance that he or she is unable to react to the questions, suggestions and lines of thought bubbling up from the pupils actually before him or her. Indeed the very notion of a target strikes me as antithetical to true teaching, suggesting as it does that hitting something already defined and limned before one is what education should be about. Education, rather than being constrained by and directed towards prescribed targets, is more like a civilised conversation, with guidelines and criteria of value, to be sure, but with no antecedently defined end (in both senses of 'end').

Slightly before Burke was speaking of the contract between the living the dead and the as-yet unborn, Hume gave expression to what has come to be called the test of time, the way in which truly worthwhile works from the past – those that should feature prominently in an educational programme – are those which have a resonance beyond their own place and time:

> The same Homer, who pleased at Athens and Rome two thousand years ago is still admired at Paris and at London. All the changes of climate, government, religion and language, have not been able to obscure his glory. Authority or prejudice may give a temporary vogue to a bad poet or orator; but his reputation will never be durable or general. When his compositions are examined by posterity or foreigners, the enchantment is dissipated and his faults appear in their true colours. On the contrary, a real genius, the longer his works endure, and the more wide they are spread, the more sincere is the admiration which he meets with.

This is a good way to think of works from the past which have endured, of their universality and why they have endured, and also why they are worth teaching to our young. It might be thought that what Hume says applies more directly to works of art and literature than to science. To an extent this is true. The theories of science which have endured may not be as ancient as Homer and Plato, but they are still the theories which have survived testing in different times and places and with different experimenters, and these are the ones we should in the first instance teach our young. But there is a more obvious problem with what Hume says when we come to works of art and literature.

It is that the same Homer that was admired at Paris and London in Hume's time is, in our time, hardly known at Paris or at London, let alone admired. This is deeply sad. It is sad because Homer is intrinsically worth reading or listening to, in the original Greek or in translation, if only because of the unsparing accounts he gives of the deepest human emotions, whether in war or in peace, because of his masterful telling and weaving of story and myth, because of the unforgettable characters he gives us, often in a few lines, because of the poignancy of the stories he tells, of the destruction of Troy and also of Odysseus's homecoming. Perhaps above all we should admire Homer because in his re-telling of what became the founding myth of Greece, he is, uniquely for a founding myth, utterly even-handed between the Greeks and the Trojans they trick and whose great civilisation they destroy.

But it is not only the intrinsic value of *The Iliad* and *The Odyssey* that makes them worthy of attention. Perhaps even more, it is because of the way they and what they tell us become re-told and re-used over and over again in Western literature, as a kind of poetic quarry endlessly mined and recast: Virgil, Ovid, Dante, Chaucer, Shakespeare, Camões, Milton, Goethe, Tennyson, and, of course, Eliot, Pound, Yeats, and James Joyce, to name but a few of the many great writers who have drawn on and from Homer.

But, as I say, he is no longer admired at Paris or at London, which saddens me. It is part of my reason for writing, teaching and campaigning for what I call liberal education, as I will explain in the succeeding chapters of this book. Liberal education is an education firmly rooted, though not exclusively so, in what Matthew Arnold called the best that has been thought and known. For us, and for obvious reasons, this best of what has been thought and known will be predominantly that of the Western tradition, for that tradition is part of our own covenant with the dead, the dead who are our own ancestors and who have bequeathed to us a literary and cultural inheritance, and have thus shaped our culture.

In saying that I have campaigned for liberal education, and indeed that this book is part of that campaign, it may be asked why a campaign is necessary, and why now. The answer will be found spelled out in the essays which follow. Here it will be enough to point out that there are contemporary trends in education which see education in quite other terms than that of transmitting and developing the best that has been thought and known, and would resist the sort of focus on past knowledge and experience I am advocating. And, from my own experience in the educational world, these trends seem to be winning, which is partly why Homer is no longer appreciated even in polite circles in London and Paris.

Thus, particularly among those who wield power and influence in our educational universe, there are many who see education simply in equipping young people for work in the world as it is to-day, so in terms of skills that might equip them for this work and for living in the modern world; talk of targets might be appropriate here, but this would simply be to underline the distinction between the open-endedness of education and training in the acquisition of clearly defined skills. Then there are those who would see education primarily in terms of the child's own growth and maturation, largely self-directed and untouched by influences from outside. There are those – and more than one might think – who believe that presenting children with the artistic and literary giants of the past will stunt their innate creativity. There are those who see education in largely political terms, as aiming to deal with contemporary problems and issues of relevance to-day. There are those who think that what matters in education is the happiness and self-esteem of the child, and that forcing them to learn difficult things and procedures is to oppress them; and going on in that vein, that teaching children the works and values of the high culture of the past is to deny them the validity of their own contemporary culture and enjoyments. There are those who see education as a fundamentally political project, addressing and compensating for past injustices, racism, ideological oppression, and inequality. And there are those who think that educators in the contemporary world have no need to focus on content in their teaching, and especially not content based on past writing and history, because in the age of electronic media everything can be looked up and accessed with the flick of a mouse.

All the trends I have just listed, which will seek to replace what I am calling liberal education with their own approaches, will be touched on in the essays which follow, and criticized. I do not deny that some of what opponents of the liberal education I am advocating hold has a point, or that some of their aims may not be worthwhile. But what I do think is that the cultural transmission inherent in liberal education must be seen as worthwhile in and of itself. It has no other end than what it is in itself, as a valuable part of the life-world of those who have access to it, as an integral part of a fulfilled life. It is something we have a duty to transmit to our children, to open their minds and feelings to it, to give them the chance to live in that world to the extent that they can, so as to give them the chance of entering or at least listening to the conversations of humanity at their richest and deepest.

Other benefits may accrue from a liberal education, such as skills, employment, a sense of social and political decency, and perhaps even happiness and self-esteem. But these must be the by-products of a liberal education, carried on in and for itself, having no end other than those internal to its studies and demanded by the requirements of the discipline in question, whether it is scientific or in the humanities. We may learn about justice and injustice from reading Shakespeare, but if we approach, say, *Macbeth* or *Troilus and Cressida,* as lessons in injustice or social order and disorder, we will miss much else in them, and probably distort what they have to tell us about politics to boot. Geography, to take another example, is compromised if the subject is taken, as it often is, as a pretext for getting pupils to pronounce on the supposed fairness or unfairness of global arrangements. An education in science should focus on the theories of science, their empirical basis and validity, and the horizons they open up, rather than on the political and technological uses to which scientific ideas are put. And, as far as happiness goes, we will always have to ask ourselves whether it is better to have the higher aspirations such an education might kindle in us, with the discontent inherent in their non-achievement, or to rest self-satisfiedly clicking on to whatever the mass media and the internet might throw at us, without any sense that these things might not be the best that *could* be thought and said, or even true.

All the points mentioned in this preamble will be covered in what follows. There are two chapters focusing on liberal education, defining what I am taking it to mean, and considering some of the barriers to its application in the contemporary world. There is a chapter considering the educational views of Rousseau and Dewey, which I see as the root of much of the contemporary discontent with liberal education and its replacement by what would be seen as more progressive approaches. This is followed by a chapter on the need for the inculcation of habits of virtue as the foundation of moral education, and a criticism of so-called 'critical thinking' before one has had experience or a chance to acquire wisdom morally. There is also a chapter on parental rights in education, arguing against much current orthodoxy, that as far as possible the views of parents as to what is desirable for their children should be recognized in the schooling given to their children.

Then there is a succession of shorter pieces criticizing what I see as common but unfortunate trends in contemporary educational practice, something which I am well aware of from having read and marked literally hundreds of essays from trainee teachers over the last few years. Many of these essays uncritically parrot questionable views on education, usually without considering their implications. The trainees find these views in the reading they are often encouraged to read in their training, and take this as an endorsement of the views in question, especially as counter-views are few and far between, and rarely feature on education departments' reading lists. In deference to Daisy Christodoulou's *Seven Myths About Education* I refer to the views in prescribed educational texts as myths, because many of them have come to bask in an atmosphere of quasi-religious reverence among those who write and teach about education. I am here a demythologizer, a heretic. By contrast with the mythologizers of current education, though, many of those who in my view have pondered seriously about education within the last century are not discussed in the right places or recommended on education course reading lists (C.S. Lewis, T.S. Eliot, Leo Strauss, F.R. Leavis, Iris Murdoch, Michael Oakeshott, Allan Bloom, Charles Murray).

The myths I criticize here include the idea that pupils construct their own knowledge; that (Benjamin) Bloom's so-called taxonomy should be taken as a map as to where good teaching should aim; that pupils should be categorized according to their background and ethnicity rather than treated as the individuals they are (what I call identity politics); that the curriculum should be 'decolonised'; that children are naturally creative; that learning should be 'independent' and 'active' rather than 'passive' (i.e. pupils listening to an inspiring teacher about things they do not yet know). In a separate chapter, I also contest the view that instead of seeking truth as something independent of who is speaking, we should always consider ideas or opinions in terms of who is proposing them (with the corollary that if they are proposed by the 'privileged' they should be rejected and shouted down). All these views militate against the spirit of liberal education, so my criticisms of them will be part of my defence and elaboration of what I am proposing. Finally, in an intentionally unacademic conclusion, I describe how the University of Buckingham Faculty of Education came about, what its rationale was when it was founded, and my own part in its founding.

To provide a brief preamble to that conclusion, and also to this collection as a whole, I will now briefly explain how I, as an academic philosopher, came to be involved in educational controversies and politics. That ought not to seem so surprising: after all, education and the care of the soul from its infancy was one of Plato's major concerns, so right from the beginning education has been seen as a philosophical matter: and Aristotle, Augustine, Aquinas, Locke, Rousseau, J.S. Mill, and Dewey, to name only some of the most famous, have all made major philosophical contributions to educational thought and practice. But with the growing cult of specialization within all academic areas, in recent times professional philosophers have not bothered themselves much with education, nor indeed have educationalists with philosophy. This is a pity, because in one way or another, as human beings, we are all involved in education, and should all have thoughts about it. So should philosophers as philosophers, while educationalists should be more aware than they often are that their views on education, mythologies of not, have their roots in philosophical conceptions of human nature.

My own involvement in what we have to call the philosophy of education began when I was invited to lead summer school courses in the subject for the University of Jos in Plateau State, Central Nigeria. I did this twice, in 1978 and 1979, and on the basis of my teaching there I produced a book entitled *Education, Society and Human Nature* in 1981. I still agree with a fair amount of what the book says, but my attitude to education was enriched, to put it mildly, by the experience of my own children beginning to go through the education system, initially in state primary schools. Some of what they were being taught, and rather more perhaps, some of the ideas about how they should be taught rather surprised me. Realising that the delightful people who were teaching my children had imbibed the ideas I found surprising in colleges or university departments of education led me to question what was happening in teacher training. I began to think that teacher training would be better done in schools than in taking university courses of dubious value and ideology. Teaching, I thought, against the prevailing consensus in these matters, was a craft, requiring practical rather than theoretical knowledge, so best acquired in practice by people who already had good knowledge of what was to be taught, good subject knowledge in other words, and enthusiasm for it. I was thus coming to favour what has come to be known as school-based training, where would-be teachers acquire their craft and professional expertise under the direction of experienced teachers in schools which valued the type of knowledge that would form the basis of what I have been calling liberal education.

In 1989 I wrote a pamphlet on teacher training, laying out my contrarian views, which found support among people with traditional ideas on education, notably with John Clare, the education editor of *The Daily Telegraph*, for whom I then started writing. Another who liked my ideas was Kenneth Clarke, the Secretary of

State for Education at the time, who, provocatively as it seemed to many, put me on the government quango in charge of the training all teachers in state schools had to have. This is not the place to go into any detail on any of this – it is too boring anyway – save to say that, against often bitter opposition, the quango did move to instituting a more school-based approach to teacher training. In 1993 I was put on another educational quango charged with overseeing both public examinations and the national curriculum (which had been introduced in 1989), where we were involved in re-drafting that curriculum. I pressed hard to put more stress on knowledge and teaching, and less on pupil-based activity and 'discovery', again often against opposition. There was, though, support as well, which simply underlined in my mind the way in which education is what philosophers call an essentially contested concept. I refer to these experiences occasionally in the papers which follow, but I mention these things here simply to explain how I, as an academic philosopher, came to be involved in education in a professional, even in a philosophical, way, and why, over the years, I was moved to lay out my views in the writings which follow in this book.

Chapter 1

LIBERAL EDUCATION; WHERE COULD, AND WHERE SHOULD IT BE?

Three Questions

Most of this chapter was written in the USA in 2010, which explains some of the references, in particular the discussion in the final section of home schooling and fundamentalist Christian Schools, as these things were at the time. Nevertheless the educational concerns in question and even the implications involved in a certain view of Christian schooling do have a timeless dimension, as will emerge. However I am also interested in the way these ideas might be implemented in a particular historical moment, a moment which, as we will see, may not be propitious for their implementation, either in Britain or in the USA. So my argument here is not wholly or primarily a conceptual one; it may be that under some political dispensations what I am calling liberal education could thrive – but not, I am arguing for both practical and ideological reasons, under the type of political dispensation we have currently in the West. In the concluding pages of this essay, I will also look at a recent approach to education which might at first sight look similar to what I am proposing, but which turns out to be something of a delusion.

One theme which underlies quite a lot of the subsequent discussion is sometimes put in the following terms. In considering education, and this is my first question, for whom is the process conducted, for the state, or for the family of the pupil? More crudely, who do children belong to, the state, that is the collective, or to their parents, a point I take up again more directly in considering parental rights in Chapter 7. To anticipate what I argue there and also here, liberal education envisages a situation in which both these options will come to seem ill-formed. Children, even as children, belong to no entity or group of people; liberal education educates for freedom from any such notion of ownership.

There is, though, a second and different question: would liberal education and its aims be best served by an education run, controlled and/or regulated by the state, or by a system in which parents have the ultimate responsibility? And if, in the twenty-first century, I say the second, I should not be taken to imply that I would favour all the ways in which parents might choose to discharge that responsibility. Indeed, as will become apparent, I most certainly do not. It is, though, another (and a third) question as to how far parents should be regulated or restricted by the state in exercising choice over the schooling of their children so as to prevent them from imposing on their children an education which I or others might disapprove of. During the course of this essay, I will attempt to deal with all three of these questions.

In order to clarify my purpose and strategy, it may be helpful at the outset to point out the logic and direction of the argument. My main concern is with liberal education, and with how its promotion might best be served in current circumstances in Western democracies. So, my advocacy of a radical deregulation of education is offered in the first instance as an answer to what I see as a problem arising from the concept of a liberal education. However, as will become apparent, I also think there are independent reasons of principle for the deregulation of education, and in the second stage of the argument I touch on them. I also look at a number of objections to deregulation, which take us beyond anything specifically to do with liberal education. And, to clarify (or complicate) things a bit more, I should point out from the outset that it is not part of my argument that a deregulated system of education will expose all children to the sort of liberal education which I find desirable. It will not; but I suggest that a deregulated system is the best chance that liberal education has in to-day's world, and probably for the greatest number of pupils.

Education for Freedom: the Child

Liberal education, as I am understanding it, is an education for freedom. 'Liberal' in the phrase 'liberal education' derives from the Latin 'liber' = free (rather than 'liberi' = children, which would be tautologous, or 'liber' = book, which will certainly be involved in any course of liberal education, but only as a part of the whole thing). An education stressing or aiming at freedom can, however, be seen in rather different and incompatible ways. At one extreme, at the progressive end, there would be the typical 'free' school, of which A.S. Neill's Summerhill (in Leiston, Suffolk) would be a famous example, or in the USA the type of thing advocated by John Holt in his book *How Children Fail*. (1)

Summerhill was, and to an extent still is, a school in which children do not attend lessons if they do not feel like it; they study the things they want as and when they feel ready for it; and, with teachers and other members of the school community, they collectively decide on the rules to be imposed in the school. In Neill's own words (on the School's website), at Summerhill 'we had to renounce all discipline, all direction, all suggestion, all moral training, all religious instruction. We have been called brave, but it did not require courage. All it required was what we had – a complete belief in the child as a good, not an evil, being.' Notably absent from this type of free school will be any form of external discipline, either in the conduct of lessons and the structuring of curricula, or, more generally, in the ethos or conduct of the school as an institution. The underlying thought here is that there is something dehumanising in imposing external curricula and controls even on young children. According to Holt, 'nobody starts off stupid', yet schools are no more than places in which pupils are coerced according to external social goals, with the result that in them 'children learn to be stupid'. (2)

By contrast, in the type of liberal education I am interested in here, discipline and externally imposed curricula will play a major role. There is an understanding that children – pupils – are not when young fully human, and only become human in the full sense by being initiated into various practices and forms of knowledge and experience in which one's humanity achieves its full embodiment and articulation. I have put this bluntly and starkly because I think it needs stating clearly and emphatically in these post-Rousseauan and possibly post-Freudian days when childhood is seen, sentimentally, as a paradise from which we adults have been excluded by the forces of civilization: 'Les seules vrais paradis sont les paradis perdus' – true enough, but I don't think that Proust (from whom I am quoting here) would have foregone his Ruskinian initiation into culture and its mysteries for a permanent holiday in his aunt's house. If we are taking the lost paradise to be, platonically, that from which we descended *before* we were born, then childhood is actually the start of our descent *into* the Cave. For Plato, of course, human existence is an uphill struggle to rise above our humanity, in which we attempt to control the two horses we set astride, one that would fly up and one that would drag us down. Plato's metaphor seems to me to be a more accurate representation of our life in general and of childhood in particular than seeing childhood as simply a time of innocence.

Actually claiming that the child is not fully human is not as extreme as it might appear at first sight. It is simply recognizing the fact of what biologists call neoteny, that when we are born we are very immature and unformed, in comparison to most other species, and remain immature for a long time. When we are young, our instincts on their own will not take us very far. The great distinction between humans and other animals is the way in which, in all cultures, human beings pass on to their young by education and training, formal and informal, immense tracts of what they need to know and do in order to survive and flourish in both natural and social worlds. During the Enlightenment many thinkers – and not just Rousseau – were fascinated by the prospect of *l'enfant sauvage*, the child who had not had a human upbringing, and who was raised in nature, among the beasts. As is well known from the eponymous film of François Truffaut, when such a child was actually found in the Auvergne (the wild boy of Aveyron), sadly, tragically, even despite all the efforts of the well-meaning doctor who fostered him, he never succeeded in becoming (dare I say?) fully human, and actually ended up as an exhibit in Paris. But, whether or not acculturation is possible for children or young people after a certain age, which is what the film seems to argue, what *l'enfant sauvage* graphically illustrates is the significance and extent of learning and acculturation in human life.

Marx was wrong when he famously spoke of humans having no nature, but only history, because part of our nature is precisely to live our lives in the *polis* where we will flourish in and through what we learn and are taught – and this (Aristotelian) view is quite compatible with thinking that there are eternal truths about what does and does not contribute to human flourishing. But because flourishing involves acculturation in a human society, with its traditions and history, education, both formal and informal, becomes critical.

The proponent of liberal education takes a view of childhood which has its roots in the thought of the classical Greek philosophies of Plato and Aristotle. Pace Holt, who thinks that 'children are by nature not only kind and loving but serious and purposeful', (3) for the philosophers of classical antiquity the child is unhabituated in desirable traits either of character or of intellect, and so is in no position to exercise the type of freedom accorded to children in A.S. Neill's school or as advocated by Holt. It is not that children are evil or malignant (though some might have evil and malignant tendencies and original sin weighs on us all), so much as that they are unformed. And this lack of formation goes through all dimensions of our existence, intellectual, physical, moral, and in terms of character. So, famously, the ancient Greeks emphasized the need in education for gymnastic (the training of the body) and music (the training of sensibility through music and the other arts), while Aristotle stressed the way in which a virtuous character can emerge only from an habituation in virtuous acts, which will, if things go well, lead to a love of virtue itself. We will have more to say about the acquisition of virtuous habits in Chapter 4.

As far as the intellect goes, what the young need above all is initiation into disciplines and traditions in which reason is exercised. None of these things are instinctive; hence the need for discipline and training. I will leave it to those who have had experience of young children to judge between the Greeks and the likes of Holt and Neill. Here I will restrict myself to the comment that even if Holt is right in thinking that schools actually *produce* the sort of malice and stupidity we see in pupils in many secondary schools these days, what this would show is that the good qualities he discerns in very young children are not strongly embedded, and need careful nurturing, just as the Greeks thought and Christians think. A similar point could be made about Rousseau, who also puts the blame for our evil inclinations on the social world, and to whom many of our current sentimental notions of childhood can be traced, but who in *Émile* requires an astonishingly *artificial* set up in order that Émile's natural goodness should develop *naturally* (It is perhaps worth underlining here that Rousseau's idea of childhood, as being a stage in which children should develop naturally and in interaction between the natural world and their childhood inclinations, is the source not only of much current thinking about primary and early years education, but also, as we will see in Chapter 3, of a powerful strand of opposition to the type of education I am here advocating).

True Enlargement of Mind

From the perspective of the liberal educator (as represented by, say, Cardinal Newman and Matthew Arnold in the nineteenth century), in an education which truly frees the mind, a key element will be initiation into the best that has been thought and known (or said); (4) as a result of such an initiation there will develop that 'true enlargement of mind which is the power of viewing many things at once as one whole, of understanding their respective values, and determining their mutual dependence', as Newman has it. (5) Here teaching and discipline are essential because the 'best' in whatever field is not going to be picked up randomly. Much of it will be hard and different from anything the pupil will be familiar with or will pick up in their ordinary life. It will require a grounding of knowledge and vocabulary and reference beyond what the pupil will meet in everyday life.

The subject matter of liberal education will include science and mathematics, treated in a serious way, as inquiries for their own sakes, examining the fundamental nature of reality from both a physical and an abstract mathematical point of view. This enterprise will remind us of both of Aristotle's view that part of wisdom is the pure desire to know the causes of things and also of the Pythagorean-Platonic sense of number as a realm of its own, adamantine in its certainty and proof, arguably penetrating to the essence of the world. But over and above science and maths, liberal education will involve an encounter with our cultural roots. Like Odysseus in Book XI of *The Odyssey*, we will, in a sense, enter Hades to converse with the dead and to discover who we and they are. Like Odysseus, each one of us has to 'sail after knowledge', or else we will be in a state 'knowing less than drugged beasts', in thrall to the clamour, mindlessness and superficiality of the present when we have nothing with which to compare or judge it.

Liberal education, then, involves an orderly and disciplined initiation into the best that has been thought and known in various dimensions, as well as an education in sensibility and in habits of virtue. In this process the learner will be introduced to various traditions and canons of thought, sensibility, and behaviour (the best that has been thought and known) as streams of experience and conversations through the ages, which of necessity have a longevity and an authority far more extensive and commanding than anything which could be produced by any groups or individuals making things anew to-day. In that sense we will, all of us, be dwarves sitting on the shoulders of giants, as John of Salisbury and later Newton put it. Of course we know more than those earlier in the conversation, as T.S. Eliot observed, and a key part of what we know is precisely those who have gone before us and their achievements. The thought, though, is that this initiation, disciplined as it is, is actually the precondition of true intellectual and moral freedom. Without this grounding there will always be an element of the barbarian at a loss in a temple whose meaning he does not understand, or of the untrained would-be artist cut off from subtlety and depth of expression by his lack of knowledge and consequent incompetence in the medium.

Much modern education is predicated on just such models. For example, as we will see in Chapter 6, 'creativity' without training is valued; pupils are expected to express a reaction to poems whose context is deliberately hidden from them, and they are envisaged as working out for themselves a type of social contract for their school just in the way Rousseau envisaged the noble savage moving the state of nature into a state of social organization. All this underlines the difference between the conception of freedom at work in liberal education and that envisaged in the progressive free school. To put it broadly and bluntly, the liberal educator sees freedom in terms of the ability of the learner to participate in and add to the conversations of mankind, in Michael Oakeshott's phrase. By contrast, as Oakeshott himself points out, the freedom envisaged by the progressive is that championed by Francis Bacon right at the start of the modern era in the early seventeenth century, the freedom of the man who dives into the River Lethe, erasing from his soul the memory of all knowledge, all art, all poetry, to re-emerge on the opposite shore, naked and glorious like the first man. (6)

It might seem a cheap shot to point out that in expressing his vision so beautifully Bacon is relying on classical and biblical imagery, but it would not be a cheap shot to point out that Bacon was the advocate of a new science, based solely on observation and experiment, which was supposed to look at the world anew and without preconception or influence from past authorities. Bacon was a polemicist who referred to the knowledge of the middle ages and of the renaissance as consisting of idols, and who excoriated the intellectual influence of Aristotle. Bacon's own contributions to the actual new science of his day were less than nugatory, and he misunderstood the mathematical and theoretical nature of the new science he was supposedly advocating, which was actually very far from addressing nature without preconceptions. Much indeed was based on the Pythagorean outlook of Kepler and Galileo, who saw mathematics as the key to scientific understanding of the world, in opposition to a method based on unstructured observation. Nevertheless, none of this has prevented the Baconian ideal of science, and his rewriting of its history (in effect wiping out the contribution of the medieval to empirical knowledge) from exercising a dominance in the popular (and even not so popular) mind ever since.

Nor should we overlook the way in which the Baconian conception of science is a thoroughly utilitarian one, in contrast to the view of Aristotle, in which knowledge of causes is a species of wisdom, good in and for itself, an aspect of mental and moral liberation. For Bacon, the true and only point of science is to improve man's estate, and the liberation is one afforded (if at all) by technique and technology. It is not, then, surprising that Bacon should have been an opponent of liberal education, to the extent that he opposed the foundation of Charterhouse because its curriculum was to be based on the Greek and Roman classics. As things have turned out, Bacon can be seen to be one of the first of many who have opposed liberal education on grounds of economic and scientific utility, including John Locke, Newman's *bête noire* in this respect (In his *Some Thoughts on Education* of 1693, Locke was firmly of the view that the academic side of education should eschew the classics and concentrate on what would be useful in the emerging economies and sciences of the 16th and 17th centuries). We stand here at the point of one of the big divides in educational thought, that between the followers of Aristotle and Cicero, the liberal educators, who see a virtue in knowledge for its own sake and the rational life as an end in itself, and the utilitarians, Bacon, Locke, and their followers, who see education and indeed knowledge itself primarily as means to ulterior practical ends, with reason the slave of the passions, rather than their master. (To avoid confusion, I should underline here that the greatest of the so-called utilitarian philosophers, John Stuart Mill, was actually a doughty defender of the ideals of liberal education; but then the happiness he defended in *Utilitarianism* was the philosophic happiness, or perhaps unhappiness, of a Socrates, as opposed to the cruder pleasures envisaged in the philosophies of his father and Jeremy Bentham).

A further element is added to the utilitarianism of Bacon and Locke by John Dewey. According to Dewey's pragmatist philosophy the key notions for any human activity are problem solving and growth. Dewey had an in-built hostility to the past because, in his denial that there were any eternal or permanent verities, the legacy of the past was that of yesterday's solutions to yesterday's problems. Explicitly linking his thought to Darwin's theory of evolution – the 'greatest dissolvent in contemporary thought of old questions' (7) – Dewey wanted everything, including philosophy and education, to address 'the intelligent administration of existent conditions', without being tied to what he saw as the absolutism and authoritarianism of the idea that the essences of things could be or had been discovered. Moreover, in contrast to the Aristotelian notion that different modes of inquiry were appropriate for different areas of life, Dewey insisted that the methods of the physical sciences, of observation and, above all, experiment, were suitable for all our endeavours. In the continuous flow of life in which we are all swimming, we must always be ready for new problems and ready – through our education – to experiment with new solutions.

For all Dewey's occasional nod towards great minds of the past, there is in his educational thinking and, even more, in that of his followers, a relentless focus on the modern and the demands (or what they take to be the demands) of the present, which cannot but be suspicious of any Arnoldian lingering over the best that *has* been thought and known. For Dewey, not only should education be directed at practical ends – to-day's practical ends and to-day's problems – approached in a technologico-scientific spirit, but it will be collectivized. As is clear from his Chicago school experiments of the 1890s, Dewey saw education in highly politicized terms, in which the community as a whole will participate in solving its problems. The school would be part of the local democratic community, and its activities would focus on projects which grew out of the concerns and interests of the people in the locality. At the same time the classroom itself would be run as a democracy in miniature, with the teacher no 'external boss or dictator', but a moderator or co-ordinator of the activities of the group (facilitator in to-day's jargon); to this fundamentally democratic enterprise all pupils would be encouraged to contribute their own individual slants on whatever topic was being investigated. And to hammer home his message that education was to be a socialized activity, as early as 1889 Dewey said this: 'What the best and wisest parent wants for his own child, that must the community want for all its children.' (8)

Education and 'The Community'

This is a temptingly tantalizing vision. Suppose that I or you or Matthew Arnold were this best and wisest parent, and had the power to enforce our vision of teaching the best that had been thought and known. Actually Matthew Arnold, convinced statist and Germanophile that he was, might, for the best of reasons, have applauded. An education focusing on the best that had been thought and known, lavished on the whole community... At least two members of the Conservative-coalition

British government of 2010 expressed to me just such a vision as their political ideal, and they thought that they might be able to implement it. But what if Dewey rather than they were the 'best and wisest parent' and had the power? Something very different would emerge, and indeed did emerge under the New Labour government of 1997-2010 after an earlier Conservative attempt to impose a knowledge-based national curriculum. Actually, what emerged between 1989 and 1997, when New Labour came in, was a rather watered down though nonetheless onerous curriculum, which was the focus of endless wrangles and controversy. New Labour's own curriculum, post 1997 was far more child-centred. In the traditional sense it was light on content, though heavily invested in citizenship and the attempt to address every perceived social problem, from obesity through smoking, alcohol and drug misuse to paedophilia, 'homophobia', global warming, inequality and racism – anything and everything that was part of that government's agenda of social engineering. All this was encapsulated in the breathtakingly banal strap-line 'every child matters', which was the keystone of all their policies, and in the equally breathtaking presumption, enunciated by one Labour Secretary of State for Children, Families and Schools (as the Department for Education was then re-branded) that the outcome would be to make Britain the best place in the world to bring up children. Anything and everything, then, was to go into schooling, apart from concentrated focus on the best that had been thought and known, which had been sneeringly caricatured by one professor of education of the time as 'the curriculum of the dead'.

Well, let us take the sneer as a compliment. Why not the curriculum of the dead, if it involves the Odyssean conversation with our great forbears? These forbears may indeed have articulated eternal truths about man and the universe, and they will certainly have looked at things in ways which enable us to put current trends and fashions into some sort of perspective. But, in the recent history of education in England it was not to be, except in a rather half-hearted way even when those in power wanted a more rigorous and traditional approach. The most basic reason is that you cannot by central government edict force some 400,000 state-certified teachers to do something. In my view, as we will see, this would be the wrong way to go about things anyway. But the problem is only compounded when what you are trying to enforce is something which significant numbers of them are opposed to, and if not opposed to, then certainly untrained for and, in many cases, probably ignorant of as well. Even the government of 1997–2010, which they and their trade unions were rather more keen on than the various Conservative administrations before and after, in the end struggled to get them to carry out a couple of simple basic tests of reading and mathematics.

But even if the teachers were more malleable than they are, there would still be the normal bureaucratic inertia to overcome in attempting so radical an ideological change, to say nothing of the downright opposition there would be within the educational establishment to it, reared as its leaders are on fundamentally opposing views of education. This establishment – government officials, local administrators, teacher trainers, university departments of education, inspectors, teacher unions, and so-called subject associations – would undoubtedly prove massively obstructive in the endless stages of consultation and pre-implementation discussion which nowadays seem inevitably to accompany any major governmental policy change in education, as indeed they did over the 1989 curriculum and its first revision in 1993-4 (in which I took part as a government appointed board member of the quango charged with writing and administering that curriculum). It was only when this establishment started getting what they wanted under the Labour

government of 1997 that a semblance of educational sweetness and light descended, and what they wanted had nothing
to do with anything Matthew Arnold might have regarded as
ideal. Considering this history, all of which is well within living
memory, I am at a loss to know why politicians still think that
the key to educational reform still lies in central government
diktat, as evidenced most recently and notably in the ultimately
abortive attempt by the then (Conservative) Secretary of State
for Education to enact a bill which would have tied state education in England up completely in a web of top-down regulation
from the Department of Education, working through licensed
and heavily administered trusts.

However, aside from what might look like local and historic
conditions peculiar to Britain, there is a more fundamental
reason for thinking that liberal education is going to sit uneas-
ily within a state system. It derives from the tension which is
inevitably going to exist between the notion of freedom implicit
in liberal education and the aims a state will have in a system of
education it is running. We have already seen Dewey speaking
of something 'the community' must want for all its children.
As if Dewey's invocation of the will of 'the best and wisest
parent' in connection with some community wide imposition
weren't ominous enough, he goes on to say that 'any other
ideal for our schools is narrow and unlovely; acted upon it
destroys our democracy.' So, according to Dewey, democracy
will be *destroyed* unless the community has a single system of
education, predicated on the will of the best and wisest parent.

Let us suppose what actually seems most unlikely, that the
parent nominated 'best and wisest' is Matthew Arnold and not
John Dewey, and the 'community' initiated an Arnoldian curriculum, how stable would this be? For who is going to regulate
and control this community-wide system? The only agency
capable of ensuring that all children received the same education

is the state. But once the state started running education on behalf of 'the community', the temptation for it to interfere in order to promote its own and different interests would prove irresistible. These interests would doubtless include such things as nation building, social cohesion, economic viability, technological utility, a healthy population and, more controversially, social justice. Not all these things are necessarily undesirable and several might be produced as by-products of an education conducted in a liberal spirit, but if they became the focus or goal of education, they would distort its character.

The Interests of the State

There is no need here to go into great detail as to the ways in which ends such as the ones just mentioned have become prominent in state run systems of education. Nor is this a new phenomenon. As long ago as 1796, Benjamin Rush, one of the signatories of the American Constitution, said this: 'Each youth does not belong to himself, but is public property and a warrior in the cause of liberty.' (9) Paradoxical as it may be to think of someone being public property in the cause of liberty, in the century following Rush's statement public education, as far as it existed, was designed not only to prepare populations for work, whether manual or mental (in most industrialized countries), but also to promote such causes as Evangelical Christianity against Catholicism (the USA), nation building in general (Prussia and Germany), the values of the secular state (France) and the production of a cadre of young people fit and apt for military service and running an over-extended empire (Britain in the late 19th century, under the Conservatives, and opposed by the churches for what they saw as glorification of war), to take but four typical examples. In the twentieth century, in addition to some or all of these there has been a stress in many places on education as an agent of social mobility, and latterly of equality.

In each case the policy in question would be defended by claiming that education is a social concern. As such it should reflect social needs and values, and moreover as a state education will necessarily be paid for out of the public purse, the state has a very direct interest in what it does and what it is for. (The fact that the public purse is involved here only because the state has taken money from individual parents who would otherwise have been able to educate their children themselves is generally overlooked at this point in the argument). Further, as societies have become more democratic, and democracy itself more populist, there is also a move to make education more egalitarian, shunning élitism (as it would be called) and those elements of the curriculum which cannot be shared by all, a theme characteristically prominent in the writings of Dewey and his followers, for whom what is now known as inclusiveness or inclusion, along with equality and diversity, is to be the very touchstone of a healthily democratic system of education.

'A Despotism Over the Mind'

The liberal educator need not deny that education is in some sense a social concern, nor that society as a whole has an interest and even a paternalistic duty in seeing that its members are educated. Both Newman and Arnold, in their different ways, saw an educated population as a good in itself, something that would leaven and civilize the society it made up, and so did Mill. But as Mill saw with compelling clarity, saying that is one thing; saying (as is almost taken as axiomatic these days) that therefore the state should take charge of education is quite another. In Chapter V of *On Liberty,* Mill warned that 'a general state education is a mere contrivance for moulding people to be exactly like one another', and that 'in proportion as it is efficient and successful, it establishes a despotism over the mind, leading to one over the body'. (10) One may, of course, have doubts about the efficiency of the enterprise, but looking at the materials of the English National Curriculum as it was from the late 1990s until 2010, there can be no doubt about an intention of just the kind Mill feared: an overwhelming and overweening drive within it to produce a certain set of attitudes on topics such as multiculturalism, environmentalism, citizenship, social justice, and even, as things were then, the European Union (amazingly, according to the Single European Act of 1986 we in Britain were bound by law to bring out the [pro] European dimension of every topic in the curriculum). Nor have such attitudinal ambitions disappeared since 2010. Some are more or less the same, some have changed, and new ones, such as forcing all pupils to do economically productive maths until the age of 18, have been mooted.

As is well known, Mill objected to any attempt centrally to impose a single view on any topic because of his belief that it was only in an atmosphere of intellectual freedom that the truth would out, a sense very much in accord with the general spirit of liberal education which would be fatally compromised were some form of intellectual or political correctness imposed from outside. And he goes on to make the pertinent point that if there were sufficient numbers of teachers within a state sector of education to run that system, there is no sound reason for their not being able and willing to teach in a deregulated system, providing education were compulsory and there was state aid for those unable to pay for education themselves (On this last point, he does, though, go on to make some sharp and currently unfashionable comments about parents who bring children into the world without the means to provide for them; unfashionable this thought may be, but it is all of a piece with Mill's fundamental premise that the education of children is first and foremost the prerogative and duty of parents as opposed to the state, both as a matter of individual and intellectual freedom, but also as an index of individual responsibility. We will have more to say on Mill on these points in Chapter 5). We could add here to Mill's observations that even if, as is currently the case, there are not enough properly educated teachers in the state sector, the best way of remedying this deficiency would be the normal market one of supply and demand – and also of opening up teaching to well-qualified would-be teachers who are currently prevented from teaching in state schools by the monopolistic system of state accreditation of teachers.

Over and above what Mill argues, we need to add that the ends of liberal education – knowledge for its own sake, the inculcation of moral and intellectual freedom, participation in the conversation of mankind (including the dead) – are not ends which sit easily with what any modern state is likely to decide are its priorities, if only because these are ends which are separate from those to which states characteristically devote themselves and independent of them. This is because they can be realized only in the intellectual and spiritual formation of individuals qua individuals, individuals who are assumed to have their own formation and individual goals, which may or may not coincide with those of the population as a whole at any given time. Indeed, to be blunt, in the age of the mass media they are almost certain not to coincide. So can a state in to-day's world not just tolerate such a form of education, but actually be its provider and guardian?

We have so far been treating the question of the influence of the state and its bureaucracies as if they were in a sense neutral phenomena, simply administering policies laid down by rulers and politicians in a disinterested way. In practice, though, we know both from experience and from the findings of public choice theory that bureaucracies are never disinterested players. They always have their own interests to pursue, their own empires to build up, their own influence and power to expand. While this need not be sinister in itself, no bureaucracy is likely to favour an activity whose aims and rationale are essentially in tension with a managerial, bureaucratic approach and also essentially to place its adherents at least one mental remove from the state. The aims of liberal education certainly are, in that they involve values which are unquantifiable, and which will seem to the managerial mind to be unaccountable, and aims which may well be critical of the forms of economic utility and social levelling beloved of the politician and the bureaucrat. No one in to-day's world should be surprised to learn what underpinned the English National Curriculum under the government of 1997-2010. In its statement of the values we were told that education is 'a route to equality of opportunity for all, a healthy and just democracy, a productive economy and sustainable development... valuing diversity in our society and the environment in which we live'. Given that any genuine equality of opportunity will necessarily involve a continuous discounting of unequal outcomes at any stage (a direction the British government is already moving in with regard to university admissions, where pupils from poorly achieving schools are to have their grades artificially enhanced), and given that the politics of diversity amount in practice to a refusal to admit differences of quality between, say, the art of the streets and that of Bach and Rembrandt, as well as a repudiation of the idea of culture as one inclusive conversation, these are anything but neutral requirements.

Though the liberal educator may hope from his work for a social leavening and other desirable social ends (though not, one hopes, the delusory and ultimately totalitarian 'equality of opportunity'), it is a leavening which will occur, if at all, through the care and nurture of the soul of the individual (Plato) and by the cultivation of the *best* that has been thought and known, and of those who are the best. This aristocracy of talent need not and should not imply a regime of social barriers; but the alternative is the situation dreaded by both Plato and Matthew Arnold in which those with most talent track down to the level of the lowest tastes, keeping those from educationally under-privileged backgrounds firmly in their place by flattering them into believing that there is nothing better to aspire to than their own uneducated tastes (rather how the mass media work in to-day's world, in fact).

Nor should we forget that the modern world and the politics of the modern state above all are aspects of what Plato called the great beast. The great beast is the public world which can be pulled in any direction by the force of public opinion, without regard to truth or justice. In a populist democracy public opin-ion is easily manipulated by propaganda, the mass media and now increasingly by what are known as social media. Political leaders are demagogues, and they in turn are in thrall to all sorts of other interests and powers. Political parties exist, but as mass movements, concerned only with growing and further-ing their own power. All this is highly corrosive of the type of serene individualism the liberal educator endeavours to foster. So we should not be surprised if the modern state hardly wants to cherish institutions of liberal education.

A Transcendent Dimension

But over and above all this, there is yet another aspect to liberal education which would make its promotion problematic for the modern state. As will be evident from a glance at its history, (11) there are, among its devotees and forbears, both Christian and pre-Christian, a striking number of thinkers who are explicitly committed to a belief in the supernatural destiny of mankind, from Plato, Aristotle, and Cicero through to Ruskin, Newman, Tawney, T.S. Eliot, C.S. Lewis, and Dorothy L. Sayers in more modern times. From the point of view of these thinkers, the formation involved in a programme of liberal education is part of the way we would respond to our nature as having a destiny not confined to this world.

At the very least, liberal education leaves open the possibility that human beings have a calling which is open and not confined to any ulterior ends, economic, political, social or, as Newman stressed, even moral. Our intellectual and aesthetic sensibilities are treated as ends in themselves, worthwhile in themselves. A full analysis of these faculties may well see them as having a transcendent aspect, not just worthwhile in themselves, which they are, but as crucial aspects of our spiritual nature. Aristotle and Newman would have analysed our intellectual faculties in these terms. In Newman's case, as we see from *The Idea of a University*, 1873, Discourse V, what liberal education aims at is that 'illuminative reason and true philosophy' which is 'the power of viewing many things at once as one whole, of referring them severally to their true place in the universal system, of understanding their respective values, and determining their mutual dependence.' But if this power is not to be a mere intellectual fastidiousness, which is often found among the highly educated and can be little more than a form of snobbery, it will need a context against which to make these judgements. Secular reason has proved incapable of overcoming the fissiparous nature of intellectual disciplines, and the 'unity of the sciences', much trumpeted in the 1920s and 1930s, remains as elusive as ever it was, as in the modern university does any uncontentious way of relating the sciences to other aspects of human nature. Newman's conclusion is that universalizing and synthesising aspirations of intellectual endeavour which he is seeking makes sense only against the background of a unifying and legitimating order, itself upheld by a divine Being. (12)

Plato and Ruskin, and a host of neo-Platonists, saw beauty and our perception of it as a bridge to the divine. Clearly a significant element of liberal education will be what the Greeks called music, things to do with the muses, perhaps, so not just music in the strict sense, but also literature and the other arts and humanities. One could argue, as did Simone Weil, that all art of the first order is essentially religious, and not just because of the obvious but often overlooked fact that so much of the greatest art is an articulation of religious feelings. But even in art which is not on the surface religious, both creators and listeners sense that in much of it there is a reaching out to something beyond us, or perhaps more accurately, a reaching down of the divine to us, that in great art there is often a sense, hard to express but definitely there, that in it the veil which separates life on earth from its ultimate source is for a time drawn aside.

Whether either of those aspects of the mind and feelings with which liberal education deals are actually rooted in the spiritual or not – and there are plenty of people who would see themselves as defenders of liberal education who would stringently deny any such thing – still in liberal education we are treating of things of intrinsic value and independent from all other concerns; by virtue of these facts the devotees of liberal education, whether teachers or students, are going to put the more quantifiable and basic concerns of the community to one side, at least for a time. Even if liberal education does not presuppose a transcendent context, in its pursuit of the best that has been thought and known, it will be fairly naturally predisposed to the idea that there are truths about humanity and nature which are timeless, which transcend time and fashion; whereas, as we have seen with Dewey, the whole drift of modern politics is towards a progressive pragmatism, the idea that there is no ultimate truth, but

IN DEFENCE OF LIBERAL EDUCATION

that each generation has to work out for itself its own solutions to its own problems, leaving behind what it would see as a dead past, offering only old solutions to yesterday's problems. Add to that the point that liberal education aims at the nurturing of mentally free individuals, independent of and not beholden to the great beast in its collective manifestations, and the inevitable conclusion is that it would be very unwise to rely on the modern state for a system of liberal education or for any defence of those bits of liberal education which have managed to survive within its systems of education and training.

Indeed, far from expecting the state to defend liberal education, we should expect hostility, overt or covert, in so far as the state will inevitably have a collectivist agenda in its educational agenda: citizenship, social equality, and no-borders internationalism for the leftists (who are dominant in the field), a countervailing nationalism and traditionalism for the conservatives, basic skills for economic productivity for the marketeers and wealth creators, or maybe a combination of bits of all three in to-day's typical social democracy. In a certain sense some or all of these purposes might be served by a course of liberal education, but only as by-products of a system with quite other ends in view.

Well-meaning liberals (in the political sense), some of whom have visions of Arnoldian forms of education, continue to profess surprise and dismay at the fact that state initiatives, such as 'Every child matters' in Britain and 'No child left behind' in the USA, routinely fail and routinely push education in more utilitarian directions, *notwithstanding*, as these critics would have it, the often huge amounts of state money that goes into these programmes. Actually it is precisely because of the 'investment' that the pressure to ratchet up testable outcomes becomes ever more imperative from a bureaucratic and political standpoint, and it is precisely because education is conceived in terms of a national investment that managerial approaches are well-nigh irresistible in these times when accountability is a guiding principle politically. Furthermore, the first interest of the managerial state, whether ostensibly socialist or conservative, is always going to be to produce a body of compliant 'citizens', economically capable and motivated, ready to play their role in the 'big society' (or whatever term is used by politicians to describe their ideal of each individual making their individual contributions to the collective goals), all of which is at cross purposes with the aims and spirit of a liberal education.

So, it is no surprise to find (as in Britain) that state introduced programmes in schools in 'citizenship' and 'critical thinking' look to the dispassionate observer as little more than attempts to reinforce the prevailing consensus on such matters as global justice, the environment, sexual morality, and racism. It would be an interesting test of a class in critical thinking to see just how far a pupil got who suggested that, let us say, the ideas of Ayn Rand be given a dispassionate consideration in the class, or that it was about time that it was about time that intellectuals started giving war a chance. Actually I don't think that either of these things would be a particularly good idea pedagogically, because I follow Aristotle in believing that more experience and maturity than the average 16 year old has is needed to make sensible judgements on matters such as individual liberty vis-à-vis the state or on war and peace; but it is just these sorts of judgement which are the staple of 'citizenship' and 'critical thinking', my point here being only that the critical part of critical thinking will characteristically be more honoured in the breach than in the observance. If a teacher were seriously interested in considering war and peace, then he or she might start by looking at Thucydides' *Melian Dialogue*, while Sophocles' *Antigone* would be a good place to start a consideration of the relation between the individual and the state. At least then the pupils will engage with perspectives which are not those of to-day's politicians and columnists (the staple fare of citizenship and critical thinking classes), and they will begin to engage with perspectives which might help them to see the partiality and limitations of our own. Unfortunately, any such study is highly unlikely.

'The Strange Death of Liberal Education'

It is not necessary here to spell out in any detail the extent to which education in the Western democracies has moved from any serious engagement with the material or concerns of liberal education; suffice it here to point out that in Britain, along with the continual erosion of content in such subjects as English, History, and the Sciences, in 2003 in the GCSE examination taken by all 16 year olds 0.2% were in Latin and less than 0.1% in ancient Greek. In 2006 in the whole country 183 took ancient Greek in A level, the pre-university exam for 18 year olds, and 927 Latin. That year 6,186 papers in total were taken in any form of classical study, compared to 30,964 in Media Studies and 21,834 in Sports Studies. These figures are a few years old, and while there has been a small resurgence in Latin (1121 A level entries in 2019), the situation in Greek remains dire. In 2019, while 86 independent schools offered Ancient Greek at A level, only 8 state schools did, with 213 pupils doing the subject in total. One wonders whether the subject can survive in school.

It was against this background that Dr Martin Stephen, High Master of St Paul's School in London, where liberal education and the classics are still very much alive, was driven to entitling his introduction to *The School of Freedom* 'The Strange Death of Liberal Education'. (13) St Paul's had been founded in 1512 by John Colet, Dean of St Paul's Cathedral and a notable Renaissance humanist and friend of Erasmus and Thomas More. Colet charged the school with teaching 153 boys 'of all naciuons and countries indifferently... in good literature both Laten and Greke, and good autors such as have the verrye Romayne eloquence joined with wisdom, specially Chisten aŭtors...'; still in the twenty-first century St Paul's holds true to Colet's spirit, and Colet's inscription appears on its door. But, perhaps that is what is strange, rather than liberal education's death elsewhere, given that, as Stephen says that 'like lacrosse liberal education is a game with no boundaries, but the urge of all but the most enlightened governments to slap border controls on at every opportunity condemns the two to a long-standing war', adding that many of our politicians would not know what a liberal education was, never mind having the will to bring it back into our national culture. What, then, is to be done, if we are in favour of liberal education?

It is a striking fact that in Britain at least the spirit of liberal education, where it is alive, is predominantly based in the independent sector of schooling (accounting in Britain for about 7% of the total number of pupils). At one level this might seem strange. Will not many parents who are prepared to pay for their children's education, over and above what they have already paid in taxes for the state system, often have other ideas about the purpose of education? In the case of many of those who send their children to the expensive so-called public schools, it might be what Stephen calls 'social laundering' – preparing them to live in the upper echelons of society and providing these children of the social elite with a social cordon sanitaire keeping them apart from the masses. Others who send their children to private schools will want a pragmatically useful education for them, focusing on marketable skills, and still others will be looking for a tightly controlled upbringing for their children within a narrow religious environment. All these motives are undoubtedly present among parents who send their children to independent schools, and none is particularly conducive to the generosity of spirit and openness of mind which characterizes the liberal ideal.

On the other hand, there are parents who positively want their children liberally educated, and there are others who like what they see of its ethos when they visit a place such as St Paul's, even if they know little of John Colet or of his ideals. The problem for liberal education in the current situation is that within the state sector there are few examples of such schools for parents to send their children to, which is hardly surprising given the drift of state-run education. Where oases of liberal education do exist within the state sector, in schools such as the London Oratory (where, alongside the Blairs and a number of other Labour grandees, many of the parents are poor Filipinos and working class Irish) and in the 160 or so grammar schools remaining within the sector (where many of the parents are newly arrived Asians), they are extremely popular and heavily oversubscribed. (Grammar schools were – and are – schools catering to the academic elite, and for historical reasons tend towards something like the form of liberal education we are here advocating). The ineluctable conclusion is that if there were more schools offering both the curriculum and the disciplinary and work ethos of liberal education, they would be popular, as the state grammar schools were when they existed in large numbers until the 1960s, at which time in England liberal education experienced something of a late flowering, rather to the consternation of the independent schools at that time, who saw themselves losing their academic superiority – and many of their pupils, who could get as good an education within the state sector for nothing.

This is not, by the way, a plea for a return to the old system where there was strict demarcation between grammar schools and the rest, based on a rather brutal and inflexible selection process for pupils at the age of 11, which, despite or perhaps because of the benefits of the system for those who went to the grammars engendered considerable bitterness and acrimony among the rest. At least, that is how the collective memory of these things would have it; though a strong case for an alternative perspective has been made by the left-wing sociologist Frank Musgrove in his book *School and the Social Order* (14), in which he argues that the best way of preserving the class and educational privileges of the independent schools in Britain was precisely to remove the possibility of grammar school education from the 25% of the middle and working class children who went to them before the system was largely dismantled. But, as I say, I am not arguing for a return to the old bi-partite system, but rather for a far more varied system in which schools should be free from state control so they could offer the type of education they believed in and which parents wanted, and that parents should be able to choose according to their own wishes and what they perceived as the needs of their children. In such an environment, it is reasonable to expect that schools based on the values of liberal education would be set up, and that they would be reasonably able to hold their own in the marketplace.

An Unregulated System: Parental Choice

This is not the place to discuss the mechanics of an unregulated system in any detail, though some form of voucher system has occasionally received support from the political left as well as from the political right. Parents would receive in the form of vouchers what they paid in taxes for the education of their children with various top-ups in the case of poor parents and handicapped children. Such a system could be a godsend to the poor – for it is poor parents in poor areas who are most trapped in the monolithic and unresponsive state system, in which they have no option but to send their children to the poorly performing and undisciplined state schools which constitute their community schools. In the few places where vouchers have been tried in the USA, they have been popular with inner city parents, though rather less popular with the middle classes outside the inner cities who are not given vouchers and who do not have access to the sort of choice afforded by vouchers, who see their taxes going to fund to others advantages they themselves do not have. (It should be noted that currently in Britain this whole discussion remains somewhat academic. In 2010, when the Conservatives came to power in Britain, a proposal from the Independent Association of Preparatory Schools [IAPS] for a means-tested voucher scheme [what they called a Personal Education Grant] was firmly rebuffed by the Conservative party which declared that it had no intention to introduce anything of the sort).

In a system of education not run or controlled by the state, even if supported by state taxes in the form of vouchers, should the state have a regulatory role? Here, along with its artificial restriction to areas of high deprivation, is the Achilles heel of the voucher system, for the state will find it very hard not to place restrictions on the use to which vouchers can be put. Many who could see some virtue in a voucher based system would fear the consequences of an unregulated system. Schools they did not like may well appear within it. It is tempting to think that some form of central regulation could guard against the worst excesses, and so the freedom the state gives in doling out vouchers, it then takes away through regulation.

Those defending liberal education should steel themselves against the temptation to go down the road of protection through state regulation – even for the best of reasons. Not only would centralised state regulation simply be the device by which the state re-invented its own system, which would not favour the liberal approach for all the reasons we have already examined, but those very reasons furnish strong grounds for thinking that the state should be as little involved in education as possible. If we want to avoid all the evils of state interference in education, we have to go down the road mapped so clearly by Mill. If the state is to have a role at all, it should be the minimal paternalism envisaged in *On Liberty*. There Mill argues that for both individual and social reasons the state has a duty to protect children who cannot protect themselves, so it should see that all children are given an education. So it could and perhaps should ensure that all parents have the means to pay for their children's education and, more fundamentally, that parents do not so neglect the children they have brought into the world so as to give them no education at all. But these interventions should not go beyond a minimal supervision guarding against only the most blatant and obvious forms of child abuse and neglect, and seen very much in that light, again not as a pretext for imposing on parents and schools the plethora of regulations, petty and not so petty, which state authorities typically insist on to-day.

Indeed, apart from ensuring that all children are being educated, the state should not go much beyond requiring that any schools which exist stay within the law (that is, they do not advocate or foster law-breaking, for example, and they satisfy basic safety requirements). There could also, quite reasonably, be a requirement that in the interests of transparency schools, being public enterprises, publish certain basic information about their curriculum, their staffing, their school rules, and their performance in public examinations.

Whether it would be possible within a voucher system for the state to manage to confine its role in the way just suggested is, of course, an empirical matter. Economists and public choice theorists who are highly sensitive to the self-aggrandising tendencies of state bureaucracies point out that vouchers are just too much of a Trojan horse, because they require both that the state takes the money away from taxpayers in the first place, and then dishes it out again (as well as deciding on the amount). Both the collection and the distribution of the money will be costly, quite apart from any less neutral accompanying intervention. Maybe tax-credits, where people are simply allowed to set school fees against tax, would be a more efficient and more genuinely liberal way. Or maybe, most radical of all, education should simply be left entirely to the private decisions of private individuals. In such a world, no doubt charities would provide education for the very poor, but also, as the work of James Tooley in India, Africa, and China has demonstrated, small schools would spring up even in the poorest areas from the private initiative of groups of parents and educational entrepreneurs, who, in those third world settings, often provide a better level of education than the competing state schools. (15)

In advocating in whatever form the deregulation of education, the defender of liberal education will have to take on board the fact that there will undoubtedly be schools they disapprove of. Here the position will be liberal in a wider sense. We can all think of examples of schools which might crop up in a deregulated system; schools for Scientologists or creationists or Islamists and the rest, which doubtless some will object to strongly. On this general point, I will say two things.

First, freedom in whatever sphere will always involve outcomes some disapprove of, but this does not mean that those making those choices do not have the right to make them. This is what freedom means, and in the case of schooling there is the further point that many parents are tax-payers, from whom the state actually takes the money in order to impose on them and their children the model of schooling it and its bureaucracies prefer. Against this I would urge that, on balance, parents will know more about the educational needs of their children than bureaucrats, motivated by bureaucratic imperatives with little regard for the individual child. Of course, some parents will make choices others find unfortunate (the price of freedom), but apart from the point of principle at stake we in the Western world are not in a situation in which bureaucratic management of schools is a roaring success. To put it bluntly, large numbers of children are failed by this system in the most callous way. There is no reason to suppose that more children would be failed were their parents to have some genuine control over their education, however bizarre some of their choices might look to others.

But then, secondly, let us suppose that we have a traditionalist Muslim school, for example. In a context of parental choice it would be supported by the parents who sent their children there, otherwise it would not exist, which would be important educationally and in other ways. It would certainly be a big advantage over the present situation in which many parents are unhappy with the schools the state forcers their children to go to; but over and above that, the Muslim school would have to be a pretty dreadful place to be worse that many of the state schools which so signally fail so many children as it is. Of course it would teach things some people did not like, but again many state schools do just that, and from them there is currently no exit for the vast majority. As far as the teaching of what is disliked goes, there would, of course, be the normal application of the law to prevent incitements to violence, suppression of the rights of girls and women, vilification of minorities, and the rest. So long as a school remained within the law, it is hard to see by what right even the best meaning of authorities could forbid the teaching of specific doctrines or world views; but equally the vast majority of parents do want their children to enter mainstream society, whatever their own particular beliefs, and so there would be pressure there for an education which was not so bizarre as to make that impossible. And even where that was not the case – as with the Amish in parts of the USA

– other things being equal, tolerance by society as a whole would seem more fair, more constructive, and more genuinely liberal in spirit than attempts to suppress minorities by force (which is what external intervention would amount to).

As to whether an Islamic school would increase religious intolerance and social divisions, which many of the opponents of faith schools allege, it is by no means clear that it would be worse in this respect than the invisible madrassas which many Muslim children currently attend *after* their days in state schools. Publicly visible, properly and transparently run and accountable religious schools might actually do more for religious tolerance and understanding than forcing members of religious minorities to go to secular schools in which their religion was not taken seriously, to which the main counter-balance would be extremist preaching in the home and the church or mosque (which would inevitably occur were there no school the parents and community leaders approved of). Interestingly, in the Netherlands, religious groups were initially allowed to set up their own schools within the state system in the early part of the twentieth century precisely to defuse the bitter conflicts between Catholics and Protestants and between secularists and religious groups which were occurring in the state schools over just what should be taught in those schools (the so-called 'Battle of the Schools'); and now that under the same law Islamic schools are being set up, there is no evidence in those schools of the promotion of radical or extremist views. And, just to underline the point about where religious tolerance is most likely to be found, in secular France the hijab is forbidden in state schools – which seems to me to be illiberal, but which I suspect quite a number of secularists in Britain would approve of – but it is permitted in Catholic schools.

In sum, then, supporters of liberal education ought to favour a system of genuine parental choice stimulating diversity of provision, with the state playing as small a role in educations as is consistent with it ensuring that all children are educated and that in their education the law is upheld in a general sense and that children are not subject to obvious physical or moral danger in schools. Not only does liberal education view education as autonomous in principle, but for the practical reasons just considered it is most likely to thrive where education is not run by the state.

It is true that both Plato and Aristotle, who in many ways shared the attitudes of the liberal educator, thought that the state should run education. In Plato's case every element of education was to enable the good running of the state, though this did require the Guardians to engage in philosophical contemplation of the Good for its own sake for many years, after which they would be forced, kicking and screaming one imagines and as Socrates envisaged, to re-enter the Cave. In *Politics* Book VIII, Section 1, Aristotle for once follows very much in his master's footsteps: 'It is a lawgiver's prime duty to arrange for the education of the young... Education must be related to the particular constitution (of each state)... education must be one and the same for all, and the responsibility for it must be a public one, not the private affair it now is, each man teaching them privately whatever curriculum he thinks they ought to study... all citizens belong to the state.' (16) He does, though, go on to concede that in education there will be both liberal and illiberal elements. Notoriously both Plato and Aristotle were admirers of Spartan attitudes to education.

A short response would be to say that although I have drawn on some of the things Plato and Aristotle said about education in exploring what liberal education might be, neither was in the modern sense a liberal educationalist, and that there is in any case a degree of anachronism in discussing systems of thought and education from two and a half millennia ago in terms appropriate to to-day's schools and to-day's state. Moreover, the education Plato describes in *The Republic* is, of course, education in the *ideal* city, to which real cities bore little resemblance. Of education in real cities, Plato says that it is so dominated by public opinion, that 'you'd be quite right to see God at work when anything does retain its integrity and fulfil its potential within current political systems.' (17) At the very least, then, in 'the present state of society' Plato would seem to be conceiving a good education as one which liberates the pupil from the moods of the great beast that is liberal education. Further, one cannot help wondering just how what both Plato and Aristotle thought about the need for education to develop the higher and contemplative aspects of one's soul would have worked out in practice in any actual state intent, like Creon in Sophocles' *Antigone,* on pursuing its own ends in conflict with those of the higher law. My feeling is that both would have been tempted to put the care of the soul, if one may so put it, above the demands of any realpolitik, Theban or Spartan, and that they would in the end have been driven to concede at least a degree of autonomy for education (See the further discussion of both Plato and Aristotle in Chapter 5).

Given, though, that education in most Western democracies is run predominantly by the state, and in many cases increasingly intrusively, and that we do not have a voucher system or anything permitting genuine parental choice for the vast majority of parents (who cannot afford private schooling), the best hope for liberal education would seem to lie in whatever private sector of education is allowed to exist. Meanwhile, as things stand, the best plan for liberal educators who want to do more than simply teach in whatever setting they can would be to campaign for greater levels of autonomy within their national systems of education.

Home Schooling

A question I would like to consider briefly at this point is whether this desirable autonomy should be taken to include home schooling. Home schooling has always, in a sense, existed, in various forms. Most people throughout history did not go to school, so whatever education they received, they must have got at least in large part at home. Even where there are schools, children learn a lot at home, and in many cases are taught basic academic skills such as reading as well. Among the aristocracy it was and may still be true that children are sometimes taught by tutors at home hired for the purpose. The home schooling phenomenon which is relevant here, however, is different from any of these conceptions. It is where within a modern society parents have taken a conscious decision to keep their children away from schools, whether public or private, and to give them their education within the home or a group of co-operating homes, almost invariably as a result of dissatisfaction with what is on offer in the schools to which their children would otherwise have gone (which inevitably means in most cases the available state schools).

In the USA in particular home schooling has grown dramatically in the last two or three decades, particularly since home schoolers have become more skilled in fighting off the inevitable legal challenges they have had to face from state authorities interpreting legal requirements for the education of children as meaning that they have to go to officially recognized schools. The bureaucratic attitude is neatly captured by what one official is said to have told some home schooling parents: 'No matter how enriching the home environment, the public schools still know best how to educate your child.' But do they, even in the terms laid down by the public schools? To the consternation of educational researchers and others professionally ill-disposed, there is now considerable evidence to show that children who are home schooled do at least as well as their schooled contemporaries not just in terms of academic knowledge and ability (as measured by public examinations and tests), but also in terms of whatever measures are employed to assess socialization and affective development.

This point is worth underlining, particularly perhaps in Britain, where home schooling is beginning to take a bit of a hold, and where there are ominous signs that politicians are speaking of the need to regulate it in the interests of child protection. But where is the evidence that home schooling *per se* raises issues of child protection, to a greater degree than, say, bullying and sexual immorality in state schools? *Home Schooling: Political, Historical and Pedagogical Perspectives,* edited by Jane van Galen and Mary Anne Pitman, (18) provides a useful overview of the evidence on the reasonable outcomes of home schooling, though the somewhat sniffy attitude of many of the authors to what they describe fairly enough is neatly encapsulated by the conclusion of one of the essays which says that 'we continue to posit that humans are learners and that they cannot be prevented from learning, even in their own homes.'

Anyway, whatever the authors of the essay, Mary Anne Pitman and M. Lynne Smith, continue to posit, in 2007 there were 1.5 million children in the USA being home schooled, or about 2.9% of the school age population, according to a report from the US Department of Education's Institute of Education Sciences National Center for Education Statistics from December 2008. This was up from 850,000 in 1999 and just over one million in 2003. In 2020 the total had reached 2.65 million, and the following year it is said to have reached a staggering 3.7 million, though whether some of this increase is temporary due to COVID restrictions is unclear. With the rapid growth in numbers there definitely has been over the past two decades, there are also increasingly extensive support networks and a plethora of materials for parents to use, as well as an effective and well-staffed legal defence body based just outside Washington DC (The Home School Legal Defense Association, or HSLDA). From the IES survey we learn that 88% of home schooling parents had concerns about the environments of schools and 73% were dissatisfied with the instruction schools provided. Positively, 83% wanted to provide their own religious or moral instruction, while 65% had an interest in a 'non-traditional approach to a child's education'. From this data it is pretty safe to conclude that there are two main groups of home schoolers, among whom there could be some significant overlap: conservative Christians on the one hand and, on the other, educational 'progressives' who believe that a child's education should be firmly centred on the interests and life of the child. Interestingly in this context John Holt, the scourge of anything to do with traditional forms of education, in his later years became a strong advocate of home schooling, his last book being entitled *Teach Your Own: A Hopeful Path For Education* (19). And the most famous of all educational experiments (a thought experiment, admittedly) was Rousseau's *Émile*, the *fons et origo* of progressive deschooling, in which Émile was deliberately kept away from all social influences in order that he could develop naturally, at his own pace, according to the rhythms of nature and childhood (or, more accurately, what Jean-Jacques imagined those rhythms to be).

'Christian-Classical' Schools

The obvious conclusion to draw is that, as things stand, home schooling is not likely to be propitious to liberal education. Fundamentalist Christianity is anything but liberal in an intellectual sense, while Holtian progressivism seems to be the antithesis of any structured initiation into the best that has been thought and known.

But maybe this is a bit too quick. Home schooling curriculum materials often contain plenty of coverage of that core of liberal education, the great books, considerably more in many cases than pupils will encounter in state run schools. And for many home schoolers, or at least for those helping and influencing them, Dorothy L. Sayers's *The Lost Tools of Learning*, which advocates a Christian-classical education, appears to be an inspiration, if not actually a manifesto. 'Let us amuse ourselves', she said in 1947, 'by imagining that (a) progressive retrogression is possible. Let us make a clean sweep of all educational authorities, and furnish ourselves with a nice little school of boys and girls whom we may experimentally equip for the intellectual conflict along lines chosen by ourselves. We will endow them with exceptionally docile parents; we will staff our school with teachers who are themselves perfectly familiar with the aims and methods of the Trivium...' (20)

It seems that many not so docile parents are doing more these days than amusing themselves. Bypassing teachers, they are actually putting into effect in their own homes something like Sayers's interpretation of the Trivium. This is a rather generous one which has the Trivium encompassing most of what followers of Newman and Arnold would hope to include in a decent liberal education for children under the medieval headings of Grammar, Dialectic (or Logic), and Rhetoric. The Trivium will then lead, Sayers hopes, to the mental liberation and ability to go further in whatever sphere which comes about through having a mind prepared in this way. One key aspect of Sayers's proposal is that in it she distinguishes three stages in a child's development, which she characterises as Poll-Parrot, Pert and Poetic, and to each of which one of the three elements of the correspond. Learning by heart (grammar) is appropriate to the first stage, in areas such as foreign languages (including Latin), poetry, mathematical tables, scientific and historical facts, and the basic elements of the Christian story. In the Pert stage, the pupil begins to analyse and argue about what is learned (dialectic), while elements of self-expression enter in the third – Poetic – stage (rhetoric), which coincides with adolescence and which pedagogically speaking culminates in Sayers's vision in the presentation of some topic in which the pupil has taken a particular interest. With this background – to be completed by the age of 16 – Sayers argues that pupils would be as well prepared as their medieval predecessors of the same age to enter university and move on to the Quadrivium (more advanced study of arithmetic, geometry, music, and astronomy, leading on, in the medieval scheme of things, to philosophy and theology).

Tongue-in-cheek as some of Sayers's proposals may be, and irritatingly arch as some will find her style, the spirit of what she has to say has certainly informally enthused many home schoolers too. Formally, 'The Lost Tools of Learning' has become the peda-gogical bible for the Association of Christian Classical Schools (ACCS), on whose website the article can be found. The ACCS was started in 1994 and as of 2023 comprises over 400 schools, educating more than 40,000 pupils. There is considerable overlap in motivation between ACCS and home schooling, as many ACCS schools were started by parents who began by meeting together with the same sort of inspiration as many home schooling parents.

What might well seem strange to the outsider is that Dorothy Sayers's dream of a revived medievalism, whose highest fruits were Chartres Cathedral, the great universities of Oxford, Cambridge, Paris and Bologna, the theology of Thomas and Scotus, the painting of Cimabue and Giotto, and the *Divine Comedy* should go hand in hand with a narrow and intolerant approach to religion and a literalistic approach to Scripture, as well as a formal rejection of 'the follies of ancient paganism', yet this is precisely what would appear to happen in the ACCS, and, one would guess from anecdotal evidence, among many home schoolers as well. The ACCS was set up as a result of the publicity given to a book published in the year of its founding called *Recovering the Lost Tools of Learning*. (21) Its author was Douglas Wilson, who ten years before had set up the Logos School in Moscow, Idaho, supposedly on Sayersian lines, which he describes in the book, and the Logos School remains the flagship institution of the ACCS. Wilson himself has gone on to gain national fame (or notoriety) for his uncompromisingly fierce Old Testamental views on homosexuality and adultery.

The ACCS has powerfully resounding statements of what their Christianity means. Some flavour of what it might come to in detail is suggested by the following statement from Wilson himself: 'It is said among us, "If we continue to maintain that God created the world in six days, we will not be granted academic respectability," To which we must reply, well, who cares? Why should we care that the guardians of the academy believe we are not intellectually respectable? They believe that the moose, the sperm whale and the mongoose are all blood relatives. Why do we want their seal of approval? It is like asking Fidel Castro to comment on the economic viability of Microsoft.' (22) And New St Andrew's College, like the Logos School associated with Wilson, has as part of its 'Statement of Faith' the proposition that 'God created the material universe from nothing in six ordinary days.'

As far as I can make out, the ACCS itself does not explicitly require its members to subscribe to creationism, although they are expected to affirm that 'the Bible is the only inerrant and infallible Word of God' and 'our ultimate and final authoritative rule for faith and practice'. This is not the case with Patrick Henry College, which makes all its trustees, administrators, and faculty attest to the proposition that 'humans and each

kind of organism resulted from God's distinct and supernatural creative intervention and did not result from a natural
evolutionary process; *nor from an evolutionary process God
secretly directed*'(My italics – so even a fairly standard attempt
to reconcile evolution and a literalist Christianity is blocked off).
They also do not like homosexuals and many others: 'any sexual
conduct outside the parameters of marriage is sin.' And in the
College's 'Biblical World-View Applications', the teaching of
six-day creationism alongside Darwinism is explicitly mandated,
even in biology courses, with faculty being selected on the basis
of their 'personal adherence' to six day creationism. They are
expected to expound opposing views, but 'in the end, to teach
creation as both biblically true and as the best fit to observed
data.' The relevance of this to the current discussion is that
Patrick Henry College – which has had considerable academic
and debating success, and also with getting its graduates intern-
ships in Washington DC – was set up in 2000 by the HSDA as
a university which would cater specifically for home schooled
students, and it prides itself on following a classical liberal arts
curriculum. Wheaton College, to take a further example of an
institution favoured by home schoolers, while also being committed to 'Christian liberal arts', requires its faculty and staff to
affirm annually that 'God directly created Adam and Eve, the
historical parents of the entire human race'. Sex outside marriage, with homosexual relations explicitly mentioned as well
as alcohol and tobacco, are off limits for undergraduates, while
the righteous are commended to 'confront' backsliders 'in love'.

A True Conversation

While it is more than possible that liberal education could be
associated with Christianity in some form, while it is certain
that a liberal education here and now will have for its subject

matter many works produced within a Christian context, and while I have already argued that liberal education may well have a religious dimension, it is impossible to reconcile the spirit of liberal education – its spirit of liberal generosity – with the hectoring and dogmatic tone of the institutions we have been looking at. I said earlier that liberal education involves conversations and also that conversations develop. I do not know whether the statements and attitudes we have been considering represent Christianity in a certain moment in the past – I suspect they do not, and that, like contemporary radical Islam, they might be a peculiarly modern phenomenon – but whether they do or not, they are certainly in no sense part of a conversation. They are conversation blockers, thought stoppers, and even if they do have some historical provenance, a genuine conversation cannot be stuck in a moment in the past, nor in a genuine conversation can dogmatic formulae be treated as the last word on anything.

Late in his life, Newman watched with dismay the promulgation of the doctrine of the infallibility of the Pope and the narrow-mindedness of the first Vatican Council. But then, shortly before he had turned his mind to educational topics, he had argued for the idea of the development of doctrine, (23) an idea which both Protestants and Catholics of certain bents might find difficult, but which might well serve as a model for liberal education itself. For a doctrine that develops is one which is essentially open-ended, unfinished, not necessarily fully articulated or even anticipated in its first formulations, receptive to shaping by new (and old) voices, unpredictable, requiring on the part of its adherents a knowledge of and love for its earlier moments and contributions and a sense of being true to their spirit. And as far as the earlier history of a doctrine goes, Newman is happy to talk of its later development as being in the early time 'unperceived', and he also makes considerable play of the way new circumstances and influences will motivate later development.

In his own analysis Newman gives seven 'notes' or criteria by which a genuinely developing doctrine can be distinguished from a doctrinal corruption. These are: 1) that in the development there is 'preservation of its type' (preservation, that is, rather than eradication); 2) that in a genuine development there is continuity of principles (as, when for example a newly discovered work is judged by its stylistic similarity to be the work of some known author); 3) that a genuinely developing doctrine is one which has 'assimilative power' (that is, that it can incorporate new influences and respond to new circumstances, without being engulfed by them); 4) that there is a logical sequence to the development, with one element leading to another; 5) that the doctrine has 'anticipation of its future' (that is, its later developments can be seen as being in a sense implicit in the earlier stages); 6) that a genuine development manifests conservative action on its past (that is that it does not destroy its past meaning); and 7) that the doctrine itself and its developments manifest 'chronic vigour' (that is, they survive over time, and do so vigorously – which is rather in the spirit of Hume's 'test of time'; that is the sense that a genuinely canonical work has the power to appeal in different times and places, and to different audiences, and are even refreshed and renewed in the process, rather than turning out to be an artifact of a temporary vogue or fashion).

The notion that doctrines can and should develop runs counter to the idea of their being a once and for all statement of faith (as we get from ACCS, and would, of course, preclude the Marian doctrines Newman was keen to defend as being Christian), but it is also against the idea that each man is his own Pope. Faith, in Newman's view, is the prerogative of the community of believers over time. Doctrines are not explicitly realized once and for all, but they develop, tried and tested in what, in another context, F.R. Leavis referred to as a continuing 'collaborative-critical dialogue'. As Newman pointed out, the doctrines of the Trinity and the Incarnation had emerged over centuries in just such a way (and, we might add, can hardly be said to have been exhaustively analysed even now). Not surprisingly Newman's doctrine came under inquisitorial fire when it was invoked, quite reasonably, by the unfortunate modernists of the early twentieth century, but that says more about the attitude of the Vatican bureaucracy than it does about Newman's vision. In all these aspects, though, Newman's analysis of the development of doctrine would seem to be a very good model for the spirit of liberal education itself and of the conversations over time and over generations which such an education should foster, which is partly why I have spent a little time looking at what Newman has to say. But if any of this is correct, on either the side of religious doctrine or on the side of the conversation of mankind, it becomes hard to see the attitude to religion of the forms of contemporary conservative Christianity in the USA which we have been looking at as being compatible with what one might hope for in a liberal education.

Reluctantly I am forced to see Patrick Henry College and the rest as at best parasitic simulacra of liberal education, despite their invocation of Dorothy Sayers and their profession of adherence to what they call the Christian-Classical tradition. If one were to be cynical, one might take the inclusion of 'classical' in the 'Christian-classical' school movement as being an attempt to mask what is really going on in those schools, and to gain a form of intellectual respectability for something which is not respectable at all. This would be too cynical of a movement which doubtless involves many sincere and well-meaning teachers and parents, but I wonder what the students (or teachers) in the institutions we have been examining make of the classical part of what they study: Homer? Horace? Ovid? Lucan? Virgil? – all admired by the Christian Dante, to say nothing of Sappho, Plato (of the poetry and the *Symposium*), Anakreon, Catullus, and Propertius, who are all certainly part of the classical tradition, and from whom even (or perhaps especially) Christian fundamentalists might learn more about themselves than perhaps they wanted. It is often remarked that there was something strange about the admixture of muscular Christianity with the Greek and Roman love poets in the English public schools of the nineteenth century. I would prefer to take an Arnoldian view, and say that it was precisely this mixture of Hellenism and Hebraism – and the necessary tension between the two – which was their strength. Maybe this will prove, ultimately, to be the strength of the Christian-classical movement as well, its pupils emerging as somewhat more rounded and open-minded than their founders' statements of faith; at least within the curricula themselves this possibility is implicit, and for that they should be given some credit.

As far as home schooling goes, there is, of course, no reason why it could not accommodate any form of education, including an unadulterated form of liberal education. Maybe in to-day's circumstances and for many people this would be the best that could be done. It could certainly be better than much of what is on offer in many schools, state and independent. Had I not been able to send my children to well-established and venerable schools offering a genuine liberal education, it is an option I might well have considered myself. However, I would just want to underline the conversational aspect of liberal education. In a good school there would be many voices and many teachers. It is highly likely that the conversation in a good school would be broader and richer than what could be provided in even the best home, and there is or should be in a school a sense that one is in an institution with its own history and tradition, extending over more than one generation, which is itself a living link to the voices of the past. And there is the further point that from the point of view of the pupil the aim of a liberal education is his or her mental and moral independence from the state, to be sure, but from the family too, en route to entry into a wider world of culture and sensibility. These aspects of liberal education will be hard to replicate in an education focused on the home, which, to that extent, would be the poorer for it. The shame in to-day's world is that so few children are able to go to schools where neither the spirit nor the letter of liberal education are likely to be found.

1. John Holt, *How Children Fail*, New York: Pitman, 1964, A further complication at this point is that in England we now have another sense of 'free' school, to refer to a school set up within the state sector of education, but by the direct initiative of parents or other providers, outwith the previously standard bureaucratic channels. This, of course, has nothing to do with A.S Neill's ideas, though it may be that for those interested in those ideas this other type of 'free' school might give them the best chance they are likely currently to have of putting their ideas into practice with state funding.

2. ibid, pp 207, 196

3. ibid, p 196

4. The phrase and variants of it occur many times in Matthew Arnold's *Culture and Anarchy* (London: Smith Elder, 1882).

5. John Henry Newman, *The Idea of a University* (1858) (Indiana: University of Notre Dame Press, 1982), esp Discourse V. Matthew Arnold's views on education are trenchantly and wittily expressed in his *Culture and Anarchy* of 1869, referred to in this volume in the edition published by Chelsea House, New York, 1983.

6. See Michael Oakeshott, *The Voice of Liberal Learning*, Timothy Fuller (ed.), New Haven and London: Yale University

Press, 1989, p 73, where Oakeshott discusses Bacon's views on education.

7. See 'The Influence of Darwinism on Philosophy' in John Dewey, *The Influence of Darwinism on Philosophy and Other Essays in Contemporary Thought*, New York: Henry Holt and Co, 1951

8. John Dewey, *School and Society*, Chicago: Chicago University Press, 1956 edition, p 9

9. E. Knight and C. Hall (eds), *Readings in American Educational History*, New York: Appleton, 1951, p 306

10. J. S. Mill, *On Liberty* in his *On Liberty and Other Essays*, ed John Gray, Oxford: Oxford University Press (The World's classics), 1991, pp 117-8.

11. See A. O'Hear and M. Sidwell (eds), *The School of Freedom: A Liberal Education Reader from Plato to the Present Day*, Exeter: Imprint Academic, 2009

12. See Alasdair MacIntyre, *God, Philosophy, Universities*, Lanham, Maryland: Rowman and Littlefield, 2009

13. Martin Stephen, 'The Strange Death of Liberal Education', in O'Hear and Sidwell, pp 1-3.

14. Frank Musgrove, *School and the Social Order*, Chichester and New York: John Wiley, 1979

15. See James Tooley, *The Beautiful Tree: A Personal Journey Into How The World's Poorest People Are Educating Themselves*, New Delhi: Penguin; Washington DC: Cato Institute, 2009.

16. Aristotle, *Politics*, trans. T.A. Sinclair, London: Penguin Books, 1981, 1137a11-32.

17. Plato, *Republic*, trans. R. Waterfield, Oxford: Oxford University Press (The World's Classics), 1998, 493a. It is here, by the way, that Plato speaks of the democratic state as being like a great beast.

18. J. van Galen and M. Pitman (eds), *Home Schooling: Political, Historical and Pedagogical Perspectives*, Northwood, New Jersey: Ablex Publishing Corp, 1991. The quotation is from p 97.

19. John Holt, *Teach Your Own: a Hopeful Path for Education*, New York: Delacorte Press, 1982

20. Dorothy L. Sayers, *The Lost Tools of Learning and the Mind of the Maker*, Garsington: Benediction Classics, 2010.

21. Douglas Wilson, *Recovering the Lost Tools of Learning: An Approach to Distinctively Christian Education*, Wheaton, Ill: Crossway Books, 1991.

22. Douglas Wilson, 'Sanctified Apathy', *Tabletalk Magazine*, Nov 2002, pp 60-1. The various statements of faith from the ACCS, St Andrew's College, Wheaton College and Patrick Henry College were found on the websites of the institutions concerned in 2010. They were all still there in March 2023.

23. John Henry Newman, *An Essay on the Development of Christian Doctrine*, 1845, revised 1878, (Indiana: University of Notre Dame Press, 1989).

Chapter 2

CLASSICS AND NOT HOG-WASH

> 'To have masters in village
> schools/ To teach 'em classics
> and not hog-wash'
> (Ezra Pound, Cantos, XCIX)

A number of schools in the USA, and now to a degree in
England, are following a curricular programme known as
'Core Knowledge'. The original Core Knowledge programme
(which is not to be confused with President Obama's plans for
a nation-wide set of school standards for the USA) grew out
of the notion of 'cultural literacy'. This was a term coined by
the literary critic E.D. Hirsch in the 1980s, when he realised
that what we want from literacy in young people is not just the
ability mechanically to decode written texts, though we do, of
course, want that. (1) To understand those texts fully, though,
and to be fully literate, they also need a wealth of background
cultural knowledge, which is presupposed in so much of what
we read. Some children, merely by being brought up in literate
households, will acquire much of this background knowledge
informally, but many will not.

Those who are not culturally literate will be at a constant
disadvantage educationally and in other respects as a result.
Because of the barriers resulting from their illiteracy, they will
be unwilling and unable to make progress educationally. From
his observations of undergraduates and other young people,
Hirsch realised that far too many young Americans were, in his

terms, culturally illiterate. The Core Knowledge curriculum is an attempt by Hirsch and his colleagues in the Core Knowledge Foundation to specify the things a culturally literate young person might reasonably be expected to know at a given age – things which all too often were not being taught in the schools to which they went.

In introducing the detailed subject handbooks produced by the Core Knowledge Foundation, Hirsch warns us to be sceptical about curricular documents which do not focus on content, but which highlight such aims as 'analysing patterns and data', 'working cooperatively in groups', 'thinking critically', and 'learning to learn'. These documents are typically, but not exclusively, produced by governments and bureaucracies, national, international, and local, and the education 'experts', usually in university faculties of education, which the official bodies tend to draw on. To take a typical example, in April 2013 a group of science educators, representing the (US) National Research Council, the National Science Teachers' Association and the American Association for the Advancement of Science recommended that fewer topics should be taught in school, with less rote learning and more critical thinking. And even kindergarten pupils will have to 'construct an argument supported by evidence to show how plants and animals (including humans) can change the environment to meet their needs.'

When it comes to content, in the type of education Hirsch is criticising, in which what he calls core knowledge is either absent or diminished, the emphasis will be on often disconnected and seemingly randomly chosen topics (dinosaurs, the Aztecs, African drumming, gamelan music, native American art, and a decontextualised approach to the European dictators all seem particular favourites for some reason).

There *will* be literature, but the stress will be on the modern, the undemanding, the fashionable, the demotic, the politically slanted, with interpretations often driven by feminist and post-colonial perspectives. In treatments of the arts and music there will be a promiscuous mixing of genres, media, and ambition, creating the impression that there are no judgements of quality to be made in aesthetic matters or any significant tradition to be passed on beyond what young people are already saturated with in the world of pop and rap. History will be based on discon-nected topics, often reflecting current ideological preconcep-tions in both manner and selection, no doubt nowadays heavily influenced by demands to 'decolonise' the subject as opposed to offering a straightforward narrative approach to the history of one's own country and home, whether ancestral or adopted. In science, environmental and political concerns, often anti-business and almost inevitably superficially treated, will edge out some of the harder elements of basic science (which, for those interested, will now have to be introduced in university courses). Religion, to the extent that it features at all, will be short on doctrine and dogma (particularly Christian dogma), and long on low-level comparisons of religious buildings and rituals, and discussions of values, undertaken in a relativistic spirit (so-called values clarification).

What will not be found, as we saw in Chapter 1, will be the language and literature of ancient Greece and Rome, the basis of Western culture for two millennia. Nor indeed will there be serious attention to any reasonable selection of pre-20th century literature, English or otherwise (modern languages being almost entirely devoted to learning the language in question by direct methods, without benefit of grammatical instruction). Nor will there be a disinterested or historically continuous immer-sion in the masterpieces of Western art and music. Systematic approaches to science and physical geography will be eroded in favour of modish political and ethical discussions, as will any attempt at a steady narrative history of one's country.

Anyone familiar with contemporary schooling, or indeed the university academy, will recognise the trends I am referring to, and could no doubt multiply examples of the sort of thing I have in mind, the most empty of which is perhaps a (major) US university which has prescribed 'Diversity' as one of four 'fields of enquiry' for its undergraduates.

Against the tendencies I am describing, one could begin by repeating two points made by Hirsch himself: first, that they are fundamentally undemocratic and unfair, and second, that they erode any sense of a common cultural or political inheritance among pupils who, whatever their background or ethnicity, are all living in the same country. These approaches are unfair and undemocratic because they will inevitably favour, if only by default, those pupils whose parents can supply either at home or in independent schools the culture, knowledge, and experiences which will be lacking in the schools dominated by the approaches I am describing (often the state schools the majority of the population have to attend). And far from solving problems arising from cultural and ethnic diversity, the bitty and fragmented problem-solving approach, for all its talk of critical thinking, will make their solution virtually impossible by failing to provide the basis for a common understanding of who and where we are, and how we might live together (diversity within a fundamental unity). It will in fact reinforce the very divisions and divisiveness in society which it is meant to combat by continually harping on the existence, or supposed existence, of discrete and conflicting ethnic groups living within what is supposed to be a common culture in a genuinely inclusive society, which transcends differences of heritage and background.

Because they illustrate the language and ideology which informs the sort of curricular thinking I am criticising, as well as the language typically to be found in such documents, I will now turn to some official definitions of the point of education from recent governments in the four jurisdictions in the United Kingdom (that is, England, Scotland, Wales, and Ulster [or Northern Ireland]).

In 2011 the Scottish Executive published its 'Curriculum for Excellence', outlining a number of 'capacities' which schooling was supposed to produce. These included young people who were open to new thinking, who could think creatively and independently, who could learn independently and as part of a group, and who could apply critical thinking in new contexts. There was nothing in this statement of capacities about the *content* or substance of the curriculum which was supposed to produce these results, even in broad, general terms. There were, though, the by now standard references to healthy lifestyles and emotional well-being, as well as a requirement for young people to develop 'secure values and beliefs', secure, note, not correct. A little earlier, in 2000, the Scottish Executive had also insisted that in schooling due regard be taken to the views of young people in the taking of decisions which affect them. (Ironically, of course, as anyone who has ever been involved in canvassing pupil opinion will know, what pupils think will differ from one year to the next; further, decisions based on the opinions of this year's students will actually impact more on future cohorts of pupils, who will have actually had no role in making these decisions).

A very similar approach to the Scottish was taken in Ulster, with its 'Curriculum Aims and Objectives' from 2007. There are also mentions of the inculcation of awareness of global and local imbalances in the world around us, as well as an unspecified understanding of *some* pupils' own and others' cultural understanding. Why some, one wonders, which others, and what aspects of cultural understanding?

In England, from the year 2000 for a decade or more the National Curriculum was supposed to 'provide opportunities for all pupils to learn and achieve'. Those who thought that 'learn' and 'achieve' were transitive verbs will have learned something here, but not, I think, much else, and this in a document which was supposed to answer concerns about lack of clarity in this area. Of course, everything hangs on *what* pupils are supposed to learn and achieve. But we are given no help here with the 2004 governmental initiative known tendentiously as Every Child Matters: 'Be healthy. Stay safe. Enjoy and achieve. Make a positive contribution. Achieve economic well-being.' It will be noted that acquiring worthwhile knowledge or becoming acquainted with their cultural inheritance are not among five things which matter to children in their development.

In its statement of curricular aims from 2009, the Qualifications and Curriculum Development Authority, as the English curriculum quango was then known, envisaged the results of schooling producing young people who are motivated to 'achieve the best they can', who are 'successful learners who enjoy learning, make progress and achieve', who 'have enquiring minds and think for themselves', who 'know about big ideas and events that shape our world', who appreciate the benefits of diversity (but not the disbenefits, for all the talk of critical thinking and thinking for themselves), and who are ready to 'change things for the better'. Why, one wonders, do we need a Curriculum *Development* Authority anyway, the very notion of curricular development being questionable, redolent of instruments of social engineering? In fact, and rather against trends elsewhere in Britain and indeed in agencies such as UNESCO, professing to speak on behalf of the whole world, the QCDA has now been abolished and the curriculum for England has been re-written under a secretary of state for education close in mind and spirit to E.D. Hirsch, a point to which I shall return. (2)

This is not the case in Wales, which has managed to outdo even the unlamented QCDA in vapidity. The Welsh Assembly, in its 2006 document 'The Learning Country 2: Delivering the Promise', has as its first of seven educational aims the emergence of young people who have 'a flying start in life', as well as ensuring (!) that all children in Wales 'have a safe home and a community which supports physical and emotional well-being', with their 'race and cultural identity recognised'. And to get children in Wales off the ground, so to speak, its school curriculum ('for the 21st century') 'focuses on the learner' (learner, note, not pupil), and supports government policy on Europe and the World, on equal opportunities, on food and fitness, on sustainable development and global citizenship, and on entrepreneurship, while offering what the officials themselves call 'reduced' subject content and an increased focus on skills.

Where is teaching in any of these official approaches? Where is there any sense that *before* one can think, enquire, work independently, and fly off into a lifetime of achievement and economic well-being there are things which one simply has to learn and learn systematically (because otherwise the chances are one won't)? Where is there any suggestion that the type of thinking involved in different fields is quite different, and may require quite different approaches (for example, in science and maths it is abstract, generalising and reductive, whereas in history and literature the detail and feel of each particular word and moment is all important)?

Where is there any acknowledgement that there are duties owed to the past, that we as teachers have a vocation to reveal to the young where they have come from? If we do not pass on what has gone before us, our cultural and spiritual amnesia will become ever more desolate, and we as a people ever more open to manipulation by oligarchs and smiling shucksters, only too able to seduce us with dissembling simplicities, the hog-wash of which Pound speaks in my epigraph (That Pound himself was seduced by one such, as he later came painfully to admit, serves only to underline the gravity of our situation, dominated as it is by demotic politics and media, to whose blandishments the world of education has proved itself by no means immune to).

Above all, what the legislators from the four jurisdictions failed to recognise is that there is a considerable body of knowledge and experience worth entering for its own sake, and quite independently of any political, economic, or social benefits. As for curriculum 'developments' being quite explicitly and shamelessly used to support or promote government policies, this was precisely what J.S. Mill warned against in '*On Liberty*', Chapter 5, as we have already seen in Chapter 1: a 'mere contrivance,' as Mill put it, for moulding people to be exactly like one another. They will inevitably become part of that soft despotism de Tocqueville had seen as characteristic of advanced democracy, the immense tutelary power which in its ambition to care for everyone, and hence to regulate every detail of life and activity, reduces populations to a state of perpetual infantilism from cradle to grave. (3)

Mill's warning about a despotism over the body might have seemed exaggerated in 1859 when he uttered it. But in Britain at least hardly a day passes without some celebrity cook being invited to pronounce on what can or can't be eaten in state schools, while edicts emanate continually from government departments on matters such as childhood obesity and teenage pregnancy (which never seem to prevent either). And if I had been a parent in Wales, I would have objected strenuously to my children being indoctrinated with whatever the Welsh Assembly thought about Europe (which is not the Europe of Charlemagne and St Louis, but the EU), equal opportunities, and the rest; but if I could not have paid for a private school or moved to England there would have been be nothing I could do about it. A despotism indeed, no better for being 'democratic' and not even noticed by the majority of the population, so inured are we to state interference in and control of education, as of so many aspects of our lives.

As for emotional well-being being a proper aim of schooling (particularly when interpreted as 'happiness'), as Mill also taught, being a fulfilled human being, a human being in a certain sense maximising his potential, may actually become an unhappier human being: 'It is better to be a human being dissatisfied than a pig satisfied; better to be Socrates dissatisfied than a fool satisfied.' (4) Mill was, of course, responding to Jeremy Bentham's notorious claim that, prejudice apart, pushpin is as valuable as music or poetry. Part of Mill's point was that intellectual endeavour, as represented by Socrates, may lead to dissatisfaction precisely because of the unfulfilled and possibly unfulfillable expectations it engenders. Was any great writer or composer ever satisfied that he or she had done what he or she had hoped, that there was nothing more that had to be done? We have to recognise the fact that the educated mind might well be a mind prone to unhappiness at various levels, precisely because of the education itself stoking idealistic but possibly fruitless ambition, but it might still be worthwhile, even so. Indeed (again Mill's point), to leave a mind capable of education uneducated, stuck in an atmosphere of bovine or porcine pleasures and contentments, might be far more cruel than opening that mind to educated discontents.

In calling Bentham's advocacy of pushpin notorious, we have, though, to remind ourselves that as a society we treat as serious artists rappers, pop singers, graffitists, pornographers, and so-called conceptual artists such as Tracey Emin and Gilbert and George; a recent Chairman of the Arts Council for England was the man responsible for the execrable *Big Brother* on television. He was in fact a pupil of Dulwich College and a Cambridge graduate, so no easy reassurance there, but rather an example of what might be called the oligarchic condescension of our rulers.

It will also guarantee that he will be in no position to make, promote, or defend the judgements of value which inspired the Arts Council, indeed what it was *for*, when it was set up in the 1940s by Maynard Keynes and Kenneth Clark. The slogan of that time, 'the best for the most', represented a noble ideal, to which the education of the time also aspired (in those days even at Dulwich and Cambridge), and aspired without invoking notions of happiness or emotional well-being.

One may, of course, think that educational regimes in the 1940s and 1950s were too harsh, and argue against the type of punishment and discipline which was common in the schools of the time. Indeed, in the world of 'Every Child Matters', obsessed with security, safety and so-called child protection against any and every possible danger, real or imaginary, it sometimes seems, and often against the child's own family, anything to do with physical or mental challenge, harshness, struggle, or self-overcoming is likely to be a source of suspicion and rejection, inviting the attentions of 'child protection' officers and even the police. (Contrast the attitude of the Spartan mother who ordered her son, on his returning alive from a Spartan defeat, to leave her at once and expunge the dishonour. Other attitudes to childhood, other sensibilities than our own, in which children are at once cosseted *and* sexualised, are possible, and are not always obviously demonic. Indeed, even in terms of ultimate happiness and satisfaction, there could be something to be said for turning one's attention away from 'how *I* feel' to things of value outside myself).

But what one is not at liberty to do, at least not if one wants to retain any intellectual integrity, is to assert the twenty-first century sentimentalism that children cannot learn if they are not happy. They could, they can, and in many parts of the world, they still do. No one could seriously maintain that the music and ballet schools of Eastern Europe of recent memory (and for all I know, even now) were places of ease, fostering or even interested in the emotional well-being of those being taught in them, but learning of a very high order undoubtedly took place, higher than in most comparable institutions in the West, indeed. One could argue that the personal costs were too high, which might be reasonable, but what would not be reasonable would be to assert that learning had not been happening (and similar points could be made about the grammar schools and gymnasia of nineteenth century England and Germany). So we may simply have to confront the possibility that we, as a culture, are ready to trade a certain level of excellence off against a hoped-for emotional well-being.

On the current shibboleth of laying on even young children the burden of being independent learners and critical thinkers, I would draw attention to what Ruskin had to say in his lecture on 'The Future of England' from 1869: 'The people are crying out for you to command, and you stand there at pause, and are silent... "Govern us", they cry, with one heart, though many minds... You alone can feed them and clothe, and bring into their right minds, for you only can govern... that is to say, you only can educate them.' (5) Whatever we (or Ruskin) might hope from our rulers, a teacher is not, or should not be, one who stands there at pause and is silent. A teacher should be one who (like Ruskin) has much value to impart, who has a passion for imparting it, and the belief and confidence to do so.

But, of course, there are also the many minds before the teacher, the great crux on which so many fail, and so many are broken. For the best but most cruelly deceived of motives, too many teachers are in the 'deep mess' that Ursula Brangwen was in D.H. Lawrence's *The Rainbow*, when she (like Lawrence himself) tried her hand at teaching. 'Children will never naturally acquiesce to sitting in a class and submitting to knowledge. *They must be compelled by a stronger, wiser will*. Against which they must always strive to revolt. So that the first great effort of every teacher must be to bring the will of the children into accordance with his own will. And this he can only do by an abnegation of his personal self, and an application of a system of laws, for the purpose of achieving a certain calculable result, the imparting of certain knowledge. Whereas Ursula thought that she was going to be the first wise teacher by making the whole business personal...' (6) And, while we are turning to Lawrence, there is also Lawrence's Jimmy Shepherd: 'We have assumed that we could educate Jimmy Shepherd and make him a Shelley or an Isaac Newton. At the very least we were sure we could make him a highly intelligent being. And we're just beginning to find our mistake. We can't make a highly intelligent being out of Jimmy Shepherd. Why should we, if the Lord had created him only moderately intelligent? Why do we always want to go one better than the Creator?' (7)

Because of our sentimental attitude to children and to ourselves, we don't like all this talk of stronger, wiser wills and knowledge and results. Nor do we like to admit that there are children who cannot achieve much or even anything in the academic line, but however it is dressed up, this is the underlying reality of the classroom. This does not mean being brutal, but it does mean recognising, genuinely recognising, differences between pupils, and not in a misguided spirit of egalitarianism trying to give all the same, best, worst, and middle, which will not help either the best or the worst, and will probably not do much for the middle either. Too much talk of 'differentiation', to use the current jargon word, is actually a way of avoiding serious attempts to cater for real and ineradicable differences between pupils. The upshot of vainly trying to educate pupils beyond their real abilities is simply to turn out 'a lot of half-informed youth who despise the whole business of understanding and wisdom', as Lawrence predicted in the writing of Jimmy

Shepherd. The Welsh Assembly may believe it can 'ensure' safe homes and communities for all the children in the Principality, but even it cannot do what God has ordained cannot be done. If we are truly concerned about education rather than the pursuit of a humanly destructive egalitarian utopianism, we must work out forms of schooling suitable for the pupils before us.

We should recognise equal legal and political rights, and we should extend and challenge all pupils, to be sure, but we should not, in deference to a false notion of equality, continually humiliate the unacademic, the Jimmy Shepherds who do (still) exist and in significant numbers, (8) by giving them material that simply rams home their limitations in the theoretic and abstract spheres. Rather, we should really recognise difference (as we are constantly urged to do by progressive educationalists, for whom 'differentiation' is currently an obsession) and develop forms of education for the non-academic which respond to their often considerable potential for activities of a practical nature. Rather than paying lip-service to the indefensible notion of an equal capacity to benefit from academic education, we should set about devising serious practical courses, involving apprenticeships and the like, for the less or non-academic, certainly for those in their early and mid-teenage years. The more academic should then be released into the challenge of serious academic study.

We must also recognise, as Aristotle did long ago, that in matters of behaviour generally, and in matters of learning more specifically, 'it makes no small difference, then, whether we form habits of one kind or another from our very youth, it makes a very great difference, or rather all the difference.' (9) Further, in human development, reasoning is not the first capacity we acquire: 'Just as the body comes into existence earlier than the soul, so also the unreasoning is prior to that which possesses reason... while passion and will and desire are to be found in children even right from birth, reasoning and intelligence come into their possession as they grow older. Therefore care of the body must begin before care of the soul, then the training of the appetitive element.' (10) All parents and teachers of young children will recognise the need for what Aristotle calls the training of the appetitive element, the directing of the will and desire into habits of virtue. For, unless we have some inclination towards virtue, reasoning on its own will not make us moral (which is part of what we hope from a good education). So, as we will argue further in Chapter 4, a lot of education is, or should be, to do with the development of a virtuous character, which, because it is not purely natural, is not something which will develop without the habituation which comes from training, habit and perception. *Pace* the Scottish Executive, secure values and beliefs are not enough; they have to be correct values and true beliefs, rooted in virtuous dispositions.

If Aristotle is right that we cannot reason well about morality without having virtuous dispositions, then the sort of critical thinking which might be desirable must follow on from this training of the appetitive element, as he puts it, or training of character, as we might put it. And we could add to that, that experience too is part of the wisdom required in genuinely critical thinking, and one reason that I am cautious about the value of 'independent' reasoning at too young an age. It is rarely actually independent, and can all too often degenerate into jejune logic-chopping, subsiding into a simplistic consequentialism unless informed by some relevant knowledge and experience, enabling us to distinguish between the long-term results we might desire and the likelihood of them actually occurring as a matter of practical policy. As Aristotle puts it, 'we ought to attend to the undemonstrated sayings and opinions of experienced and older people or of people of practical wisdom not less than to demonstrations; for because experience has given them an eye, they see aright.' (11) The point here is that experience, and experience alone, gives us the basis we need to judge sensibly in actual, complicated situations, situations where there is no clear-cut application of first principles, but rather a question of weighing and assessing competing factors and considerations, and often in the process modifying our original ends to boot.

I have criticised the curricular documents we have been examining for the absence in them of any sense that there might be things worth learning for their own sake. Part of the burden of my argument is that the teacher has his or her authority because he or she knows things which the pupils do not, and that these things are important for pupils to become acquainted with, either because they are necessary means to desirable ends or because they are valuable in themselves. I will say little on the first element (means to other ends), beyond a general caution in this area. Because of the universal and compulsory nature of schooling, a very good case would have to be made out for including a utilitarian item on the curriculum. Is this x essential for future well-being? Is it going to be available only in school? Is it best imparted in school? So basic literacy and numeracy would qualify here, but we should be very sceptical of lobbyists who are constantly urging that their speciality be on the curriculum (e.g. cooking, personal finance, local politics, computing technology). These things are often a) a matter of fashion or in other ways transient, b) easily and often better picked up elsewhere, and c) may not be really necessary anyway. By contrast, we cannot emphasise too often that unless pupils are introduced to the best that has been thought and known in key areas in their formal schooling, they will never meet them, to their considerable loss.

So we turn to things valuable in themselves, and the learning of which should (could) be itself an advancement in life, and not a means to some further advancement (even if it is).

In a way we are back with Socrates and the fool, and what is particularly difficult here is that the uneducated person, being uneducated and therefore without the knowledge a Socrates has, is in no position to make a sensible choice as to the value of a Socratic existence. Mill: 'And if the fool or the pig is of a different opinion, it is because they only know their own side of the question.' (12) So there is something amiss with the thought of the Scottish Executive that in these matters the views of pupils should be taken into account. The burden and the faith rests with the teacher; so is it an unreasonable faith? Are we dealing here with mere prejudice, as Bentham (and anyone who repudiates judgements of value in this area) would have it?

What this question comes down to is whether the things of which education and, by extension, culture deal with are important and worthwhile, which is partly why, in distinction from our legislative documents, it is as well to be somewhat specific about the putative content of any liberal curriculum (liberal=knowledge which is *liberating* in a human sense, knowledge which is worth having for its own sake). It would certainly, as Newman proposed in the 1852 addresses now known as *The Idea of a University*, (13) involve studying what is worth studying for its own sake; and it would also have as a goal producing in pupils the ability to see the different elements of knowledge and culture as they stand in relation to each other, and as they each, in their own way, contribute to the whole of human thought and experience. More specifically, again following Newman in essence, but drawing on the categorisation proposed by Kant, we could say that the substance of a liberal education deals with what concerns the world, the soul and God (taking the soul to cover humanity in its history and in its attempts to come to terms with its condition, and God to involve reflecting on ultimate realities). Put in this way, it would probably be hard to find anyone who might not find something valuable, something worthwhile in these studies. After all, we are not just machines for survival and reproduction, though if we were, coming to this conclusion would be part of what emerged from the study of the world, the soul and God. It would thus be one of the results of a liberal study (though, in my view, an unfortunate result, because if all our activity is simply geared to promoting survival and reproduction this would undermine the claims of any of our beliefs, including our belief in the theory of evolution, to be *true* as opposed to merely survival-promoting).

What is involved in the traditional liberal curriculum is what is or hopes to be (in Matthew Arnold's phrase) the best that has been thought and known (or said) on these matters, and it is here particularly that judgements will tend to be internal to the particular form of knowledge or experience. For example, no one as a ten or even a sixteen year old pupil outside Italy, or indeed as anyone who had not read and given serious attention to the *Divine Comedy,* could have any real sense of the value of the poetry of Dante. Here, as in science, as in maths, as in history, as in music, I will have, to a greater or lesser extent to rely on the judgements of those who have gone before me, who have studied these things and made themselves expert in them, and who have seen these things surviving the test of time: that is that they are not merely the taste or expertise of one generation or culture, but have appealed and appealed deeply to different people in different times and places. There is, of course, room for movement and adjustment in all of this, and in the case of science, a degree of progressive increments of knowledge and certainty and displacement of failed ideas. But, for anyone not attracted to a modish relativism, works such as those of Homer, Virgil, Shakespeare, Milton, Goethe, Pushkin, Racine, Proust, and so on in literature, and similar lists from other fields are going to remain central and touchstones of what can and has been done. It was, I think, F.H. Bradley who opined that the man to whom ring a' ring a' roses is as good as a Shakespeare sonnet is 'either a fool or an advanced thinker.' Unfortunately for far too many of our children, the world of education, particularly in so called schools of education, but also in university literature departments, contains within it large numbers of noisily advanced thinkers.

There is nothing in fact very new in this. As Jonathan Rose reports (14), even in the 1960s the social historian Richard Hoggart was inveighing against what he called 'the Beatles are in their own way as good as Beethoven nonsense', and despairing at hearing an Oxbridge academic proclaiming that 'lavatorial graffiti are not to be distinguished in any qualitative way from the drawings of Rembrandt' and a BBC executive declaring that 'there is no longer art. There is only culture – of all kinds.' This is significant, poignant even, because Hoggart had himself been a pioneer of the study of popular culture which had led to the very erosion of judgement he is here deploring. That this abandonment of discrimination has only grown in influence and significance in the subsequent half century or so does not make it any the less deplorable, or any the less of a betrayal of generations of children, particularly of children from backgrounds of illiteracy, poverty, and deprivation, where school is probably going to be the only place where they might be able to receive any sort of cultural or intellectual stimulation.

Over and above coining the phrase 'the best that has been thought and known', Matthew Arnold said this: 'Plenty of people will try to give the masses, as they call them, an intellectual food prepared and adapted in the way they think proper for the actual condition of the masses. The ordinary popular literature (read: television, pop music, computer games) is an example of this way of working on the masses... but culture works differently. It does not try to teach down to the level of inferior classes... (it seeks) to make the best that has been thought and known in the world current everywhere, to make all men live in an atmosphere of sweetness and light, where they may use ideas, as it sees them itself, freely – nourished, and not bound by them.' (15)

Personally I would resile from the unfortunate phrase 'sweetness and light': I do not find sweetness in the *Iliad* or the *Oresteia* – light maybe, but a steady, unwavering light, illuminating the darkness of our condition. Moreover, I doubt very much that 'sweetness and light', however generously construed, will on their own be enough to counter the effects of original sin, to which we are all continuously prone and whose effects are dramatically and unpityingly revealed in Homer and Aeschylus. But these reservations aside, I find Arnold's vision of the teacher (for that is what it is) both uplifting and (in the true sense) challenging. It is the possession of such a vision in his or her chosen subject, together with the craft and strength to transmit it to those unacquainted with what it consists in (and who in all probability will not otherwise become acquainted) which makes a good teacher.

In England in 2012 some new governmental standards for teachers were introduced, following drafting from a small committee, of which I was a member. (16) Against the prevailing governmental and bureaucratic trends, in them there is a vision of the teacher not too far distant from Arnold's. There is a strong focus on the practice of teaching itself, on subject knowledge and understanding, on love of learning and engagement with one's subject, on scholarship and on intellectual curiosity, on stretching pupils of all backgrounds, and also on rules for behaviour and the appropriate exercise of authority, which is not just about behaviour, narrowly conceived, but which is about one's authority as a teacher, but also – in the spirit of liberal education – about not exploiting vulnerabilities of pupils thorough misuse of that authority. Perhaps more important, and in line with Hirsch's strictures, there are significant omissions (significant, that is, in to-day's world of education). There are no such creatures as 'learners' (though plenty of teachers and pupils), there is no talk of independent or personalised learning, no talk of pupils discovering things themselves, nor of learning styles or multiple intelligences, nor is there obeisance to the great idol of group work or mention of ICT. Teachers are expected to have skills of their own, but these are not to include equipping pupils with skills, as opposed to developing and extending the knowledge and understanding of pupils in the subjects they will study (study, note, not 'research').

What these subjects will be, and how delineated, was outlined for England in a new national curriculum framework in 2013, under the direction of Michael Gove, who was Secretary of State for Education at the time, and determined to move towards a knowledge based approach in the spirit of Hirsch (Despite my Millian strictures earlier about a general state education, given that the political reality is that we do have a national curriculum, and will almost certainly continue to have one in some form or other, it is crucial that such a curriculum should reflect the best that has been thought and known, rather than be an instrument of social and economic engineering, as it all too often is and even in England could all too easily be again). As already mentioned, this new curriculum for England is to an extent in the spirit of Hirsch's Core Knowledge initiative, with a sense of 'the best that has been thought and known' strongly in the background, though with little detail as to what is to count as 'high-quality works' or 'seminal' literature or the 'greatest artists, architects and designers in history' or 'great' musicians and composers. There is considerably more detail in the areas of science and mathematics and in the original draft was in history, at the core of which was a sequential narrative account of the history of Britain and the British Isles (though not omitting the American Revolution!). It is this largely schematic attempt to give British children some sense of their identity and history which prompted Sir Richard Evans, the then Regius Professor of History at Cambridge, not to praise the curriculum, as one might have expected, but to dismiss it. According to Evans, it focused on the rote learning of facts, to form a celebratory national narrative, amounting to 'a preparation for Mastermind or a pub quiz', rather than an education. (17) One might reply that it was precisely the abandonment of any attempt in school history teaching to give an overview of British history that led to the subject becoming, for the ordinary reader anyway, dominated by vastly popular books, written in the main by non-academics, no doubt to the chagrin of the academics. This aside, though, I could not myself see any demand for rote learning or indeed of mention of dates in the new history curriculum (maybe there should actually have been something more in these respects than the rather vague references there are to 'essential chronology'!).

Nor do I accept the view of Simon Schama, expressed in a speech at the Hay Literary Festival, that this 'insulting and offensive' curriculum was a 'ridiculous shopping list' simply or mainly about national self-congratulation. (18) The narrative history of these isles could and perhaps should be as much a source of weeping and despair at human cruelty and stupidity as of self-congratulation – the Norman conquest, the peasants revolt, Ireland over the centuries, religious strife in the Tudor period, the slave trade, aspects of imperialism, Peterloo, the Tolpuddle martyrs and chartism, nineteenth century industrialisation, the Indian mutiny, the Boer War, the 1914-8 War. All these things were indeed mentioned in the original 2013 curriculum, as things about which pupils should be taught, and of course many of the other things stipulated can or even should be treated dispassionately, even as having negative aspects. Thus, for example, Clive of India is mentioned as a figure to be discussed, which seems particularly to have rankled Sir Richard for being potentially offensive to pupils of Indian descent. To them no hero he – but not to many even in his time, for whom he was no hero either. He was actually attacked in Parliament and by Dr Johnson for his adventures in India, and died in suspicious circumstances, which would surely have been mentioned in any relevant history lesson.

But alongside the negative aspects of our British history, there should also be a degree of justified self-congratulation in certain respects, which possibly Professor Schama would himself admit, such as the development of the rule of law, religious toleration, democracy and liberal values, Churchill and the Second World War, and our peerless literary heritage, to name only some of the most obvious. A degree of affection for one's country, and pride in its achievements, is surely not to be disparaged. Indeed it is one of the things which binds a people together, even if, as George Orwell mentioned more than once, it is something which left-wing intellectuals seem determined to stamp out and to sneer at on every possible occasion. (19)

Regrettably, on history Michael Gove gave way to the critics, which itself says something about the way democratic processes of lobbying and 'consultation' worked against a Secretary of State for Education attempting to row back against pedagogical orthodoxy. In the final statutory version of the history curriculum, most of the names of the actual historical figures originally mentioned were relegated to the non-statutory part. Let us hope that those teaching the curriculum do follow the hint they are given by this *volte face* and play down any attempt to equip young people with a knowledge of the main events and people in the history of their own country.

But Sir Richard Evans and Professor Schama were not the only critics of the 2013 curriculum, and history was not the only source of academic discontent. The whole curriculum and its underlying direction are deeply misguided in the opinion of 100 'leading' academics in education, all working in publicly funded universities (including Oxford, Cambridge, and London), who sent a letter on the subject to the now defunct *Independent* newspaper. According to the 100, 'this mountain of data will not develop children's abilities to think, including problem-solving, critical understanding and creativity... Little account is taken of children's potential, interests and capacities, or that young children need to relate abstract ideas to their experience, lives and activity', in place of which there are what the letter describes as 'endless lists' of spellings, facts and rules. (20)

In terms of numbers anyway, the 100 academics of *The Independent* were outdone by a group of 200, mainly academics, but including writers like the Poet Laureate and the so-called Children's Laureate of the time, who wrote to *The Times* on October 1st, expressing their 'grave concern' about recent reforms of the curriculum and education in England. They too spoke of the 'incessant' testing to which children in England were now (apparently) to be subjected, and the competitiveness and sense of failure this testing engenders in the vast majority of children. In the view of the Laureates and their associates, 'childhood is too important to be squandered or exploited'. Children are 'natural learners who deserve an abundance of new experience', the 'straightjacket' the government is imposing on them is destroying 'the educational richness' that should be their 'birthright'. Narrowing the range of 'learning experiences', as the government is doing, 'will lead to 'damaging consequences for children's mental health and for the quality of childhood itself.'

The spirit of Rousseau clearly continues to walk in the columns of *The Times* (whether the signatories of the letter appreciated this or not). But leaving the sentimentality, hyperbole, and invective aside, what the government actually demanded was a simple test of reading at the age of 6, tests of English and maths and 7 and 11, with science added at 11, and public exams at the ages of 16 and 18. Far from this being a diet of 'incessant' testing, the government is actually abolishing the otiose 17 year old public exam, and cutting down on coursework in exams. And how can a curriculum beefing up English and Maths, and going some tentative way in the direction of Hirsch's Core Knowledge, amount to narrowing the range of learning experiences?

These two letters are symbolically useful in that they exemplifies perfectly the kind of thinking – and writing – Hirsch was warning us against, and also the weight and type of opinion would-be reformers will inevitably have to confront Not surprisingly the second letter ends by calling for arresting change and seeking a 'consensus' on education (code for maintaining the status quo). We can note both letters hyperbole (*mountain* of data, *endless* lists, *incessant* testing) and flailing invective (singling out spellings, facts, and rules for special opprobrium, as if these were in some way obviously objectionable and in tension with 'thinking', and talking about a little bit of rigour and content in education 'damaging children's mental health').

But my objection to the letters go far deeper. England has recently gone above the average on international comparisons among developed countries for standards in language, maths, and science, on a level with Denmark, Australia, Japan, and the US in the 2018 PISA rankings for the OECD, but still well below Singapore, China, and Estonia. But while this is gratifying, and says something about the work done in England since the change of government in 2010, once one gets beyond the basics to what is done in more cultural areas such as literature, history, foreign literature and the like the situation is not so good, due in part to the erosion of content and ambition since the days of the O level, which was abolished in the 1980s. Then 15 and 16 year old pupils were regularly doing the sort of work now required at A level, as any inspection of O level papers from that era will confirm, and as I remember from my own O levels in Latin, Greek, and History.

Even on basic skills, employers still regularly complain that too many of the poorest children, educated under the dispensation our Laureates do not want to change, fail to achieve the benchmark educational qualifications at the age of 16 (whereas practically everyone educated in fee-paying schools does). For many children, including those (some of whom I know) who live in circumstances of violence, crime, poverty, and neglect, far from education needing to relate to their circumstances, as our experts would have it, a good school can be an oasis of civilization. It can be this precisely because it is taking pupils away from the circumstances of their lives, which they leave behind at the school gate, into a different and a better, a more peaceful and a more orderly world. But school as an oasis of sorts is not the case only for pupils coming from difficult or deprived circumstances. For most, if not all, pupils entering into the worlds of science, mathematics, history, classical music, and great art and literature – entering into the best that has been thought and known – ought to be a prime way of transcending their immediate circumstances, and affording them visions of enduring value and endless possibility which even from situations of affluence they could not otherwise imagine or dream of. But I am afraid that too many of them are being offered too much hog-wash and too little of the classics. Even where genuinely worthwhile material is studied, public exams remain resolutely inclusive of the mediocre and the transient – no doubt in the name of inclusivity, which of course deprives those who need it most of any chance of transcending their circumstances.

Simone Weil once rather plaintively said 'I do not mind having no visible successes, but what does grieve me is the idea of being excluded from that transcendent kingdom to which only the truly great have access and wherein truth abides.' (21) And in order to open that transcendent kingdom to others she famously wrote and spoke about *Antigone* for factory workers. Without hoping to emulate that great spirit in any other way, we educators can at least emulate her in this. In their own different ways, such was also the ideal of Arnold, of Newman, of Ruskin and of Mill, all of whom I have mentioned here, eminent Victorians all, in whose footsteps I humbly follow.

1. See E.D. Hirsch, *Cultural Literacy: What Every American Needs To Know*, New York: Knopf Doubleday Publishing Group, 1988. Although the book mentions 5,000 facts that every literate American should know, it has been criticised for what it omits! Doubtless any such attempt will be so criticised, which does not mean that what it includes should not be there, or, more fundamentally, that a notion of core knowledge, however imperfect, is not something educators should not refer to in their teaching. As will be shown below, too many curricular initiatives are sadly deficient in this respect, to the detriment of the pupils being taught under their wing.

2. The new spirit in question is nicely encapsulated by Michael Gove, the then Secretary of State for Education, in his speech 'The Importance of Teaching', from October 5th, 2013 (available on the gov.uk website, under Department of Education).

3. See J.S. Mill, *On Liberty and Other Essays*, edited by John Gray, Oxford: Oxford University Press (The World's Classics), 1991, p 117-8; Alexis de Tocqueville's views on the enervating effect of welfarist democracy are to be found in Part 4, Ch 6 of Vol 2 of his *Democracy in America* (from 1840): A de Tocqueville, *Democracy in America*, trans. G. Lawrence, London: Fontana Press, 1994, pp 691-3.

4. In *Utilitarianism* (1861, Ch 2), Mill, *op cit*, p 140.

5. John Ruskin, 'The Future of England', Ch 4 of *The Crown of Wild Olive*, in *The Works of John Ruskin*, edited by E.T. Cook and Alexander Wedderburn, London: George Allen, 1905, Vol XVIII, pp 500-2.

6. D.H. Lawrence, *The Rainbow*, New York: The Modern Library, 2002, p 371.

7. D.H. Lawrence, 'The Education of the People' (1918), in *Lawrence on Education*, edited by Joy and Raymond Williams, Harmondsworth: Penguin Education, 1973, p 133.

8. See Charles Murray, *Real Education*, New York: Crown Forum, 2008, Ch 2.

9. Aristotle, *Nicomachean Ethics*, 1103a33, as translated by Sir David Ross, Oxford: Oxford University Press, The World's Classics, 1966.

10. Aristotle*, Politics*, 1334b27-8, as translated by T.A. Sinclair, revised by T.J. Saunders, London: Penguin Books, 1981.

11. Aristotle, *Nicomachean Ethics*, 1143a31.

12. J.S. Mill, *Utilitarianism*, p 140.

13. J.H. Newman, *The Idea of a University*, Notre Dame Indiana: University of Notre Dame Press, 1982. See especially Discourse V, 'Knowledge Its Own End'.

14. Jonathan Rose, *The Intellectual Life of the British Working Classes*, Yale University Press, 2001, p 366.

15. Matthew Arnold, *Culture and Anarchy* (1869), in the edition of New York: Chelsea House, 1983, p 31. This is one of the places where Arnold talks of 'the best that has been thought and known'.

16. *Teacher Standards 2012* , available on the Department for Education website, https://education.gov.uk/publications/

17. Richard J. Evans, 'Michael Gove's history curriculum is a pub quiz not an education', New Statesman, 21/3/2013, accessed at http://historyworks.tv>news>2013/031

18. Reported in *The Daily Telegraph*, 30/5/2013.

19. See, for example, Orwell's essays 'Inside the Whale' and 'Wells, Hitler and the World State', in *The Penguin Essays of George Orwell*, London: Penguin Books, 1984, pp 107-138 and 194-8.
20. The letter was published in *The Independent* for March 20th, 2013, where it was accompanied by a favourable leading article.
21. Simone Weil, *Waiting on God*, trans. E. Craufurd, London: Routledge, 1951, pp 15-9.

Chapter 3

PHILOSOPHY AND EDUCATIONAL POLICY: ROUSSEAU AND DEWEY

Probably everyone reading this book will have an idea of what has come to seem a perennial battle in schools and in education more generally between a traditional vision of education, such as the one being argued for here, and an alternative 'progressive' compendium of ideas and practices, which finds favour with many well-meaning people. The reason it finds favour is because it seems to promise a more humane practice, more caring of the individual child and his or her needs than the traditional view that, whatever a child wants or feels, there just are things that have to be taught and learned. While not necessarily a Gradgrindian harping on 'Facts, facts, facts', and at its best certainly no such thing, this is often how traditional education is caricatured by its critics. Instead they propose and often practice a method which allows children, especially young children, to play, as opposed to being taught directly. They are supposed to discover what they need to learn from their own play and what is often called their 'research', that is looking things up for themselves and going where their interests might be kindled. Pupil choice is valued, over-valued from the perspective of traditional practice. In general, teachers schooled in the progressive mentality will often say that they see themselves as teaching children, not subjects, and their own role as facilitating the efforts of pupils (learners in the current jargon) rather than focusing those efforts on the subject knowledge the teacher sees as their duty to impart. It is also believed that individual pupils have their own learning styles and different intelligences, all of which teachers should be aware of and cater for. But possibly somewhat in conflict with treating children as individual learners rather than as members of whole classes moving forward together, there is in progressive thinking a rooted antipathy to selecting and grading according to ability, 'symbolically violent', according to one professor of education. Above all, lessons should focus more on what is relevant to pupils' needs and interests than to a syllabus imposed from above. And schools and classrooms should in their practice model democratic procedures and practices, with pupil voice, as it is called, being a major element in the life of a school.

Probably anyone with any experience of recent trends in education, as pupil, parent, or even teacher will recognise the progressive picture, which is not, of course, new. As long ago as 1990, in *The Guardian* for 4th of December of that year, the journalist Edward Pilkington reported vividly on a visit he made to the School of Education at the then Roehampton Institute (now University, and then, as now, a major trainer of teachers):

Only four weeks into the course (students) have begun to absorb the message that will be hammered home with monotonous regularity throughout their four years at Roehampton: children should not be told what to do, but encouraged to learn for themselves. Their tutor, Graham Welch, assistant dean of education tells the class that the key to learning is play: 'You have to realise that everyone, including big kids like us, learn through play.' This approach is rapidly becoming the norm in teacher training establishments and primary schools, and stems from the idea that children learn at their own pace and according to their unique level of understanding. The traditional model of teacher standing in front of the whole class cannot work because the lesson will be too simple for some pupils, while leaving others behind. A more democratic and appropriate approach, says Roehampton, is to start with the child's understanding and develop from there. Thus the institute advocates that children should be given some control over how they spend their time in school, or Roehampton – they should be given the right to negotiate their own curriculum. 'Negotiated curriculum is an idea rooted in a concept of democracy,' says Graham Welch. There is a lot of evidence to suggest that children as young as three are better motivated if they have a say in the way their day is organized.

This report is from 1990, and in some respects things have changed since then, at least in the sense that the government and the inspectorate now insist on basic levels of literacy and numeracy even in primary schools, and will hold schools and teachers to account on this. Nevertheless, à propos of Pilkington's last point, as recently as March 2023 the Scottish Executive has issued guidelines on 'The Voice of the Infant', declaring that even with pre-linguistic babies, 'those around them… should facilitate infants to express their feelings, and consider their views, uphold their rights, and take action accordingly.' And at the other end of educational spectrum, we can still remember the notorious inspection of King Edward VI School at Stratford-upon-Avon in 1989, which criticized the school for its reliance on 'traditional methods' and didactic teaching, even though (or perhaps because?) pupils at times were listening 'attentively' and even 'with evident enjoyment', whereas the needs of pupils 'in the late twentieth century require the introduction of new procedures, new methods and new courses.' Again it may be hard to find such a blatant expression of progressivism in to-day's Ofsted reports, but even among the inspectorate one may doubt that progressive attitude in the 1989 report has completely disappeared.

However, rather than multiplying examples of progressive educational trends in the recent or not so recent past, what I want to do in this Chapter is to explore the philosophical roots of this thinking. Many who follow and endorse these trends are not aware of these roots, and hence are not in a good position to evaluate them, or the vision of humanity which underpins them. This Chapter is intended to make a contribution to this understanding by examining the educational thinking of Jean-Jacques Rousseau in the late 18th century and John Dewey in the early 20th. Our question is to consider how it is that educational thought in our country has moved so far from the traditional vision of education as being about the imparting of such skills as are necessary to live a reasonable independent life, together with an introduction to the best that has been thought and known seen as a body of knowledge and experience, existing in its own right outside of the minds of what are the philosophical current which have flown beneath these surface changes? How is it that the proper focus of education has come to be seen not as subjects to be learned and disciplines to be acquired, but the mental structure and development of the child and his or her social environment?

Any answer to this question must begin with Rousseau, whose educational doctrines are laid out mainly in *Émile* (1) which is ostensibly an account of one child's ideal upbringing by a tutor in rural isolation away from the temptations of the city and the influence of other children. It is indeed a paradox that many of Rousseau's individualistically child-centred doctrines are now dear to the heart of an educational bureaucracy which sees social integration as a prime educational aim and will go to almost any lengths to prevent parents educating their children at home.

In *Émile*, though, there are two reasons for withdrawing the pupil from society. The first is so as to remove him from the harmful influences of society in order to allow his nature to develop in its own way. If properly developed, it will develop in a good way. According to Rousseau, vice and error, alien to human nature, are introduced into it from outside.

But Émile's education in solitude is not purely negative, and this takes us to the second reason for a cloistered education. The child has its own needs and should be allowed to develop in its own way, progressively, moving from one stage to another at its own pace and in its own time. Children are not miniature adults; in Rousseau's view, nature wants children to be children before being adults. Childhood has its own way of seeing, thinking, and feeling. These childish ways are largely concrete and largely sensory. So early education will avoid books and abstract thought and reasoning in favour of direct contact with the physical world. The child should be allowed to indulge its sports, its pleasures, its delightful instincts in line with its particular stage of development. The child's needs are thus satisfied in a cocoon of self-sufficiency abandoned to play and discovery; the child is the noble savage in miniature, untroubled by the distractions and vices of society. Reasoning and socialisation, which will come, will emerge through building on the early experiences of sensation and feeling; they will occur naturally and without the strains inherent in false society if the environment is carefully controlled by the tutor. The child will begin to realise the usefulness of reasoning in its encounters with the physical world, while it will become moral when it extends its innate feelings of pity to the other people it encounters. As he develops, he begins to move from pure instinct to a rational sociability, but this should occur not through the repressions of his passions but by allowing them to express themselves gradually and harmoniously.

In order to do this, what must be avoided at all costs in education are those occasions which would promote vanity and what Rousseau calls *amour propre* in the child. Education should not corrupt a child's spirit by exciting vicious and unrealisable desires. According to Rousseau, the standard education of his time taught everything except self-knowledge and self-control, the arts of life and happiness. The self-sufficient Savoyard peasant for whom Rousseau professed unbounded admiration does not need the useless facts and dead knowledge of the arts and sciences. Indeed, in Rousseau's view, only vanity and elitism could motivate a man to spend his life studying in libraries or laboratories. Rousseau is quite prepared to accept the implication of all this, that the education he is advocating is an intellectually restricted one: 'The world of reality has its bounds, the world of imagination is boundless; as we cannot enlarge the one, let us restrict the other'.(2) We should 'desire mediocrity in all things, even in beauty'(3). Individual excellence must be sacrificed for a life and an education which brings us closer to a natural goodness and harmony.

Émile, then, is a heady brew, combining nature worship, child centredness, an emphasis on doing and discovery at the expense of reading and being taught, together with a pervasive hatred of the existing order of things, particularly its competitiveness and elitism from which the child must at all costs be protected. Émile is to be tutored, but much of the tutoring is negative – protecting against the civilised meddling in our nature which makes us evil – and what is not negative is (in today's jargon) largely a matter of 'facilitating' what ought to be natural growth of the child into adulthood.

It cannot be said that anyone – even Rousseau himself – accepted every pedagogical recommendation in *Émile*, which as a prescription for education could hardly be applied to more than a very few children. Nevertheless, the spirit of Rousseau's thought has come to infuse practice in education, particularly in early stages. The key themes are those of progressive sequential development in childhood of the child as a natural growth, potentially good if allowed to develop without social interference of the wrong sort, of the vital role of play and discovery, and finally of a roosted hostility to competition and comparison.

All these themes are taken up in one way or another by the influential theorists of early education in the nineteenth century. Johann Heinrich Pestalozzi (1746-1827), unlike Rousseau actually ran schools in his native Switzerland, schools which became a magnet for educational reformers in the years after his death, culminating in a reorganisation of American elementary schools in the 1860s. He emphasised the importance of individual differences between children and also of the role of child-initiated activity, as opposed to rote learning. Education should develop to its fullest individuality the talent nearly each person possesses by nature: each person has his or her own 'truth'. And to pass to each stage in development, the experiences and tasks of the previous stage must be fully mastered. Modern civilisation and formal education do not allow the time needed for this process of organic development replacing deep learning with shallow, unassimilated knowledge which is largely verbal in nature and turning the soul from its deeper self to false and unsatisfiable ambitions.

Similar themes are also found in the work of Friedrich Fröbel (1782-1852). Education should be seen as part of the work of cosmic evolution, with a stress on the inner development of the individual towards full self-consciousness. It should harmonise with the stage the individual has reached, starting with the youngest children with play as their first initiation into purposeful activity. He founded a kindergarten in his native Thuringia in 1837, which became a model for many similar institutions. For a time in the 1850s his kindergartens were closed on the order of the Prussian authorities (who rightly suspected Froebel of heterodox religious views and liberal political leanings). But the ban lasted only ten years, after which the kindergarten movement and its associated psychological and educational philosophy became unstoppable in the affluent countries of the West.

Maria Montessori (1870-1952), along with Fröbel, is perhaps the best known exponent of the view that in their early years children, given an environment rich in manipulative materials, would largely teach themselves. Although her work began with children with learning difficulties, her system or something like it is used in countless primary schools and colleges of teacher education in Western Europe and the USA. In writing as if each child contained within itself some special spark to be ignited into a bright glow, she certainly threw her own spark into the educational tinder box.

Pestalozzi, Fröbel, and Montessori represent what might be seen as the romantic though practical wing of child-centrism, romantic because of the highfalutin and largely idealistic philosophy guiding their thought, practical because of their interests in actually organising classrooms. In both these ways, they are precursors of much primary and early years thought and practice today, an amalgam of sentimental romanticism about the child and a practice or set of practices which is said to be justified as practice, and insulated from any whiff of criticism from other theoretical or empirical standpoints.

It is, though, with Piaget (and in moral education with his disciple Lawrence Kohlberg) that the idea of education following the sequential development of the child receives its fullest and most systematic exposition in quasi-scientific form. Piaget is mainly famous for devising a number of experiments in the 1930s which were designed to show that children developed abstract categories of thought from concrete operations according to set and predetermined patterns. For Piaget, logical and mathematical operations manifest themselves first as overt behaviour and are only later internalized in abstract thought. Time, too, is held to be grasped as time only in a relatively late stage of child development, as is the ability to 'decentre' oneself from one's own perspective. At earlier stages, there will be considerable difficulty for young children in realising that an object stays the same over time, and even more in recognising conservation of quantity as a substance like water is transferred from a vessel of one shape to a vessel of a different shape. Kohlberg advances similar theses about the development of various kinds of moral reasoning in the child, again supported by observation and experiment.

From a psychological standpoint, Piaget and Kohlberg's work has been subjected to much criticism. Interesting as it undoubtedly is, it is certainly not regarded as the final or even first truth. But in one unfortunate sense, it sits all-too well with child-centredness in education. To put it bluntly and provocatively, the prestige of Piaget particularly, and Kohlberg to a lesser degree, have licensed generations of teachers being taught to limit their expectations of and ambitions for their pupils according to what 'psychological research' has supposedly said is possible at a given age or stage. The demands of the subject are thus regarded as secondary to contested psychological theory, theory which educational practice will obviously tend to 'confirm' in so far as it is predicated on that theory.

If Rousseau is the one great source of child-centred theory, Dewey is the other. To Rousseau's romanticism and naturalism, and its concentration on individual psychology, Dewey brings the sociological element so notably absent from the thinking of Rousseau's successors, as well as a far more directly political emphasis. For Dewey, education is above all a social and political project, and he was highly critical of what he saw as the misplaced romantic individualism of Mme Montessori and her followers. As he put it as early as 1899, in *The School and Society,* 'the full meaning of any subject matter is secured only when the studies (are) presented ... from the standpoint of the relation they bear to the life of society'.(4)

Not only that, in *Experience and Education* (of 1938), Dewey conceived the school itself as a 'social enterprise in which all individuals have an opportunity to contribute'. In this social enterprise, the teacher is not an 'external boss or dictator' imposing on children curricular standards alien to their current lives. They are rather the leaders of group activities, in which their suggestions are not a mould for a cast-iron result, but are a starting point to be developed into a plan through contributions from the experience of all engaged in the learning process.(5)

So, for Dewey, it is not simply that education must shadow the natural growth of the child. There is at the same time a systematic erosion of the authority, teacher and subject, in an effort to recreate both school and curriculum as miniature democracies within, responding to social needs and influences without. These themes and their educational implications are developed at great length in *Democracy and Education,* Dewey's major educational treatise, which was published in 1916.

According to *Democracy and Education,* traditional schools substitute a bookish, pseudo-intellectual spirit for a social spirit. They may secure specialised technical abilities in algebra, Latin, or botany, but 'not the kind of intelligence which directs ability to useful ends'.(6) True learning, by contrast, produces skills which are transferable (in the modern jargon), socially useful, and eminently sharable. The value of an activity or of a form of social life is judged by how far it is shared by all members of the group in which it takes place, and by how far the group which generates it interacts with other groups.

Dewey is, in fact, fundamentally hostile to social divisions of all sorts, seeing them as barriers to that demotic sharing of interests and mutual transparency of communication which for him is characteristic of true democracy, true culture, and true education. Any division between the learned and the unlearned he sees as due to a selfish hemming-off of one class from another. Any production of works or thoughts which cannot be fully and freely communicated to all men he sees as symptomatic of a rotten, selfish, and spiritual society, 'spiritual' being for him a term of abuse. Any insistence on the singularity of a national or local culture against cosmopolitanism (multiculturalism) he sees as offending humanity, a crime of which all systems of education up to now are guilty.(7)

Education, then, is for Dewey either a means by which boundaries can be set up and reinforced, or a means of breaking them down. Education can erect boundaries of various sorts, between classes of men, between distinct subjects of study, between élites and nonélites, between nations. But if we fully appreciate our common needs as human beings and the importance of solving our problems together and of democracy as a mode of living in which experiences are shared as widely as possible, we will look to education to break down stratifications and distinctions of all sorts. While Dewey defines culture as the capacity for constantly expanding the range and accuracy of one's perceptions of meanings, it is clear that he is really more interested in the former: range in terms of the numbers of people with whom one shares perceptions, rather than accuracy.

Arguing against the identification of culture with the possession of something inner, he writes:

The idea of perfecting an 'inner' personality is a sure sign of social divisions. What is called inner is simply that which does not connect with others – which is not capable of free and full communication. What is termed spiritual culture has usually been futile, with something rotten about it, just because it has been conceived as a thing which a man might have internally – and therefore exclusively.(8)

It is hard to say whether Dewey fully realised the consequences of his view: that it would make much of the culture of the

Middle Ages futile and rotten, to say nothing of the writings of, say, Pascal, Kierkegaard, and T. S. Eliot.

He also wrote that for some (of whom he disapproves),

> feelings and ideas are turned upon themselves, instead of being methods in acts which modify conditions. Their mental life is sentimental: an enjoyment of an inner landscape. Even the pursuit of science may become an asylum of refuge from the hard conditions of life – not a temporary retreat for the sake of recuperation and clarification in future dealings with the world. The very word art may become associated not with specific transformation of things ... but with stimulations of eccentric fancy and with emotional indulgences.(9)

The conclusion to which one is inescapably drawn here is that, like Rousseau, Dewey would not have shrunk from the mediocrity which must follow upon any general acceptance of his views of democracy and education.

Dewey's reductionism regarding content is manifested in his assertion that 'in the last analysis, all that the educator can do is to modify stimuli' (10) so as to produce desirable intellectual and emotional dispositions in the pupil. We need not deny that the production of desirable dispositions is an aim of education; what is at issue here is whether they can be produced without the child being introduced to specific bodies of knowledge and experience. Can, for example, a child learn to do physics without studying the content of modern physical theory? From where else will he or she derive a sense of what a problem is in physics, or indeed, of its solution? Equally, can a child learn to draw or paint without being introduced either at first or second hand to the discoveries made by the great artists of the past in their masterpieces? Of the rules of perspective, say? The gaining of an intellectual disposition can be likened to the learning of a language in that both expression and discovery of new meanings depend on mastery of a pre-existing structure. And, as we learn from Aristotle, much the same is true of moral and emotional dispositions; it is only when we learned to love the good and honouring the noble requires that we are taught which things are good and which actions noble – a knowledge of the content of morality, in other words.

Dewey, by contrast, is insistent that the teacher or, even worse, a book, is not to 'supply solutions ready-made' to pupils.(12) His opponents would agree that there is little to be said for filling the child's mind with information just for its own sake. But Dewey would reject any knowledge which cannot be busily and quickly put to use, doing something, improving social conditions, solving problems. For him unapplied knowledge is 'static' 'cold-storage', 'miscellaneous junk' cluttering the mind and likely to impede truly educative processes.

It is hardly surprising that Dewey disparages the 'acquisition of information for purposes of reproduction in recitation and examination' (12) given his stress on what would today be called active learning, which leads him to speak of 'the child of three who discovers what can be done with blocks, or of six who finds out what he can make by five cents and five cents together' as 'really a discoverer'.(13)

All thinking, he insists, is research, and all research is original with him who carries it on, even if everyone else in the world already knows what the researcher is looking for. Dewey's critics can fairly point out that much of what on this view counts as research would be a most inefficient use of the researcher's time, forcing him to rediscover for himself myriads of things which are already known. More profoundly, they may question the possibility of conducting any research which does not emerge from a background of largely inactive knowledge against which the researcher makes his initial guesses as to the nature of a problem, the point of solving it, the likely solutions, the most economical methods for testing them.

The idea of each learner and each child as an original thinker, as a kind of miniature scientist researching into his or her own problems largely for himself or herself, will increasingly tend to upgrade the intellectual value of early learning, and therefore downgrade the very real difference between that and the true originality which can exist only at high levels of human endeavour. Dewey, in common with the romantics, underplays the role of formal instruction in the transmission of human knowledge, or at least this is how he was and is read.(14)

There is indeed a connection between Dewey's view of the child as an original thinker and his attempt to use education and the curriculum as a means of establishing a radically egalitarian version of democracy. Democracy for Dewey is not as it was for Karl Popper, say, primarily a means of removing governments regularly and peacefully; it was primarily a matter of living together, sharing experience and fraternal problem-solving. As with Rousseau and his notion of the general will, Dewey was splendidly unaware of the potential for collectivist bossiness, not to say tyranny inherent in such notions, and thus less interested than he should have been in that control of governments which is implied in the ability of the people to remove them.

Education, however, was certainly a political project for Dewey. Thereby, we are all to learn about participation and communal problem-solving: hence the attacks on the inner life and on educational authorities. In the content of education, we are to concentrate on essentials, 'the things which are socially most fundamental, which have to do with the experiences in which the widest groups share';(15) hence the attacks on educational élites and assessments. In its crudest terms, what is not part of everyone's experience and problems, including those of children, is at best inessential in a democratic education, mere dead lumber from the past, and at worst a throwback to a divided, class-ridden form of existence. But an education animated by a social spirit will be a prime means of building up a common experience in which all share, and which will break down distinctions between classes of people, between subjects of study, and between school and the world outside.

For Dewey the main aim of schooling is to build up a community life:

> In place of a school set apart from life as a place for learning lessons, we have a miniature social group in which study and growth are incidents of present shared experience. (16)

It is crucial to this project that the interests of the school connect with those of the community outside. Dewey does not seek a monastic or college atmosphere, and is wary of any adherence in the school to the culture of the past. The modern world and its problems and the concerns of the future world are where the emphasis should be. This attachment to the experience of the present and to present problems leads him to denigrate the study of history and literature, except in so far as those subjects can throw light on the present. Such stress on present relevance actually takes Dewey as close as can be to a relativistic notion of truth:

> No matter how true what is learned was to those who found it out and in whose experience it functioned, there is nothing which makes it knowledge to the pupils. It might as well be something about Mars or about some fanciful country unless it fructifies in the individual's own life. (17)

What fructifies in the life of present individuals is not that which is true in some absolute or timeless sense, but that which enables them to modify their present experiences and social conditions in response to present unsettlement. As long as a topic makes an immediate appeal to pupils, we need not ask what it is good for. It is good enough that it responds to some present interest of the pupil. To satisfy our current biological and social needs, past authorities in education must be jettisoned. They are likely to make pupils unhappy with the modern world and to distract them from it. History and literature must be displaced from the centre of the curriculum in favour of social studies: the stress on classics and masterpieces in traditional education must be replaced by a scientific and experimental attitude, in which beliefs and values formed at first hand have far more validity than anything handed down by tradition.

With Dewey, this dismissive attitude went hand in hand with a belief in the power of unfettered and contemporary human reason to solve the problems we are confronted with, and also with a belief in the need to submit our activities economic, educational, social – to collective central planning. It is impossible to over-emphasise the degree to which Dewey's educational views imply a specific view of man and of society; in criticising Dewey and the educational philosophy he has influenced, we will also be taking issue with the underlying anthropology and politics.

What is true of Dewey is true *mutatis mutandis* of Rousseau and the educational romantics. Their educational prescriptions are not and cannot be isolated from a general view of humanity and society, one which encourages free and natural individuals and which will be critical of any tendency in society which appears repressive or authoritarian. As we have suggested in considering Dewey, such an approach overlooks the extent to which knowledge, learning, and culture depend on external authority and are far removed from immediate political and social concerns. As far as society as a whole is concerned, a very real question must remain over the extent to which any society can be as egalitarian as Rousseau wanted or as democratic and multicultural as Dewey advocated without lapsing into anarchy and incoherence, if not at least into the mediocrity of TV and the mass media.

Some of these doubts become even more pronounced when we consider the way these approaches to education have been translated into the approach to psychology by Abraham Maslow, Carl Rogers, and their followers. These approaches are not only clearly influenced by the thought of Rousseau and Dewey, but they have in turn been highly influential in the world of education in Britain as well as the United States. Late in his life (significantly, in 1969) Maslow came to regret what he saw in America of the lack of a sense of evil, and among his students any sense of a distinction between who should teach and who should learn. Maslow actually wrote in his diary for 14 April 1969, that the problem with the college faculties of the day was that they lack a theory of evil and

so don't know what to do in the face of viciousness. This non-theory of evil, it occurred to me, is one peculiar version of the 'value-free' disease (which is the same as ethical relativism, of Rousseauistic optimism, of amorality, i.e., nothing is wrong or bad enough to fight against) ... What kind of educational philosophy is it that is unprepared for ill will?

The only problem with this heartfelt plea from a disillusioned educator was that for most of his career he himself had in his psychological theory and practice attempted to be a 'facilitator of learning' rather than an authority, sought to promote autonomy and self-actualisation above all else, had in Rousseauesque fashion sought to liberate feelings repressed into the unconscious, and had clung to the theory of universal benevolence – all points with obvious philosophical antecedents, and in Britain from the 1920s onwards all increasingly firmly embedded in what came to be seen as the best educational practice, in both moral and academic education.

By the late 1960s Maslow was having doubts: but doubts were only later to assail the mind of his psychological colleague Carl Rogers, the founder of what has come to be known as client-centred psychology. Central to Rogers's psychology was the notion of personal growth, a notion also central to Dewey's philosophy generally and his ideas on education in particular. Dewey had written in *Democracy and Education* that the process of education has no end beyond itself, that growth is the characteristic of life, and also that education is all one with growing. In sum, there is nothing to which education is subordinate save more education – a clear antecedent of the notion of 'life-long learning' and of the concept, dear to present day educational gurus that what is significant in education is not content, but process, problem-solving, and yet more education.

Rogers translated all this into psychological and educational practice. As he himself put it, in his system

> the teacher or professor will largely have disappeared. His place will be taken by a facilitator of learning, chosen for his facilitative attitudes as much for his knowledge ... We shall ... see the facilitator focusing his major attention on the prime period for learning – from infancy to the age of six or eight. Every child will develop confidence in his own ability to learn, since he will be rewarded for learning at his own pace.

We will be confronted again and again with the thought that what matters in education is learning not teaching, process not content. The Rogerian student

> will learn to be an individual not a faceless conformist... He will find that learning, even difficult learning, is fun, both as an individual activity and in cooperation with others ... His learning ... will be, in itself, an experience in living. Feelings

of inadequacy, hatred, a desire for power, feelings of love and awe and respect, feelings of fear and dread, unhappiness with parents and with other children – all these will be an open part of his curriculum, as worthy of exploration as history or mathematics ... the student will never be graduated. He will always be part of a 'commencement'.(18)

This is Rousseau out of Dewey, an unhappy amalgam of Dewey's growth theory and a Rousseauesque stress on the individual and his or her inner state as a subject of awe and fascination. In Rogers's own psychological practice, counselling was 'non-directive', self-directive growth from within. The psychiatrist facilitated, but made no judgement. If this non-directiveness has not yet become standard practice in education, it certainly has its toe-hold there. This is so particularly in theorising in moral education, and in the highly influential values clarification movement, where the aim is not to tell pupils what to do, but rather to enable them to recover and expound the sources and implications of the values they turn out to have on examination of their inner attitudes to various situations, real or imagined. This parody of moral education was foreshadowed as early as 1926 by Dewey's influential disciple W. H. Kilpatrick, when he wrote that

our young people face too clearly an unknown future. We dare not pretend that the old solutions will suffice for them. Our youth no longer accept authoritarian morals. We must develop then a point of view and devise a correlative educational system which shall take adequate account of this fact of ever increasing change. Otherwise civilisation itself seems threatened.(19)

Even in 1926, relativism must have seemed a curious remedy for an impending collapse of civilisation; but one cannot but be struck by how old and cliché-ridden are political and educational appeals to the pace of change. As far as moral education goes, however, value clarification proves to be the ultimate abrogation of teacherly authority:

> An increasing number of students are no longer willing to tolerate a curriculum that does not acknowledge their needs, interests and concerns... Are we to tell them what to value and how to live... in the hope that they will listen? No. None of us can be certain that our values are right for other people.(20)

There are, of course, significant differences between the various figures we have looked at in this brief survey of progressive educational thought since the time of Rousseau, not least in the differing emphases given to the social context of the school. When contrasted with a traditional approach to education – as being the teaching from without of the best that has been thought and known, regardless of the child's immediate interests, social needs in general, or immediate applications of what is learned – what the progressives have in common is far more striking and has been far more influential than what separates them. Much standard educational thought in Britain over the last half-century looks very much like an amalgam of the progressive themes together with doctrines of self-esteem; a stress on learning rather than on teaching; a disparagement of subjects without immediate interest and relevance; a hostility to hard and fast externally imposed standards (regarded as antithetical to the natural development of the child) and, conversely, an obsessive harping on the cultivation of individual difference; egalitarianism within school and without; a hostility to didactic and authoritarian approaches to education and morality; in the early stages particularly an emphasis on play, discovery, and practical activities at the expense of structured and particularly bookish approaches to learning; the notion of the child as a 'researcher', actively constructing his or her own 'knowledge'; and finally the idea of education itself as, in the large sense, a political project, having to do with the reconstruction of society and the self-discovery and self-creation of the learner.

To the amalgam of Rousseauan and Deweyesque ideas should be added two further themes which are currently highly influential in education: while not explicitly present in either thinker they certainly sit well with their ideas. The first of these is the notion of self-esteem and the hostility to sharp or externally imposed discipline. That self-esteem is an *idée fixe* in Britain of the twenty-first century, and not merely among educators, hardly needs underlining. While Dewey would doubtless have been critical of the notion as currently deployed (if it was unhealthily 'inner' and not linked to actual problem-solving) and while Rousseau was, of course, the self-critical, self-analytical author of *Confessions* (though that itself could be seen as the ultimate tribute to his own self-esteem), self-esteem can be seen as a logical extension of some of their ideas, as we have suggested in considering Maslow and Rogers.

Thus, from Rousseau we certainly derive the notion that human beings are naturally good: 'the first impulses of nature are always right'; 'God made all things good, man meddles with them and they become evil.' The child, if not exactly a noble savage, should learn that all his passions are good, provided they are not perverted or unnaturally repressed. And what is *amour propre* but an obsessive absence of self-esteem, seeking compensation and reinforcement from the ever fickle and unreliable opinions of others?

As far as Dewey is concerned, hostility to class-divisions and a stress on the contributions each individual has the power to make, however backward on conventional criteria, certainly forms the basis for the cultivation of individual self-esteem. For, without the confidence which comes from self-esteem, individuals will not play the part in group work and discussion which Dewey is hoping for, nor will they give their own growth the significance Dewey accords it.

Relativism, like self-esteem, is not explicitly part of the programmes of either Rousseau or Dewey. On the other hand, both espouse forms of egalitarianism which are conducive to relativism. Rousseau is highly critical of the pretensions of cultural, academic, and social élites; in *Émile* it is the humble Savoyard vicar whose home-grown wisdom is esteemed. Dewey regards all social groups as having a valid contribution to make to the educational project, however unqualified they may be on existing criteria. He inveighed against national sovereignty and was always in favour of the 'new and broader environment' which would result from the intermingling in schools of young people from different races, customs, and religions.

None of this is precisely relativism, but it certainly suggests that educators should not seek to impose on pupils the cultural standards of existing élites. It would provide a very good basis for the theories of thinkers such as Althusser or Foucault, for whom much of the existing school curriculum and educational organisation (including literary canons and traditional styles of assessment) are little more than the means by which those currently in power simply reinforce their position, parts of the ideological apparatus of state hegemony in Althusser's terms. It would also provide a ready foundation for feminist, decolonizing, and neo-Marxist pleas that the voices of the white middle-class males be silenced in order that we (or, more accurately, our children) attend to those of the dispossessed and of those groups which had previously been under-represented (women, ethnic minorities, homosexuals, the traditional working class). Both Rousseau and Dewey explicitly saw many judgements of cultural evaluation as little more than the positioning of those who have much to gain from refusing to admit other voices into the pantheon. Of course, as things stand now in Britain, precisely the reverse is true, as one sees in the constant complaints from influential educators and others to resist governmental attempts to prescribe such things as tests of literacy and numeracy and to move to curricula encapsulating the notion of Core Knowledge. We cannot know what exactly Rousseau or Dewey would have thought on the details of any of this, but such reactions are certainly in the spirit of their thought.

So, one suspects, is the hostility one finds in British education to objective testing, and most especially to the testing of intelligence. Such measures are decried variously as being 'unreliable', simply a measure of how far the norms of existing élites have been internalised, and, above all, divisive. While neither Rousseau nor Dewey would have gone along with the extreme environmentalism of some current thought – according to which there is no such thing as native intelligence, or if there is, it cannot be measured – there are certainly aspects of their thinking which would support attacks on any current types of test. From Rousseau, they would appear simply to reinforce existing and suspect modes of thought (analytical, life-denying, 'logocentric', in to-day's jargon); from Dewey they would reinforce undesirable divisions in society, as well as privileging the modes of thought of those already dominant. While neither Rousseau nor Dewey believed nurture was all in upbringing, they would both obviously be unsympathetic to anything (such as intelligence tests) which appeared to cast doubts on (in Rousseau's case) the spark within each child or (in Dewey's case) the validity of every perspective on a question. The way they each conceive democracy and equality would undoubtedly have made them and those influenced by them hostile to the notion that people should be graded for intellectual ability on a metric scale, particularly if there was any suggestion that there was something final and definitive about the results of such grading. The suggestion that there might be offends anyone with either sentimental or egalitarian leanings, which goes some way to explain the unprecedented disdain in which Sir Cyril Burt is currently held in educational circles. Burt claimed to have produced good evidence for innate intelligence, and evidence that it could be measured. His detractors, after his death, accused him of fraud, an accusation widely and uncritically accepted, and anyone casting doubt on it is likely to receive short shrift in most departments of education today. But the accusation is itself suspect. It has itself been trenchantly criticised, and its unqualified repetition in academic circles is to be deplored.(21) And even if it were true that Burt had simply invented his data, that would not in itself undermine the idea of native intelligence or the testing for it.

Before closing this essay on the philosophy underlying current educational orthodoxy, it is worth remarking once more that – on his own admission – Rousseau's educational proposals are hardly suited to mass education. But, perhaps more surprisingly, no more are Dewey's.

John Brubacher in his *A History of the Problems of Education* describes the laboratory school Dewey founded in Chicago in 1894 as follows:

> Dewey thought it was an archaic practice for elementary schools to spend 75 to 80 per cent of their time on verbal studies. While such a proportion might have been proper before the invention of printing, in the twentieth century it amounted to forcing a middle- and upper-class education on the mass of the population. In place of such an education Dewey substituted one centering in ... the current social occupations of the home and community with which the child was becoming increasingly familiar. Thus, Dewey's school started with household occupations. From here foods and textiles were later traced to the source of their production. Still later,

occupations were seen in their historical setting. Number work was done incidentally to occupations like carpentry and cooking. Reading and writing began in the children's keeping of their own records. These and other activities were all conceived in a social context, for it was Dewey's idea that education was the regulation of a process whereby the child came increasingly to share in the social consciousness.(22)

Much of this could have been predicted on the basis of Dewey's writings; indeed, part of the practice is actually laid out by Dewey in *The School and Society* in 1899. Equally, the extent to which Dewey's practice seems unremarkable to us today shows how far ideas of the sort which he expounded so insistently have captured the less than commanding heights of educational theory in the twentieth century and still to-day. It is thought worth observing here that Dewey's own school started with three teachers for thirty-two pupils, rose to sixteen teachers for sixty children and ended with twenty-three teachers plus ten assistants for 140 children. Whether or not a child-centred education such as Dewey advocated is a good thing, we cannot but agree with Dewey and his followers that to be successful an education based on the child, their interests, and ever-changing personality is bound to be extremely labour intensive. We should remember this point when we hear – yet again – that education is 'under-resourced'; conversely, we might observe that there must be something very peculiar about a teaching system which fails to produce some impressive results when operating with the pupil-teacher ratios Dewey allowed himself. Nor should we overlook the sheer inefficiency of teaching methods other than interactive whole-class teaching, in terms of pupil-teacher contact and pupil distraction.

What I have attempted to do in this Chapter is to bring out some of the philosophical presuppositions and political implications of progressive educational thinking. This thinking turns out to be anti-meritocratic, anti-dogmatic, collectivist, self-consciously progressive, and egalitarian, adumbrating a form of radical democracy in which notions of authority, quality, and truth itself have become suspect. Teachers may not think of themselves as political radicals or as philosophers; but the ideas which have come to dominate their profession in this country since the mid 1950s are closely linked to the politics of radical egalitarianism, and, more remotely, to the philosophical sources of that radicalism.

1. J-J Rousseau, *Émile*, (1762), quoted here in the Everyman edition, London: J.M. Dent, 1911.
2. *ibid*, p 45.
3. *ibid*, p. 372.
4. J. Dewey, *The School and Society* (1899), quoted here in the Phoenix Books edition, 1963, p 100.
5. J. Dewey, *Experience and Education* (1938), quoted here in the Collier Books edition, 1963, p 72.
6. J. Dewey, *Democracy and Education* (1916), quoted here in the Free Press edition, 1966, p 39.
7. *ibid*, pp 98ff.
8. *ibid*, p 122.
9. *ibid*, pp 135-6.
10. *ibid*, p 180.
11. *ibid*, p 157.
12. *ibid*, p 158.
13. *ibid*, p 159.
14. It is worth noting at this point that as a writer Dewey was nothing if not inclusive. If in many places he insisted on the child discovering things for him or herself, at others he also stressed the need for adult

guidance and, even if not over-enthusiastically, for bodies of existing knowledge. Nevertheless, he did say all the things that I attribute to him, and many of those who have read him (and through teacher education both in the US and here) and many who have not, have been influenced by the child-discovery aspect of his thought.

15. *Democracy and Education*, p 191.
16. *ibid*, p 358.
17. *ibid*, pp 341-2.
18. C.R. Rogers, 'Interpersonal Relationships', *Journal of Applied Behavioral Studies*, 4 (3), 1968, pp 274-5.
19. W. H. Kilpatrick, *Education for a Changing Civilization*, New York: Macmillan, 1929, pp 41, 49-50.
20. M. Harmin, H. Kirschenbaum and S. Simons, *Clarifying Values Through Subject Matter: Applications for the Classroom*, Minneapolis: Hart, 1973, p 31.
21. See Robert Joynson, *The Burt Affair*, London: Routledge, 1989.
22. John Brubacher, *A History of the Problems of Education*, New York: McGraw-Hill, 1966, p 389.

Chapter 4

REASON, VIRTUE AND CHARACTER: REFLECTIONS ON MORAL DEVELOPMENT

It is a common assumption in the educational world and elsewhere that the moral development is integrally tied up with reasoning ability, and, following on from this, that pupils in school should be encouraged from an early age to think critically about matters such as fairness, personal relationships, bullying, racism, and even more complex topics such as drugs and sexuality. I do believe that reasoning is an integral element in developing what, following Aristotle, I will call practical wisdom, and also that reasons can be given for fundamental moral positions, as indeed Aristotle does in his own writings on ethics, though how far reasons can go is a matter to which we will turn. But the relationship between reason or reasoning and morality is not a simple one. It is not one that should lead us to advocate 'critical thinking' in schools or elsewhere, divorced from the formation of character and the gaining of experience. What I want to suggest in this chapter is that the acquisition of practical wisdom requires an intertwined development of character and reason, alongside a growing and often fraught, if not actually painful, immersion in the complexities and intricacies of life. Nor, despite the authority of Laurence Kohlberg, who is often cited in these matters, is it clear that a mature moral judgement develops 'as a child's reasoning ability develops', smoothly in tandem with it, so to speak. (1)

What we say about the inter-relatedness of reasoning and moral judgement will depend to a considerable degree on how we think of reasoning. The position I am going develop here is somewhat parallel to the view espoused by Gilbert Ryle à propos of intelligent behaviour: 'intelligent behaviour is not piloted by the intellectual grasp of true propositions'. (2) I am tempted to sum up the position I am advocating by saying that moral behaviour is not piloted by the intellectual grasp of true propositions, and by adding that where Ryle saw intelligent behaviour as requiring a grasp of an unformalisable knowing-how, I see in moral behaviour a need for unformalisable elements of character and experience underlying judgement and even more practice. As Michael Oakeshott put it, what is required is an 'initiation into the moral and intellectual habits and achieve-ments of (one's) society, an entry into the partnership between past and present, a sharing of concrete knowledge', a sharing which will be compromised if education is conceived in terms of the acquisition of sets of skills divorced from immersion in the appropriate concrete knowledge, in the moral case the learning of the habits of moral feeling, response, and action. (3)

This need for a sharing of concrete knowledge is only too likely to be overlooked if, in the moral sphere, 'reasoning ability' is conceived as a kind of forensic tool, which can be developed by exercises in logic or 'thinking', that is through what is sometimes favourably described in prospectuses for philosophy courses and the like as 'the ability to form an argument'. The thought seems to be that, having acquired this ability, one is then in a position to bring it to bear in a topic-neutral way on matters which make up the stuff and practice of human life, be they ethical, political, aesthetic, nurturing, sporting, or whatever. Against this, I would urge that moral discussion and thinking is not a question of anyone at any time applying a topic neutral forensic ability in reason-ing. As Cora Diamond has pointed out, 'a clever fifteen year old could go through the logical rigmarole of what (R.M.) Hare calls reflective moral thinking', but without the experience required for feeling and understanding what the relevant arguments and considerations actually amount to, he or she will not actually be able to reason well morally. (4) Thus rationality itself, in the full human sense, is incomplete before the development within it of moral or ethical practices, experience and ideas; further, reasoning about morality requires possession of the right dispositions over and above argumentative cleverness. I will thus resist any move to think that these practices should be subject to standards extrinsic to them (what is often *referred* to as reasoning or rationality, though tendentiously in my view), in advance of the acquisition of those standards or of experience in the area in question.

So, from my point of view, the development of what might be regarded as reasoning ability in an abstract sense, even to a high degree, may actually go along with a superficial, even an immature, attitude to judgement in human affairs. Consider for a moment Gonzalo's famous speech in *The Tempest* : 'I'th'commonwealth I would by contraries/ Execute all things, for no kind of traffic/ Would I admit; no name of magistrate;/ Letters should not be known; riches, poverty,/ And use of service, none; contract, succession,/ Bourn, bound of land, tilth, vineyard, none;/ No use of metal, corn, or wine, or oil;/ No occupation, all men idle, all/ And women too, but innocent and pure... All things in common nature should produce/ Without sweat or endeavour. Treason, felony,/ Sword, pike, knife, gun, or need of any engine/ Would I not have, but nature should bring forth/ Of its own kind all foison, all abundance/ To feed my innocent people...' This speech is interesting, because it is the type of thing which would automatically commend itself to an intellectual of a certain type, 'reasoning' about society from, as it were, first principles, divorced, either perversely or naively from any real experience in the motley of human affairs.

Gonzalo is, of course, an old man, but as if to underline this point about naively immature reasoning in morality, even as I was originally writing this, the BBC read out an extremely similar vision, composed by Year 10 (i.e. 14 year old) pupils from the Lammas School in Leyton, under the direction of an artist called Ruth Ewan. In the magic world they envisaged, there would be natural plenty, no countries, no borders, no government, no violence, no gangs, education without schools, a global health service and, poignantly perhaps, 'my' parents reconciled. Now it could be argued that reason could be deployed against the Lammas pupils and against Gonzalo (as in the play Sebastian and Antonio rather cynically do); but no such reservations were offered by the BBC, which seemed to be inviting us to wonder at the adolescent wisdom on display. What is strikingly absent from both visions was any sense of how the citizens of these new commonwealths were to be made virtuous, even in the absence of scarcity. There was no recognition of the need for any habituation in virtue, or indeed of the ubiquity of vice and of the discipline and struggle needed to overcome the vicious and slothful tendencies to which we are all prone. There was no sense that in the arena of human living (ethics and politics, broadly speaking, but including the aesthetic as well) something thicker than the deployment of reasoning skills on their own is required, a context of practice, experience, moral sentiment and habituation in virtue.

That this should have been apparent from the very beginning of Western philosophy's treatment of these matters is dramatically, if unintentionally illustrated in Plato's dialogue *Euthyphro*. Because of the more or less automatic reverence accorded to the person of Socrates, particularly by those of a rationalistic temper, the most striking aspect of this dialogue is commonly overlooked. In it Socrates, *en route* for his trial for impiety, defeats in argument a young man called Euthyphro. Euthyphro is also on his way to court, but in his case to get his father prosecuted for negligently allowing a slave to die in unpleasant circumstances – at the very least a case of manslaughter, one would have thought. Socrates aims to show that Euthyphro is unjustified in what he is doing, because when he defends himself by saying that he is prosecuting his father out of a sense of piety, he is unable to define the notion of piety in a non-circular or question begging way. Euthyphro, who is admittedly something of a prig, continues on his way to the court even after his Socratic encounter, but he is regarded by most readers of the dialogue to have been worsted in the argument (and weighty conclusions about the nature of religion have often been drawn from this).

But, from my point of view, a crucial aspect of the story is that Socrates shows no interest in the dead slave, in what in the light of my earlier remarks we might call the thicker or wider human context. So, to someone not blinded by Socrates' reputation and his formidable analytical rhetoric, who is actually more moral, Socrates or Euthyphro? Socrates may have won the argument, but in a human sense, who is more right? Doesn't Euthyphro's father deserve to be called to account? Don't even slaves deserve their day in court, even if posthumously?

Aristotle, Plato's pupil, wrote that 'there is a faculty called cleverness; and this is such as to be able to do the things that tend towards the mark we have set before ourselves, and to hit it. Now if the mark be noble, the cleverness is laudable, but if the mark be bad, the cleverness is mere smartness...'? (5) *Mere smartness*: is that what Socrates is exhibiting in *Euthyphro*? We can, of course, argue about just what is meant by cleverness here, and indeed whether Aristotle's Greek is properly translated by 'cleverness', as opposed to something with a more instrumentalist connotation, maybe even 'glibness'; but the basic point is clear. *Good* reasoning about practical matters is more than a purely intellectual matter, not a matter of a topic-neutral critical rationality which can be deployed willy-nilly to any matter that comes before it, theoretical or practical, important or trivial.

To fill out Aristotle's point a bit, in more recent times, the much vaunted rationalist Christopher Hitchens may have demolished the saintly Mother Teresa, on paper. No doubt in argument Nietzsche could have chewed up Florence Nightingale for breakfast and spat her out, as Lytton Strachey attempted in *Eminent Victorians* as long ago as 1918, while mentioning Strachey leads me to ask whether I would rather be with him or General 'Chinese' Gordon, another of his targets, were I in a tight spot calling for courage, humane understanding and leadership. I know in each case whom I would trust were it to come to knowing the right thing to do, and actually doing it; and it isn't the cleverer, more articulate arguer.

If argumentative reasoning on its own is insufficient to guide morality, what else is needed? Aristotle's answer is in terms of character, specifically in terms of the development of the four cardinal virtues, moderation or temperance, courage or fortitude, practical wisdom or prudence, and justice. And these need careful nurturing from the beginning. One hardly needs to be a child psychologist or an early years specialist to know that none of these virtues come naturally or easily; being a parent or even just a moderately dispassionate observer of young children should suffice. Such was St Augustine: 'If babies are innocent, it is not for lack of will to do harm, but for lack of strength. I myself have seen jealousy in a baby and know what it means. He was not old enough to talk, but whenever he saw his foster-brother at the breast, he would grow pale with envy.' (7) Some virtuous motivation is required to counteract our other dispositions, and, while our better dispositions are not contrary to nature and may indeed have some basis in our nature, they are not purely instinctive in the sense of developing automatically without some nurturing and experience. They will need training so as to become habitual, for each virtue in its own way will involve restraint of other tendencies or vices to which we are all continually tempted: intemperance or unrestrained passion and excess; cowardice or taking the easy way out; the folly to which even the old are susceptible; self centredness and putting oneself first, rather than giving to others what they deserve or are owed. In different guises, each of these virtues appears in all the great moral traditions of the world, whether they be Graeco-Roman (in all their many streams), Hebraic, Christian, Hindu, Jain, Buddhist, Confucian, Taoist, Islamic, or indeed any other of which I am aware, including philosophical traditions, such as those stemming from the writings of Hume, Kant, and the utilitarians.

There has recently been an interesting ethnographic study pointing to the universality of certain basic values. In 'Is it Good to Co-operate? Testing the Theory of Morality as Cooperation in 60 Societies', the Oxford University team of Curry, Mullins, and Whitehouse analyse accounts of 60 highly diverse societies, and show that, despite differences in application, some basic moral principles regarding cooperation are present in all of them. These principles centre round helping one's kin and one's group, mutual honesty and trust, bravery, generosity, deference to superiors, fairness in distributing disputed resources, and recognition of prior possession. In none of the societies studied were there any counter-examples to the recognition of any of these values, which thus cannot be seen as the exclusive preserve of 'the West' or of any other specific group or religion. Indeed, one might tentatively suggest that it is only where rationalistic currents emanating from the West have had an influence that any of these values have been questioned in theory or practice. It seems that these, and maybe other values, have a pretty good claim to be genuinely universally recognised, at least in an empirical sense. (8) We can be pretty sure that in the sixty societies studied by the ethnographers the virtues in question are inculcated in the members of societies in question from a young age through example, habituation and training, no doubt including reward and punishment.

This pretty universal recognition of these and other basic virtues (and indeed of the correlative vices) makes it look as if they are somewhat more fundamental to the life of humanity than the specific intellectual and theological contexts in which they are variously embedded and from which they may seem to derive support. Actually, the process of support might go the other way round. The theological, philosophical, and other machineries of justification may in fact be built on a prior recognition of their importance and validity of these basic virtues, and the justificatory frameworks then developed as what come to be seen as implications of our starting intuitions regarding virtue, value, and character.

From a purely phenomenological point of view, Thomas Nagel may be right in seeing value as entering the world with the emergence of life, and then, as human beings develop understanding, being recognised as goods in themselves, independently of desires, individual or collective, and of any instinct we have to survive and reproduce. In this sense, virtues would become self-sustaining and objective, in contrast to the view elaborated by Richard Rorty, according to which they are only ever epiphenomena of morally neutral desires: 'There is nothing already in existence to which our moral ideals should try to correspond... The answer to the question 'are some human desires bad?' is 'no'. But some desires do get in the way of our project of maximizing the overall satisfaction of desire... There is no such thing as an intrinsically evil desire'. (9) Am I alone in finding Rorty's view of desire and the role of ethical reflection (reduced to the working out of maximal desire-satisfaction – a view he shared with Richard Hare) surprising, if not profoundly wrong? Against Rorty, we might mention Iris Murdoch's observation that 'the ordinary person does not, unless corrupted by philosophy, believe that he creates values by his choices. He thinks that some things really are better than others and that he is capable of getting it wrong.' (10). And also, no doubt, that some things are worse than others, and some simply evil. Can we not simply say that genocide and all the accompanying paraphernalia of oppression, slaughter, and torture, and the desires underlying such things, are just wrong, in these cases, actually evil? And that once there is life and the capacity to respond to its qualities and frailties, there is something already in existence to which our moral ideals should correspond.

Of course, it may be that this moral objectivity predates life on earth as something inherent in the universe, and only becomes apparent when there are living beings on whom morality bears; be that as it may, Nagel's suggestion that value, objective value, comes along with life and with conscious human life in particular is convincing. Value being conceptually linked to the requirements of life for flourishing is enough to dispel the idea that value is a just matter of choice or preference – we can, of course, choose or prefer things which may not be conducive to flourishing of ourselves or of other living creatures, but that would be wrong objectively. As human beings with self-consciousness, we are in a position where we can and indeed have to reason about where that value lies, and what is objectively demanded of us by it and beyond any purely selfish or subjective consideration. We, as reflective human beings, 'develop the collective capacity to think about reasons they may have which do not only depend on what is good or bad for themselves.. but extend to the lives of beings other than themselves'; and indeed, in Nagel's view to other conscious creatures such as animals and even to the inanimate world. (11)

The wonder, though, is that the preference view, as expressed by Rorty and Hare, passes with very little sense of surprise or comment among many contemporary moral philosophers.

Or perhaps it is not so surprising, given that it is all of a piece with the prevailing position in analytic philosophy that facts, and facts alone, are objective and to be reasoned about, while values are at bottom a matter of non-rational choice. It is this view, the so-called fact-value distinction, which underlies the view of rationality which I am here contesting.

But beyond noting the phenomenological point about the objective way virtues present themselves to us and their ubiquity, I want to say nothing more here about their provenance or ontological status. What I want to emphasise, following Aristotle, is the way they require a process of formation in young children (and adults), so as to embed these habits, rather than negative ones to which we, as naturally self-centred as well as other centred, are also prone. To quote Iris Murdoch on this point: the psyche is 'an egocentric system of quasi-mechanical energy… whose natural attachments are sexual, ambiguous, and hard for the subject to understand or control. Introspection reveals only the deep tissue of ambivalent motive, and fantasy is a stronger force than reason. Objectivity and unselfishness are not natural to human beings.' (12) But if I am arguing that these basic virtues are not purely intellectual, that they do not *depend* on some pre-moral intellectual support and also that their deployment requires struggle within, I am not saying that reasoning is not involved in their deployment and development. Reasoning will be needed to reveal just how they might be sensibly and effectively applied in practical judgements, which is actually just the way that the unjustly lampooned Florence Nightingale operated. Far from being the moralistic dullard one might have imagined from reading Strachey, in 1858 she was elected the first female member of the Royal Statistical Society, not only having developed for herself a version of the pie-chart, but also having clearly demonstrated the link between hospital hygiene and survival, something ill-understood at the time, and even now, it seems.

Reasoning will also be involved in making practical judgements and, once we have them, in refining and developing the moral standards each of us inherits in one way or another. Once we have our basic moral orientation, we can by reasoning, come to see that this should be extended or developed in directions we did not initially envisage. It is thus quite possible that the comparatively recent and growing realisation that racism is immoral and that even supposedly harmless jokes and insults are not actually so harmless, had something to do with reasoning about what Peter Singer has called the expanding circle, whereby our moral attitudes are extended to wider groups whom we come to see are not relevantly different from those to whom we originally believed we owed moral concern. It is arguable, though, that even here changes in societal attitudes may often owe as much to factors already involving feeling, sensitivity and value, as to reasoning in a narrow sense. These factors would include increases of empathy brought about by changes in the mood of a society, by religion, perhaps, or actual encounters with those from other races and cultures, which are then given intellectual backbone by reasoning of the sort we find in Singer. And then, what further reasoning is required? The medal produced by Josiah Wedgwood, with an enchained African slave, surrounded by the words 'Am I not a Man and a Brother?', contains all the philosophy needed. It remains to the eternal shame of educated Greeks like Aristotle that they were incapable of developing their insight and sympathy that far (I do not, though, think that this invalidates Aristotle's reflection on the nature of virtue and character, as opposed to implying that he himself had not developed either sufficiently).

Whatever we might say about the causes of changes in social attitudes, however, from an Aristotelian perspective it remains the case that underlying and supporting any reasoning and refining of our moral practices, the ultimate ends to and for which each of us acts depend on whether or not our basic dispositions of character and desire are initially directed towards good things or base things. So, in view of the personal discipline and parental and social support needed in acquiring and sustaining these virtues, to quote Aristotle again, 'it makes no small difference, then, whether we form habits of one kind or another from our very youth; it makes a very great difference, or rather *all* the difference.' (13)

Nor is it simply a matter of the *habits* we form in our youth. Or rather, one of the habits we should form is that of attending to the judgements of those more experienced than ourselves: 'we ought to attend to the undemonstrated sayings and opinions of experienced and older people or people of practical wisdom not less than to demonstrations because experience has given them an eye to see aright.' (14) Earlier Aristotle had written of Pericles and others who are good at managing states and households as being those who could *see* what is good for themselves and for others, but it is a type of seeing which can be obscured by pleasures and pains coming between us and the ends at which we aim. (15) Seeing aright in circumstances of complexity and doubt, where unformalisable judgement is of the essence and where temptations can deflect us, is crucial, but attending to one's elders in this way is a very hard habit for the young, especially if their elders have, like Ruth Ewan, given them an exaggerated sense of their critical abilities and thinking skills.

Aristotle goes on to develop the implications of his view in Book X, Ch 9 of the *Nicomachean Ethics*. (16) To live temperately and hardily is not pleasant to most people, especially when they are young. But without a character infused with habits of virtue and directed towards what he is unafraid to call 'nobility and goodness', base people will abstain from base acts only through fear of punishment. It is perhaps worth underlining here that by 'habit' in this context, Aristotle and his followers are not talking about mere behavioural reactions. The habits are a matter of attending to situations and seeing and reacting to them in a particular way, and so they involve thought and perception and feeling right from the start; but they are not dispositions formed through dispassionate ratiocination in the absence of a certain feeling towards what is virtuous, a sense that sympathy, say, is better than gratuitous cruelty, or that a personal relationship based on mutual exploitation is lacking something compared to one based on a wish to promote the good of the other.

Aristotle goes on to say that those with contrary habits or dispositions, those 'living by passion... pursue their own pleasures and the means to them, and avoid the opposite pains, and have not even a conception of what is noble and truly pleasant, since they have never tasted it. What argument would remould such people? It is hard, if not impossible, to remove by argument traits that have long since been incorporated in the character'. (17) Well intentioned people, particularly if of a rationalistic disposition, may find this too hard a saying. Surely, it will be said, there are things you can say to convince immoral or base or purely manipulative people of the errors of their ways. In practice, as anyone who has had dealings with aggressive or behaviourally difficult people (e.g. in a school with large numbers of pupils with little or no parental or community support) will know only too well, there often is nothing you can *say* which will bring about the necessary changes. There may be things we can *do* to turn their lives around, as it would be described, but doing here is not a matter of saying, if only because none of this is fundamentally a matter of argument, as opposed to the acquisition of a certain disposition of the soul.

Aristotle is wrong if he is taken to mean that base people cannot be turned away from their baseness, and reasoning can certainly play a role in such a turning away (though not one which will necessarily show the immoralist to be defeated in argument). Aristotle, or his transcriber, exaggerates when he says that youthful habit-formation makes *all* the difference in virtue acquisition if that is taken to mean that a good character cannot emerge after a thoroughly depraved childhood or a wholly unsatisfactory upbringing. Even in the worst of circumstances, and even given what religious people would refer to as our fallen nature, there is always within us some inkling or desire towards the good. Indeed, it could be that a morally horrible environment might itself incline a child to some sense that there is or must be something better, something more in harmony with what could be, with what he or she should be. We could also note that the very attempt of the type of immoralist Socrates and Aristotle were arguing against, Thrasymachus or Jean Genet, say, to rationalise his or her advocacy of the bad to be actually the good is, in a perverse way an acknowledgement that there is a good that we all need to conform ourselves to; to coin a phrase, rationalisation of immorality will be the tribute vice pays to virtue.

So Aristotle is wrong if his stress on upbringing is taken to imply that there is no hope for those brought up badly. Even within a bad upbringing and even within the most apparently depraved soul there will at times be glimmerings of a better, more humane, more harmonious form of life and society. This is recognised by the scholastics with their talk of synderesis, conscience maybe, which is to be found in all of us, and which may not have been given sufficient weight by Aristotle when he talks of upbringing making all the difference, as if that is inevitably the end of the story. But where he is right is in insisting that virtue and morality can never be a matter of reason on its own; an attraction to the good is required. And, further, in the normal case, what we are inclined to argue for morally will depend very largely on the dispositions and feelings we have already acquired. Schools can indeed do something here (all though too often they do not), in developing a strong ethos, with clear examples from the leadership and staff, and clear structures of reward and punishment. Then, but not before, reasoning, discussion, and reflection may be able to take root in a positive way.

For it is not as if the difficult, base people are necessarily incapable of understanding arguments. Psychopaths and other people steeped in wickedness are often good at arguing, only too able to counter the points made to them, point by point. This may even be partly precisely because of their psychopathy: they understand the moves, but lack the virtue-based empathy which motivates and directs right thinking. We hardly need Nietzsche to show us that there is nothing formally irrational or illogical in arguing in favour of immoralism. Thrasymachus in Plato's *Republic* had shown us that long ago, in cleverly and cynically defending the position that justice is what serves the interests of the stronger. Do Socrates or any of his philosophical successors ever satisfactorily answer Thrasymachus, without presupposing that there are occasions where the other has an absolute claim on me, which of course is just what is being questioned? But as G.K. Chesterton pointed out, maybe we should not be too impressed by this: 'Maniacs are commonly good reasoners... The madman is not the man who has lost his reason. The madman is the man who has lost everything except his reason.' The point is that any position needs roots and first principles, and that what Chesterton calls 'detached intellectualism' has lost its roots in imagination and experience. (18)

For the situation in logic and reasoning is that any chain of reasoning sooner or later reaches a foundation, and in the moral-ethical case, often sooner rather than later. And whatever turns out to be the rock-bottom can always itself be dialectically challenged. Doing that will hurt him, infringe his basic rights, even kill him; thankfully, good enough for most of us, most of the time – because of the way we have been brought up and have come to live and to feel; but, if I am a moral sceptic or some form of political or religious fanatic (fanatic, most of us will say, but perhaps that in itself prejudges the issue), why should any of that worry me, the sceptic or the fanatic, especially if he is standing in my way or in the way of my cause?

At this point we may seem to have reached an impasse. Only someone with the right attitudes and dispositions can reason well about morality. People without the right dispositions will not reason well. Because they do not have the right dispositions, the arguments and considerations adduced by the moral reasoner will fail to sway them. And this is not a defect of reasoning or critical thinking in the abstract sense, but a defect of attitude. The way we have set this dilemma up has been in terms of moral upbringing and training in habits of virtue. But it is not just a question of children and upbringing. From the purely argumentative point of view we have an aporia at the heart of morality itself. For the situation with children is no more than a reflection of exactly the same situation which will confront adults attempting to argue about morality.

In practice, the situation may not be as bad as has just been suggested, partly for the reasons already considered in discussing the Aristotelian claim that what happens in youth makes *all* the difference as far as moral thinking goes. Socrates does attempt to catch Thrasymachus and even more Callicles (in *Gorgias*) out by getting them to admit that, on the basis of attitudes they do actually have, some immoral ways of behaving are to be condemned. Thus, for example, Callicles is brought grudgingly to admit that, by analogy with bodily health and also for one's own state of mind, it is better for the soul to refrain from undisciplined and unrestrained desires. Moreover, a completely intemperate and tyrannical man would be incapable of any sort of fellowship or friendship, or indeed of ruling in a way that actually produced peace and public decency, as opposed to violence and unbridled luxury. (19) So it may well be that those who argue in favour of some sort of moral scepticism can actually be shown that at some level they do have attitudes which conflict with what they are claiming to believe. If we move from self-professed immoralists in our own society to other societies, the situation is perhaps less problematic than the existence of individual sceptics or psychopaths in our own society. For, as we have already noted, it would be very hard to find any society in which to some degree and in some form, at least to a limited degree, life, property, and truth telling are not valued, and appropriate attitudes taught from childhood. As with the sceptic in our own society there may well be a basis for moral discussion and for avoiding a form of relativism. We may even appeal at this point to a universally shared degree of synderesis found in everyone, a natural capacity to apprehend intuitively universal first principles of right action, despite differences of actual moral practice and despite however much personal immorality. However, encouraging as this is when faced with the aporia of the previous paragraph, these considerations actually reinforce the claim we are making in this essay that morality and moral argument have to proceed from a basis of shared attitudes and also from some sense that nearly everyone has of what is actually better and more harmonious, rather than from premises adopted on purely intellectual grounds. In this context synderesis, if we are prepared to admit such a thing, is already a disposition towards the good, and towards recognising it, and not a purely intellectual matter.

In 1367 Petrarch, in the course of his attempt to reconcile pagan and Christian thought, said this: 'the object of the will, as it pleases the wise, is to be good; that of the intellect is truth. It is better to will the good than to know what is true. The first is never without merit, the latter can often be polluted with crime and then admits no excuse, therefore those are far wrong who pursue their time in learning to know virtue instead of acquiring it'. (20) Who are the wise, in Petrarch's book? That this remark is in the course of a polemic against both Aristotle (or at least against fourteenth century Aristotelians) and Cicero need not force us to conclude that both Cicero and Aristotle would not have agreed with Petrarch on the point at issue, as would Socrates and Plato, for what is the decade and a half long preparation for philosophy in *The Republic*, but an education in sensibility and in habits of virtue *before* entering into reasoning about truth and virtue? In the nineteenth century, Ruskin put the point, 'reason can but determine what is true. It is the God-given passion of humanity which alone can recognize what God has made good'. (21) I take it that Ruskin here is speaking of reason in the limited sense recognised by the followers of Hume, that reason in the strict sense is confined to matters of fact, value being something else. And, in the last century, writing about the intellectuals of his own time, George Orwell had it, 'patriotism, religion, the Empire, the family, the sanctity of marriage, the Old School Tie, birth, breeding, honour, discipline – anyone of ordinary education could turn the whole lot of them inside out in three minutes.' He added, 'But what do you achieve, after all, by getting rid of such primal things as patriotism and religion?'. (22) Orwell's own answer was, for many intellectuals in the 1930s, entry into the communist party; but if we think that we know better than that, please don't say, critical reason, for that would simply open up once more the age old struggle between Socrates and Thrasymachus and all those who have, in one way or another, followed in their footsteps.

Simone Weil, in her great essay on *The Iliad*, pointed out that, as a primitive human reaction, I do not react to another human being as I would to a thing. Stepping aside for a person who crosses our path is not the same as stepping aside to avoid a street-sign. So this natural human reaction, what she calls 'this indefinable influence of the human presence' may well be the well-spring of moral behaviour. In this she may be echoing Montaigne and Hume, and is fairly close to Wittgenstein. But as we have already seen from Aristotle, the development of this indefinable influence is not instinctive, and not indefeasible. I *do* not react to another human being as a thing, but *can* not? There are such things as child soldiers, even more scary than adult soldiers, because of their robotic insensitivity. And after her observation about the passer-by and the street sign is taken, Simone Weil immediately goes on to describe how in war men treat other men as things, and women as booty. Homer describes Hector outside the walls of Troy as being far from the hot bath Andromache was preparing for him, and Weil comments with slight and pardonable exaggeration that most men, most of the time, are far from hot baths. 'Nearly all of human life has always passed far from hot baths.' In what sense of reasoning is this failure of recognition or of solidarity a failure of reasoning? (23)

As Wittgenstein put it, even if in a different context, after reasons come persuasion – and, unless you can draw on the indefinable influence of which Weil speaks, appealing to a living disposition to care about others, or to respect their rights, we are back in the situation Aristotle envisages: 'wickedness perverts us, and causes us to be deceived about the starting points of action. Therefore it is evident that it is impossible to be practically wise without being good.' (24) By 'practical wisdom' Aristotle means not just politically or rhetorically effective reasoning, but reasoning or judgement which produces moral outcomes. In this sense goodness then precedes practical wisdom, which will be undermined by base dispositions. But what Aristotle called the base, Nietzsche or Ayn Rand might have thought of as superior beings. Nietzsche indeed extolled the merits of Cesare Borgia, who was far from being good or practically wise. (25)

Hilary Putnam, following Robert Nozick in considering whether it might be possible to give an argument that would convince Hitler himself or some other Nazi of the wrongness of their views, wrote that 'The only answer to this demand... is to point out that probably no statement except the Principle of Contradiction has this property.' (26) This is surely too abrupt; it might be possible to persuade even a Nazi that the hardness they required was actually too hard, too corrupting to their own young people, or that the costs of the Final Solution were, even from their point of view, just too great in terms of the reaction it provoked. Richard Hare argued along these lines in *Moral Thinking*, suggesting that in the end even Nazis would realise the counter-productive effects of their policies, though one might modestly suggest to Hare that long-term unacceptable consequences were not what was really wrong with National Socialism. (27) Indeed, managing to convince a Nazi of the consequential unacceptability of his ideology would be a long way from persuading them of the intrinsic wrongness of anti-Semitism or that the conspiracy theories on which much of their position was based were insane; for such conspiracy theories have by no means disappeared in the world even to-day, nor indeed has anti-Semitism, and conspiracy theories are notoriously immune to refutation by argument – for it is of their essence that they are heavily insulated against counter-argument.

Argument on its own, reasoning seen as an exercise merely of ratiocination, is not enough in this kind of context. Something like a cultivation of Simone Weil's indefinable influence of human presence would be required, on the basis of which we could reason about how far this sense should be extended (so as to include Jews, slaves, and other outcast or scapegoated groups, etc). In an enigmatic remark at the end of the essay on *The Iliad,* Simone Weil says that only he who knows the empire of might and knows how not to respect it is capable of love and justice. (28) I think that this is actually quite profound. The indefinable influence is only the start of our moral journey, and it is in itself insufficient without a structure of moral reasoning. Having this sense of the human person affronted or ignored (knowing the empire of might) is what starts us on moral reasoning, on working out rationally what is demanded of us by the presence and existence of persons, on what a virtue like justice actually implies – or does so for those of us who do not simply succumb to the empire of might. In saying this, I am not saying that love and justice are enough to *defeat* the empire of might. At times force might be necessary (as Simone Weil must have recognised in her work for the Free French); the issue is the presupposition of love and justice themselves, in a deep sense, of moral reasoning.

On the initial acquisition of habits of virtue, Aristotle has this to say: 'Just as the body comes into existence earlier than the soul, so also the unreasoning is prior to that which possesses reason... while passion and will as well as desire are to be found in children even right from birth, reasoning and intelligence come into their possession as they grow older. Therefore the care of the body must begin before the care of the soul, then the training of the appetitive element.' (29) For the training of the body and the appetitive element, he recommends the traditional Greek programme of gymnastic and music, and in particular music which is a stimulus to virtue and which accustoms them enjoying themselves in the right way (i.e. not for Aristotle music in the Phrygian mode, which makes puts people into intemperate frenzies of excitement, and clearly not the transgressive tide of pop and rap to which our young people are exposed from an early age). And, if gymnastic is to be part of a training of character as well as of the body, I doubt that Aristotle would have had much truck with the unsporting attitudes displayed in most professional sport these days, and which are evident all too often in school sports as well (though they were not absent from the ancient Olympics either). However, leaving aside the particular details (or prejudices) involved in what an Aristotelian might say about music and gymnastic, what is clear is that from an Aristotelian point of view character must be being formed before the child can reason, both because in a child desire, passion and will precede reason and intelligence, but also because character of the right sort is necessary for reasoning of the right sort about what we should do. Of course, the perspective being proposed here would take character formation to be a life-long matter, and as one matures from the inexperience of childhood and adolescence to adulthood and middle and old age, reasoning and judgement will play an increasingly crucial role in this.

Let us assume that character has been formed, and reasoning is setting off on the right track. There is a continuing role for character as one moves through life. In a morally good life reasoning and intelligence do not, as it were, take over, having extricated themselves from their embedding in sentiment, character, and habit; The struggle against fantasy, self-centeredness, and moral blindness and the cultivation of virtue continue. That we should think in this way is suggested by the protean nature of argumentative reason, that reasoning can just as well be directed to bad ends as to good, and also by the limitations of reasoning in providing a foundation for morality. Pascal is much to the point: 'All your enlightenment can bring you only to the point at which you will find neither truth nor goodness...' (30) Part of his reason for saying this is his conviction (which he shares with Hume) that reason is no match for a determined scepticism, in either epistemological or moral areas. But he goes on to say that reason on its own, that which distinguishes us from the beasts, may in itself lead us only beastwards, to aiming at and achieving noxious pleasure, depravity, and unhappiness.

Even if, as we have done already, one rejects the claim that depravity is the only and necessary direction of an unreformed reason, Pascal is surely right to point to the potential reason has to mislead us. And his belief in original sin, even if we might demur at the theological framework, is certainly a useful corrective to unrealistic optimism about either our reasoning powers or our intrinsic goodness as human beings, a corrective with which, in different ways, both Plato and Aristotle would have taken for granted. Pascal himself develops a tripartite division of human faculties into *sens, raison,* and *coeur.* Sense and reason are necessary, but regarded in isolation suffer from inherent deficiencies, which can be remedied only through the development of *coeur,* heart, which plays the role of what we have been calling character. (31) We require *esprit de finesse* as well as *esprit de géométrie.* Elsewhere Pascal says what might be a summary of what I am trying here to argue: 'Whereas it is said that when one is speaking of human affairs that it is necessary to know them before loving them, the saints, say that in speaking of divine affairs it is necessary to love them before knowing them.' (32) Simone Weil's gloss on this might be that in speaking of human affairs we have to start from recognising the distinction between a person and a street-sign, to see them as a separate and inviolable fellow-sufferer, which is a form of selfless or self-abnegating love.

In drawing on Pascal's analysis here, I am not wanting to engage in a kind of armchair faculty psychology. It is not that sense, reason, and heart are separate or separable bits of our make-up, but rather that each of them is an element in whatever we do. Indeed I actually want to encompass morality in a suitably broad and practical conception of rationality, one which goes far wider than the purely formal elements of reasoning or informal logic. The danger which I am arguing against here is to think that one element – our reasoning faculty, conceived as a topic-neutral instrument of 'thinking', in this case – can be extracted from the mix and somehow made to rule and judge the rest of our personality. There must be intellect and indeed thought in everything we do, but it must be a feeling intellect, an intellect directed to and permeated by certain goals and dispositions we feel to be desirable.

Pascal thought that *coeur*, to be rightly directed, had to be animated by divine grace, and also, incidentally, that all human activities are fallible, doomed to failure. Even if we are more optimistic than that, we have to acknowledge with the *Pensées* that the besetting weakness of humanity was inconstancy, the endless and endlessly fruitless search for diversion, subjection to the servitude of pleasure. And Pascal himself would *certainly* have warmed to what Michael Oakeshott, a thinker of a very different stripe, said about our being prone to enthralment to 'a ceaseless flow of seductive trivialities'. (33) The temptations to which we are subject do not lessen with age, so the answer to the question about the constancy of character is that, even if we have developed habits of virtue, we must be ever watchful.

Human beings are weak and prone to all sorts of wickedness, even the best of us. One can say this without acceding to Pascal's total pessimism and ignoring the real good that people do, or the real goodness in many individuals (but never, of course, unqualified goodness, goodness *sans phrase*). Actually fully acknowledging human weakness and sinfulness – which many of us are reluctant to do for sentimental or romantic reasons – might make us less petty-mindedly censorious when we do see people fall, or their failings are brought publicly to our attention in the media, for the rest of us to gloat at in a superior way. Be that as it may, as we have already seen, some of those whom Pascal would have called pagans, such as Aristotle,

Plato, and most Hellenistic and Roman thinkers, were realistic about our potential for baseness, as Aristotle put it. Where the pagans differed from Pascal is that they did see the possibility of moulding character for the good, by good up-bringing in the first place, leading to the inculcation of habits of virtue, and then by subsequent vigilance as life goes on.

Both pagan and Christian thinkers would see character development as essential not just to right judgement and good reasoning about human life in general and morality in particular, but also as liberating, as part indeed of any education which could properly be called liberal in the sense of freeing us from servitude. The servitude in question is servitude to passion and desire and vice of all sorts, including sloth, the countervailing mastery being above all self-mastery. It is easy to see the liberating qualities of each of the cardinal virtues; temperance as freedom from excesses of all sorts and from what drives us to excess, courage as freedom to stick to our goals without being deflected by force inside or out, prudence as freedom from haste and bad judgement, and justice as freedom to enjoy the fruits of genuine community. It is far less easy, of course, to have and exercise these virtues in the face of opposition, temptation, and seduction, and, particularly when confronted with evil, all too easy to reason ourselves into acceptance of seduction of one sort and another.

Nor is it the case that possession of a virtuous character guarantees outcomes which will suit us. The gods are capricious, rain and other blessings of nature fall on the unjust as much as on the just (or sometimes, it seems, more so). In the *Nicomachean Ethics* (34) Aristotle struggles with the question of how happy a man such as Priam might be said to be who, after a period of happiness and success, faces misery and disaster. He is reduced to saying that though the happy man will have the strength to bear his misfortunes, and will never do what is hateful and mean. In that sense he can never become miserable, even though he fails to reach blessedness. Is this something of an evasion? Hector in facing fate was noble, but it is hard to say that Achilles and Athena did not make him as miserable as a man could be, in drinking the cup not just of his own degradation, but also in his knowledge of what would befall Troy and those he loved and was fighting for. One might feel that here and elsewhere Aristotle does not plumb the depths of what is involved in tragedy. Whether this is so or not, it is not coincidental that it was the people for whom tragedy was the highest art were also those who articulated most clearly the nature of the cardinal virtues. As demonstrated by 'English Gordon, stepping down sedately into the spears' (35), it is the self-mastery acquired in the possession of those virtues rather than our reasoning ability that might enable us to bear whatever the fates are preparing for us. (36)

1. This summary of Kohlberg's views is to be found in the highly influential textbook for teachers, *Learning to Teach in the Secondary School*, edited by S. Capel, M. Leask and T. Turner, fifth edition, London, Routledge, 2009, p 221. Whether or not Kohlberg would have approved of the exact formulation, it is certainly the sort of thing which is commonplace in educational circles.

2. Gilbert Ryle, *The Concept of Mind*, London, Hutchinson, 1949, p26. There is indeed an affinity between Ryle's position on the irreducible element of 'knowing-how' in most human activity (irreducible to propositional knowledge) and the position of this chapter, in that both derive from Aristotle's views on practice. There is a close point of convergence between the two in that

in neither practical activity generally nor in moral judgement more particularly can one envisage the knowledge necessary being encapsulated in anything like a manual or list of explicit instructions. Whether one is riding a bicycle down a busy street or deciding how to treat a wayward pupil, there are always far too many factors of highly variable import bearing on the situation for any such algorithmic approach. What is necessary in each case is an unformalisable sense based on experience, of how to pilot the street on this occasion or how to treat *this* child in these circumstances. In the moral case, as we will see further below, it is this unformalisable security of judgement which Florence Nightingale had and which Lytton Strachey so manifestly lacked.

3. Michael Oakeshott, *Rationalism in Politics and Other Essays*, (New and Expanded Edition), Liberty Fund, Indianapolis, 1991, p 38.

4. Cora Diamond, '"We Are Perpetually Moralists": Iris Murdoch, Fact and Value', in *Iris Murdoch and the Search for Human Goodness*, edited by Maria Antonaccio and William Schweiker, Chicago and London: Chicago University Press, 1996, 79-109, p 100.

5. Aristotle, *Nicomachean Ethics*, trans. by Sir David Ross, Oxford, Oxford University Press (World's Classics), 19 , 1144a23. Cited henceforth as *Nic Eth*.

6. C. Hitchens, *The Missionary Position: Mother Teresa in Theory and Practice*, London: Verso, 1995.

7. St Augustine, *Confessions*, trans. R.S. Pine-Coffin, Harmondsworth: Penguin Books, 1961, p 28.

8. O.S. Curry, D.A. Mullins and H. Whitehouse, 'Is it Good to Cooperate? Testing the Theory of Morality as Cooperation', in *Current Anthropology*, on line, Feb 8, 2019

9. The Rorty quote is from his *An Ethics for To-day: Finding Common Ground Between Philosophy and Religion*, New York: Columbia University Press, 2010, p 15. Nagel's views on the

status of morality are most recently expressed in his *Mind and Cosmos: Why the Materialist and Neo-Darwinian Conception of Nature is Almost Certainly False*, Oxford University Press, 2012, especially in Ch 5 at pp 120ff. R.M. Hare's on moral reasoning can be found in his *Moral Thinking*, Oxford University Press, 1981.

10. Iris Murdoch, *The Sovereignty of Good*, London: Routledge and Kegan Paul, 1970, 97.

11. Nagel, *Mind and Cosmos*, p 118.

12. *Ibid*, 51

13. *Nic Eth* 1103a33

14. *Nic Eth*, 1143a30.

15. see *Nic Eth*, 1140b6ff

16 *Nic Eth*, 1179a31-1180a14

17. *Nic Eth*, 1179-20

18. G.K. Chesterton, *Orthodoxy*, London, John Lane, the Bodley Head, Ltd, 1908, pp 9 and 14.

19. see Plato, *Gorgias*, 504-20

20. Petrarch, *On His Own Ignorance and That of Many Others*, Hillsdale College Course Outlines, p 537, lines 22ff.

21. John Ruskin, 'Of King's Treasuries', from *Sesame and Lilies*, in *The Works of John Ruskin*, Vol 18, ed E.T. Cook and Alexander Wedderburn, London: George Allen, 1905, p 80.

22. George Orwell, 'Inside the Whale', in *The Penguin Essays of George Orwell*, London: Penguin Books, 1984, 107-138, p 127.

23. See Simone Weil, 'The *Iliad*, Poem of Might' in her *Intimations of Christianity Among the Ancient Greeks*, London, Routledge, 1987, pp 24-55, esp pp 28 and 25.

24. *Nic Eth*, 1144b1

25. see F. Nietzsche, *Beyond Good and Evil*, tran. W. Kaufmann, New York: Vintage, p 197. And it is not only with immoralists that reasoning runs into the ground. One has only to think of a philosopher such as Elizabeth Anscombe, defending a particularly

uncompromising form of counter-reformation Catholicism with all her formidable reasoning powers. She was so unsettling to the secularist liberalism of most of her philosophical colleagues that it is reported that many of them ended up simply wishing that she wasn't around to show by her very presence that 'reason' did not necessarily converge on their progressivist conformism.

26. Hilary Putnam, *The Many Faces of Realism*, Open Court, 1988, p 68; see also David Wiggins, 'Truth, Pragmatism and Reality', *Philosophy, 88,* July 2013, pp 351-68.

27. R.M. Hare, *Moral Thinking: Its Levels, Method and Point*, Oxford University Press, 1981.

28. Weil, *op cit*, p53

29. Aristotle, *Politics*, trans. T.A. Sinclair, London: Penguin Books, 1981, 1334b27-8.

30. Blaise Pascal, *Pensées*, le Guern edition, Paris: Gallimard, section 139 (p 131)

31. Heart: 'We usually fall into much error by considering the intellectual powers as having dignity in themselves, and separable from the heart; whereas the truth is, that the intellect becomes noble or ignoble according to the food we give it… It is not the reasoning power which, of itself, is noble, but the reasoning power occupied with its proper objects. Half of the mistakes of metaphysicians have arisen from their not observing this; namely, that the intellect, going through the same processes, is yet mean or noble according to the matter it deals with, and wastes itself away in mere rotatory motion, if it be set to grind straws and dust. If we reason only respecting words, or lines, or any trifling and finite things, the reason becomes a contemptible faculty; but reason employed on holy and infinite things, becomes herself holy and infinite.' John Ruskin, *Stones of Venice*, Vol III, Ch IV, section VII. (*The Works of John Ruskin*, (ed) E.T. Cook and Alexander Wedderburn, London, George Allen, 1903, Vol X!, p 203) 'Mere rotatory motion': a lot of that in academic philosophy.

32. Blaise Pascal, *Opuscules et Pensées,* (ed) Léon Brunschvicg, Paris: Hachette, 1912, 185

33. Michael Oakeshott, 'A Place of Learning' in his *The Voice of Liberal Learning* (edited by Timothy Fuller), Yale University Press, 1989, pp 17-42, p 41.

34. *Nic Eth*, 1099b32-1100a30.

35. A phrase borrowed from Geoffrey Hill's poem 'The Mystery of the Charity of Charles Péguy'.

36. I am indebted here to conversations with David Wiggins, and also to his *Ethics: Twelve Lectures on the Philosophy of Morality,* London, Penguin, 2006. Candace Vogler, Anthony Price, Elizabeth Frey, and Robert Peal have also helped me in some key places in my argument. An early version of this paper was given as the Knox Memorial Lecture at the University of St Andrews, April 22, 2013. I am grateful to John Haldane, both for arranging the invitation and for discussion of many of the issues raised, and to John Kekes for helpful comments on an earlier version.

Chapter 5

FAMILY AND STATE IN EDUCATION: WHAT ROLE FOR PARENTS' RIGHTS

Parental Rights in Law and Practice

The United Nations Declaration of Human Rights was ratified in 1948. Its article 26 states in unequivocal terms that 'parents have a prior right to choose the kind of education that shall be given to their children'. Slightly earlier, in 1944, the British Parliament passed a landmark Education Act, section 76 of which stated that 'pupils (are) to be educated in accordance with the wishes of their parents'. As far as I know, the 1944 Act has not been repealed in this respect, and the United Nations declaration still holds. What I want to do in this chapter is to examine the reasons why both documents are correct in placing parental rights in educational matters above those of the state. The reason for doing this now is that it is no longer clear that parental rights are recognised in practice in many places, nor is there any general understanding of why they should.

Did they ever? The cynic would no doubt say that, even in 1948, parents quoting article 26 in the USSR would have got short shrift. They may well have found their children, enmeshed in state schools and nurseries and pioneer palaces, denouncing them to their minders. By the end of the 1950s parents wishing to invoke article 26 would have fared no better in Poland, Czechoslovakia, Hungary, East Germany, Romania, Albania, and in many other places including notably China and Cuba. But one should not be too cynical about the rest of the world. In the Britain of the 1950s and 1960s, there was some flexibility in relation to religious schools. But parents who used the state system of education (some 93% of them) who wished to exercise the right for choice of school under the 1944 Act would routinely meet massive obstacles placed in their way by the officials charged with allotting school places according to inflexible bureaucratic norms. The civil servants involved would often justify this by claiming that they knew better than parents how to fit pupils to schools and had a better understanding of what the public good required in terms of which schools should exist where.

Leaving the situation in the Eastern bloc before the fall of the Berlin wall, we should note there are currently in this country disturbing signs that parental wishes may be being flouted in ways undreamed of back in the 1940s and 1950s. It is not just that parents in Britain still have extremely limited choice over which schools their children will go to, but more that within schools doctrines and ideologies which many parents would object to are being promulgated and enforced through state directives and inspectorates. I say 'would object to' here because it is not always easy for parents nowadays to find out exactly what is being taught and advocated in their children's schools on such sensitive and disputed matters as sexuality, race, and climate. This itself says something about the way some of those in charge of education, including some head teachers, view the rights of the parents of the pupils.

So why are parental rights in education important? The UN declaration talks about parents having rights over the education of 'their' children. Does this imply that the mere fact of propagating children gives the parents something akin to possession of children they bring into the world? Children do not *belong* to their parents as a car or a house might. Children are living human beings, increasingly with minds of their own, moving towards autonomy and independence, which is part of what a civilized upbringing should be directed towards. Nevertheless the intimate relationship between parents and their children means that parents are best placed to make certain decisions over the way their children should be reared and educated, and in this sense parents have rights over and above any we may think belong to the state in this respect.

So, although I disagree with St Thomas Aquinas when he says that children belong to their parents before they reach the age of free will, I do agree with the Thomistic view on parental rights, as expressed by the landmark papal encyclical *Rerum Novarum* from 1891. (1) *Rerum Novarum* – 'Of New Things' – is an attempt by the Catholic Church to spell out what the new social order arising from industrialization should be, and what attitude should be taken to workers' rights and the rise of socialism. In section 14 of the encyclical parental rights are directly addressed: parental authority cannot be abolished or absorbed by the state, for parental authority has the same source as human life itself. A state setting aside the parent and setting up state supervision over the home and the family would act against natural justice. It is this view which I will expound and defend in what follows. I will show that it relies on general truths about human nature, rather than on anything peculiar to Catholic social teaching or dogma. Part of what is at issue here is the principle of subsidiarity, that is wherever possible devolving decision making to the smallest units in society, in this case the family. Referring here to the principle of subsidiarity may have a wider significance, as this principle, and indeed aspects of Catholic social teaching more generally, have from time to time been influential in the relevant policies of the European Union.

However, there have been societies in which a very different view of parental rights from the Thomistic one was taken, and there have been distinguished thinkers who have dismissed such rights entirely. We will now look at ancient Sparta and Plato as paradigmatic examples of a society and a thinker in each case.

Parental Rights in Sparta and in Plato

According to Plutarch in his biography of Lycurgus, the legislator credited with the development of ancient Sparta, Spartan children were held not to 'belong' to their fathers, but 'to the state in common'. (2) They belonged to the state in the sense that boys and men were bred to fight for Sparta, while girls and women were to produce offspring for the purposes of fighting and propagating for the common good. Belonging to the state in common entailed that on birth, a new-born child would be examined by tribal elders. If they were flawed or deformed, they were left out on one of the surrounding mountains to die of exposure. At the age of seven healthy boys were taken from their parents and placed in herds, as Plutarch called them, to be brutally trained and toughened up for military service under the control of sergeant-major-ish figures called boy-herders. Girls were also trained in physical exercise so as to develop their capacity to bear children healthily, and also in useful domestic pursuits. It is not necessary to go into further detail here, save to say that existence in Sparta was, as Plutarch remarks, tantamount to living in an armed camp. Everything in Sparta was subordinated to this, which explains why the ancient Spartans were such indomitable and courageous soldiers, feared throughout the Hellenic world and beyond.

If in ancient Sparta citizens belonged to the state in common, this is even more dramatically the case in Plato's *The Republic*. (3) The Athenian Plato was in fact strongly influenced by what he knew and liked of Sparta in his picture of the ideal state. Like George Orwell in *1984*, Plato was not very interested in the proletarians, and what he recommends as far as education and upbringing are concerned is focused on the ruling élites, the guardians of the state, and the actual rulers.

Because the lives of the ruling echelons of the ideal society are to be directed and devoted solely to the public good, Plato will remove from them everything which might encourage or permit any kind of self-interest as far as is possible, though interestingly, unlike Orwell, he does not seem sensitive to the way that sheer love of power can corrupt rulers as much as material wealth. However, he is very sensitive to the dangers and 'dissensions that arise among men from the possession of property, children and kin' which would no doubt include striving to give one's own children a better life and inheritance than those of others. Indeed, in later discussing disordered states, Plato inveighs about the way the rich pamper their offspring and make of them 'spoiled wantons'. (4) Whether this is entirely fair or not, in families there will inevitably be a tendency to favour of one's children in aiding their ascent to status and position, amounting at times to nepotism.

Thus, to avoid the many abuses which Plato sees as arising from inequalities of wealth, often centred on one's family, the guardians in the Republic will have all their possessions in common. Their mode of life will be rigorously egalitarian. They will live entirely in common, including in their personal lives. Women will be on the same level as the men, and, as far as possible, equal in roles. As Plato sees families as giving people private, selfish, and particular concerns and interests, drawing them away from the communistic way of life, there will be no families. Men and women will, of course, have to copulate so as to produce children, but this will be by means of communal orgies to be held at set times, after which the pairing couples will disperse. Children will be brought up in communal pens or crèches, taken by state officials from the mothers at birth, so that parents and children will not be able to recognize each other as such (The men, of course, may not know that they have actually impregnated a woman, or indeed, if they have, which woman). In the communal nurseries and schools, children will then be given the type of education Plato thinks will fit them for guarding and ruling the state, though taking care to ensure that those who advance to the higher stages of contemplative philosophy do not forget that they are to return to duties in the state.

What Plato is doing here is to build on those aspects of Spartan life which he finds attractive, and to push them to the limit. Plato's own attitude to what he calls kallipolis, the beautiful city, is not altogether clear – did he really believe it to be beautiful, or was he proposing it as a dreadful warning to utopians? Whatever Plato's own position here, and most scholars have taken *The Republic* at face value, there is no doubt that many subsequent readers have found, and still do find, aspects of it appealing: its kibbutz-like equality, its armed readiness, its proto-feminism, its egalitarianism, and, perhaps most insidiously, its implied critique of the autonomy and privacy, even insularity, of the family. To see why Plato is wrong on this last point particularly, we cannot do better than turn to Plato's own pupil, Aristotle. In his *Nicomachean Ethics* and his *Politics,* Aristotle shows us a sense in which the family is both a natural institution and a beneficial one, generating affections, loyalties, and virtues which utopian visionaries hostile to the family either wrongly dismiss or overlook completely. (5)

Aristotle on the Family and the Household

Human beings, as Aristotle tells us, are naturally disposed to form couples, not only as animals do, for reproduction, but also 'for the various purposes of life', with each partner bringing particular goods to the union and fulfilling different functions. The children of such unions will naturally be loved by their parents, as being a part of themselves, while the children will love the parents as having originated from them. Because of the ties of blood, children will start life with a natural affection for their parents, and a disposition to obey. In this environment children will learn the habits of virtue, without which any moral or reflective ethical life is impossible. Aristotle strongly and correctly believes that in order to reason well about morality, you must already have dispositions to love and respect the good and be shamed by the bad, dispositions which are best nurtured in the family. (6) Crucial to the question of education is the fact that the bonds linking parents and children mean that parents will know their children and what suits them better than those outside the family, so 'private education has an advantage over public'. And the ties of blood, which exist between parents and children, will also extend to siblings, cousins, grandparents, grandchildren, and so on. Thus the family engenders a small community, with links to the past and the future, ideally inculcating loyalty, virtue, and love in a way that would not be possible in a larger, more impersonal and less naturally related setting. (7)

These considerations in the *Ethics* are resumed and developed in the *Politics*. If the union of man and woman is natural, as being required for propagation, other needs are fulfilled in the family, as we have seen, but to fulfil the needs and promote the success of single families, villages will be formed, and then, in order to deal with matters of justice, states. In this sense the state is natural and man is naturally a political animal. Aristotle develops this point by saying that there is a sense in which the state is prior to the individual, or indeed the family, who are not fully self-sufficient. In particular, it is only in a state, with laws and systems of justice and order beyond personal self-defence and revenge that individuals and families can lead peaceful and productive lives. (8) However, against Plato, that does not mean that property and marriage should be abolished. Ownership produces care and responsibility over what one owns, and also pleasure or enjoyment, including that of exercising generosity. Common or free sexual relationships would undermine the special affection which comes from marriage, and the bonds and loyalties which come therefrom, which are of benefit to the state. In general, and in opposition to Plato's general line on equality and lack of differentiation among the guardian classes, too much uniformity in a society would be 'to reduce concord to unison or rhythm to a single beat'. (9) We will have more to say later on the benefits of difference and dispersed initiative within society in general and in education in particular, for this will turn out to be one of the most important values in and brought about by parental choice. However, we do have to note that, seemingly against the general line he is taking and against what he says in the *Ethics*, at the end of *Politics*, Aristotle insists that education, being a public concern, the responsibility for the curriculum and education generally must be that of the state: 'education must be one and the same for all.' (10) We will suggest in what follows that Aristotle is right in saying that the state does have a responsibility for education, but that this does not require that it should lay down a universally mandatory curriculum, or that it should monopolistically provide education itself. Indeed, the state would better discharge its own responsibilities if it facilitated the parental choice recommended in the 1940s.

In pitting Aristotle against Plato on the family, and in endorsing Aristotle's position, I am not claiming that Aristotle is completely correct on all points here or elsewhere. Notoriously, in discussing the family, or what he tends to refer to as the household, Aristotle speaks approvingly of the possession of slaves, and also about the dominant role of the father. What he says about slavery should be emphatically rejected; however, what he implies about households can be fruitful in suggesting that one positive feature of the immediate family may be the way in which others not related to the family by blood may be drawn positively into its orbit, friends and others helping with child-care, school journeys, games and sports, sharing holidays and the like. In other words, families have a natural tendency to branch out to and even create other small communities, with their own virtues and sense of belonging. As far as the father is concerned, we can, of course, take issue with the Aristotelian idea that the father is or should be the ruler of the household. But there may still be virtue in seeing a degree of differentiation of role as being one of the benefits of living in a family/household – differentiation which can in part stem from basic biological differences, which it is unnecessary to spell out here. In any case, what I see, following Aristotle, as the virtue of the family does not depend on any hard and fast doctrine of role differentiation among the parents.

What it does depend on is the thought that the family is essentially a household, as Aristotle says, a household of a specific sort. It is a home, a place of belonging, and as such it has beneficial characteristics which will not be otherwise attainable elsewhere. We have already touched on the intimate ties of affection, dependence, and care which exist, or should exist, between parents and children, and the way in which they cannot be replicated in more impersonal and less intimate settings. Building on this, we can also consider the way in which basic habits of civilized life are engendered unreflectively, quasi-naturally within a family upbringing, such as language, norms of behaviour, moral attitudes and feelings, and a sense of loyalty and belonging. This is not to deny that these habits might not be produced in other settings, but only to insist on the seamless way they will be produced in a well-functioning family. Nor is it to deny that not all families are well-functioning. Some may function hardly at all, with the result that their children may reach school age without the most basic dispositions and skills. But this will be by contrast with the vast majority of families which do function well, and points to the need in the sadly deficient families for support and guidance, rather than being an argument against families as such. It also underlines the way that in most families the beneficial effects of that form of life continue to be produced, in part because parents and grandparents feel instinctively what needs to be done, often despite difficulty and struggle, but with a sense of reward for the unique type of success inherent in family life. As Aristotle points out at length, happiness should be seen as a by-product of virtuous activities done well, rather than something like pleasure, which we can or should aim at directly. (11) In this way, for very many people, living and working at family life is one of the deepest sources of happiness, and not just for parents and children as related to each other, but for other relations such as grandparents, siblings, cousins, aunts, uncles and the like.

Family Life: Wider Considerations

In defending and advocating family life, as we are, we do not need to deny that families can be prone to abuses of various sorts. The very intimacy which is a crucial part of good family life can lead to child abuse. It can, but again, this is not the norm, and is regarded by most people and in most families as the more heinous as a desecration of a sacred bond and as exploitation of those who are innocent and defenceless. Families can also be a source of corruption, as Plato suggests, from the familial possession of property and wealth. But again, we can agree with Aristotle, and many other subsequent thinkers, that owning property is a benefit and a bulwark. It is a benefit because it enables the possessors to lead their own lives in freedom and security, prey neither to violent seizure nor confiscation by an over-mighty state, though for both of these to be prevented, a state with a legal system is necessary, as Aristotle says. In addition, getting and having property inculcates habits of work, responsibility, and foresight, virtues integral to family life. But again in Aristotelian mode, good things and institutions can lead to excess. Excessive wealth may be a bad thing; excessive pursuit of wealth certainly is, especially when it leads to corruption and nepotism. We can note that in Dante's *Purgatorio* (Canto XX), Hugh Capet is being punished for avarice. He tried too hard and too deviously to secure riches for his descendants who went on to form the Capetian dynasty which ruled France for more than three centuries. In Dante these Capetian rulers are themselves denounced for similar sins by their ancestors. So avarice and nepotism are vices, worthy of punishment in the next world if not in this, but that does not mean that a responsible attitude to family property and a moderate and prudential concern for the material and social well-being of one's children and descendants are not virtuous expressions of natural family love, stemming from bonds which are fundamental to a good society. And it is clearly of benefit to society in general that there should be families who provide and care for their young, and instil in them dispositions to work, be responsible, and care for their children.

Roger Scruton follows Aristotle in pointing to one very important and unique aspect of family life, one which recognises the social quality of the family and implicitly its extension through generations. Being a member of a family not only gives us a home, metaphorically if not literally speaking. It also gives us an identity and a motive for staying together. Well functioning families may disagree within themselves, but they will discuss matters of general concern among themselves, and the members of the family will accept to be bound by the final decision, even if they disagree individually. The family is part of their identity, and that does not change even if there are conflicting views. This 'shared identity takes the sting from disagreement. It is what makes opposition, and therefore rational discussion possible; and it is the foundation of any way of life in which compromise, rather than dictatorship, is the norm.' (12)

So the family is a group within the wider society. It has its own ineffaceable bonds arising from blood and birth. In the family important values and virtues are nurtured and fostered in a strikingly effective way. This is not to say that these values cannot be developed in other contexts; but it is notable that many surveys show that children not brought up in stable two parent families on average do worse on many counts, psychological, moral, educational, and even in liability to be abused, than those who are. (13) In giving its members a sense of home, belonging, and identity, the family is not against the state or the wider society. Indeed, as already observed, for its flourishing it needs the state with its framework of defence, order, and legality. But it is not the same as the state or to be subsumed within it. Even while recognising the legal and other benefits of the state and benefitting from them, it may disagree with aspects of state policy or with the views of the majority in a state. It may take its own path. The family is thus autonomous, one of those little platoons which Burke saw as essential to a free society, if not the basic little platoon.

So, within a state, the family is prior, naturally and socially, for both biological and political reasons. Where it exists, or is allowed to exist, its bonds will be stronger than those of any other institution, as well as in principle affording home, belonging, and upbringing of a uniquely beneficial type to its members. The family will not be hostile to the state, but it will be in important respects more cohesive than the state, and autonomous of it. It is precisely because of this last point, from which its private and partial interests and loyalties stem, that utopians like Plato, the admirer of Sparta, will tend to be hostile to the family and even want to abolish it altogether. And it is not just out and out utopians who want to minimize the reach and influence of the family. Remarkably, in 1796 in the wake of the American revolution, Benjamin Rush, one of the original signatories of the Declaration of Independence, said that 'each youth does not belong to himself, but is public property in the cause of liberty'. (14) It is remarkable that Dr Rush thought that liberty would be served by a regime owing more to Sparta than to what the USA was becoming at the turn of the nineteenth century. And he was also remarkably wrong if he thought that thinking of youths as public property, and hence presumably, leaving their families with little or no say in their education or development, would serve the cause of liberty. To see why this is so, we can do no better than turn to what J.S. Mill, the great nineteenth century advocate of liberty, had to say on education in his classic *On Liberty* from 1859. (15)

The Family and Liberty: J.S. Mill

Mill's discussion of education in Chapter V of *On Liberty* may well surprise those who are not familiar with its arguments. Mill begins by asking if it is not almost 'a self-evident axiom' that the State should 'require and compel the education, up to a certain standard, of every human being who is born its citizen'. Answering in the affirmative, he goes on to say that it is also a 'sacred' duty of parents to give to their offspring 'an education fitting him to perform his part well in life towards others and himself'. How are these two principles to be reconciled? Mill is clear that no one should bring a child into the world without having some prospect of feeding and educating it, but that if these duties are not fulfilled by parents, the state should step in and supply them, both for the good of the child – paternalism – and for the good of society in general. And this intervention on the part of the state should be effected as far as possible at the expense of the parent.

Mill's robustness on parental responsibility may be unfashionable in 2023, at least among public commentators and officials, though it has something to be said for it, and is probably in practice accepted by many of those about to become parents even in 2023. However, Mill's next point is the crucial one, and it is one which can and should be defended quite independently of whether we agree with Mill on the parent's initial duty. While Mill accepts that it is the duty of the State to enforce universal education, he insists that is quite different from saying that the State should provide this education. In Mill's own words, the reason for making this distinction is that

> a general State education is a mere contrivance for moulding people to be exactly like one another; and as the mould in which it casts them is that which please the predominant power in the government, whether this be a monarch, a priesthood, an aristocracy, or the majority of the existing generation in proportion as it is efficient and successful, it establishes a despotism over the mind, leading by natural tendency to one over the body.

Every one of Mill's words here is worth pondering. Mill is as passionate and eloquent a defender of liberty as any. The whole argument of *On Liberty* is that liberty in a society depends on the possibility of a diversity of view, of disagreement and discussion, and that it is only through disagreement and discussion that truth will emerge. Even, or perhaps especially, the most widely held and apparently irrefutable opinion should be tested by critical reflection, if only to bring out its true strength and validity. I suspect that Socrates might agree, although Plato, his pupil, would not. As we have seen, Plato wanted a unified state, a super-Sparta, unified in thought as much as in behaviour. But given that no one, not even a Platonic guardian, can have the whole truth on anything, as Socrates would have insisted, and given that dissent or question-free unity of this sort will be achieved only by compulsion, a state unified in the way Plato wants will indeed be a despotism. Against Plato, and against all those who dislike difference and diversity of view in a society, or faction, as they might disparagingly call it, it is worth recalling the words of James Madison who, like Rush, was an American founding father. In *The Federalist Papers* (No 10) he says:

> Liberty is to faction, what air is to fire, an aliment without which it instantly expires. But it could not be a less folly to abolish liberty, which is essential to political life, because it nourishes faction, than it would be to wish the annihilation of air, which is essential to animal life, because it imparts to fire its destructive agency.

And in *Federalist* 51, Madison goes on to insist that the rights of minorities, civil and religious, will be best secured against majority oppression by numbers of different interests and sects being present in a society. Justice, he says, is the end of government, which will ever be pursued until it is obtained or 'until liberty be lost in the pursuit.' (16)

To return directly to Mill and education, the general state education he deplores, one where liberty is lost, would to-day be one arising from a democratic 'majority of the existing population'. Assuming what we may doubt in practice to be the case, that the majority is having its wishes enforced on the system of education, could such a thing truly be said to be 'despotic', as Mill says? Madison has given us reasons to think it could be in practice, and as Thomas Jefferson observed, an elective despotism is still a despotism: '173 despots would surely be as oppressive as one... As little will it avail us that they are chosen by ourselves. An elective despotism was not the government we fought for.' (17) A majority government would certainly be illiberal to the extent that it admits of no divergence or exit from its methods and curricula for parents who dislike what the state is offering.

That there can be such a thing as a democratic despotism, a soft despotism, has been tellingly suggested by de Tocqueville in the second volume of his *Democracy in America* from 1840. (18) In such a society, the leaders will be not tyrants, but rather schoolmasters. Over the whole of society, there will stand an immense tutelary power, resembling parental authority, or rather would do, if its aim was not that of normal parents, but rather that its subjects should be kept in *perpetual* childhood. This power 'covers the whole of social life with a network of petty, complicated rules that are both minute and uniform', and which relieve individuals of the need to think or provide for themselves. They will, in effect, be infantilized, as de Tocqueville said, from cradle to grave, we might add. It is easy to see that in such a society, parents would have no rights over the education of their children. Their say, if any, will be limited to what they might be able to persuade their elected representatives to push for within the state bureaucracy, which will amount in practice to very little. As Mill says, this will amount to a despotism over the mind, over what can be taught or thought in school, but in such a way that it may not be recognized as such. Will it establish a despotism over the body? Well, it may certainly try to, with directives about what children are allowed to eat in school, about how much exercise they must take, and about how their social and personal development is to be conducted outside the home and in school.

These reflections on liberty, both in general and specifically on educational provision, suggest that parental rights in education are not just what would be good from the point of view of the family, but they are also good from the point of view of the society as a whole, if that society has liberty as a core good. Against this, it could still be urged that it would be best for children, for all children, to have the best education possible, and some or even many parents may not understand what this is. As Dewey memorably and somewhat sententiously put it back in 1889, 'what the best and wisest parent wants for his own child, that must the community want for all its children.' (19) Dewey does not, of course, say who he thinks the best and wisest parent might be, though one might have a suspicion as to who it is, and if it were John Dewey, it is not what I would want for my child. It would be 'the community' that imposed whatever it and Dewey wanted on my child and on all other children, so we are back in effect with a Millian despotism.

Public Education Policy and the Family

No doubt too, as experience with state direction of has shown, the mechanics of 'the community' coming to a view on what the best and wisest parent might want or who that best parent might be would not be altogether disinterested or transparent. I write here from experience, dispassionately I hope, as having served from 1993-7 on the British government quango charged with re-drafting the National Curriculum for England and Wales, and overseeing public exams. First, the opinions or prejudices of the legislators involved will deeply affect educational policies on matters such as curricula and examinations and school inspection, as they certainly did from 1993-7 and subsequently, when a change of government reversed much of what had been done earlier. Then there will be special interest groups lobbying for their particular causes, in many cases with some success, given the way these things work. There will, in addition, by the interest of the providers, as represented by teacher trade unions and their supporters in academia who continually lobbied for particular notions of how teaching should be conducted. Nor, to be totally honest, should we discount here the way advisors such as myself come to be chosen and actually influence policy. As I say, from my own experience I know the tortuous and indirect way government policy on education (and other matters) actually comes to fruition, and, even though it arises through 'democratic' processes, the results, even where they may be desirable, may have little to do with what the majority in the country actually want.

Nor should we discount the bureaucratic interest; civil servants may be personally incorrupt and government departments functioning impeccably, but, as in allotting school places, bureaucracies and those running them always have their own agenda. For good reasons or bad they may have their own ideas on what a smoothly running education system should be, one which may naturally and for convenience give rather more attention to the interests and wishes of the providers than they should. They will often, and in a way understandably, prioritize administrative convenience – the smooth running of a vast system dealing with millions of children and half a million or so teachers – over and above the wishes or interests of individuals, in this case, individual parents and children. As already observed, families will undoubtedly know more about the needs and interests of their children than will civil servants at some remove from them. Family wishes should not be overridden simply to stop good schools being oversubscribed and poor schools not having enough pupils to keep going, as happens all too often when bureaucrats have charge of school places, and typically see their role as one of maintaining the status quo as regards school

IN DEFENCE OF LIBERAL EDUCATION

provision. Things are quite different here in the independent sector where schools which not enough parents want will, in very short order, reform themselves or have to close. But most parents will not be able to exercise that freedom; exit from the state system is just too expensive for most, and all too often poor schools are kept open with pupils in effect forced to go to them.

It might, though, be said that in a system where parental choice was the ultimate determining factor there would be schools which taught things which were out of tune with the norm or with what had come to be generally acceptable in a society. Here we have to allow that parental choice should up to a point be constrained by law. That is, schools which mal-treated children physically or which indulged in practices which seriously infringed children's basic rights in other ways, would not be permitted and would be closed down by law. As already observed, families can flourish only in societies in which there are legal systems upholding basic rights and administering justice. So one of the conditions of living a reasonable family life is to be in a society in which family members have to accept certain legal constraints, including up to a point, on education. Beyond very basic decencies and rights, though, it is not hard to envisage cases where some families and some members of some families hold beliefs which appear to contravene gener-ally held principles or norms of conduct, and wish to have their children educated in conformity with their minority beliefs and principles. Should such schools be permitted to exist? Should the mere fact that schools might be teaching minority religious beliefs or operating on extreme progressive lines, or even on very traditional lines, be closed down by the state? On this ques-tion, from the perspective of what is required by liberty, Mill is emphatic: 'All attempts by the State to bias the conclusions of its citizens on disputed subjects, are evil.' (20) There could surely be no more blatant attempt by a State to bias the conclusions of its citizens on disputed subjects than by preventing parents with dissenting but not inhuman views from educating their children as they see fit.

Parental Rights and Pluralism

In order to see what might be involved here, and how respecting parental rights might work in difficult cases, I now turn to William Galston's article 'Value Pluralism and Political Liberalism'. (21) It is relevant to note here that Galston is not only a distinguished American academic (senior fellow at the Brookings Institution), but has also served as a Presidential Advisor to President Clinton and has worked in no fewer than six US presidential campaigns. In the article Galston considers the attitude governments should take to communities such as the Amish, Mormons, and some minority Christian Churches when parents in those communities wish to educate their children according to their own principles rather than according to state norms, and who are taken to court as a result. Of course these cases are difficult, because in the cases in question the states will be using the law to do what they believe to be in the children's interests. Here there is a clear conflict between parental rights and what the legislators and officials deem to be the state rights, acting paternalistically on behalf of the children.

The beleaguered communities in question are in general law-abiding and, as Galston notes, often score highly on political engagement and education; he concludes that respecting value pluralism in liberal societies (that defended by Madison and Mill) requires that liberal societies should not 'casually interfere with organisations that don't conduct their internal affairs in conformity with broader political norms.' (22) Galston argues that there is a baseline minimum which everyone in a liberal society must conform to. So no community would be permitted to engage in human sacrifice, for example, and less unrealistically Galston would deny Jehovah's Witnesses the right to withhold blood transfusions from their children in life threatening situations. He also concedes that there is room for reasonable disagreement about where that baseline should be drawn, 'but the moral philosophy of pluralism should make us very cautious about expanding the scope of state power in ways that coerce uniformity.' (23) In line with his theoretical stance, Galston supports the parental rights of the groups he considers against legal attempts to coerce them and their children into the state schools or in attempts to make their own schools follow the state norms where these are matters of dispute.

Galston points out that in the cases in question there are conflicts between religious faith, tradition and authority, on the one hand, and what might be called Enlightenment values, on the other. He (and I) would defend the rights of the religious parents in such cases. Unfortunately, and against Galston's caution about expanding state power in these matters, in Britain anyway the state is increasingly using a combination of the law, regulation and compulsory inspection regimes to force all schools, including independent schools, to teach its own, or what may be majority, beliefs. These include beliefs on such matters as sexuality and climate change, and may well soon include beliefs on race and colonialism, with others to come. In each of these cases, present and to come, the positions taken up or maybe to be taken up, by the state are on what Mill rightly calls disputed subjects. In saying this, I am not saying where I stand on any of these matters, nor am I saying that the preponderance of argument may be on one side rather than the other, nor, incidentally does Galston in the cases he considers.

But what both Galston and I are saying is that the state should not abuse its power by enforcing its own view, or the view of those who have captured the state mechanisms in this respect, on those who disagree. It should not prevent parents from educating their children as they see fit. Galston argues his position from the point of view of political liberalism and value pluralism; I do so both from that point of view and from an analysis of the family which sees the family as a basic component of the liberal society, valuable in itself, but in its autonomy and separation from the state, a key element in a society which is essentially liberal. Liberal societies should uphold and defend parental rights in education, rather than undermining them by imposing its own views on education. Education is in itself a fundamentally contested area, so I would not, for example, as was attempted by a recent Secretary of State for Education, try to close down Summerhill. Nor would I insist, as some ethically conservative activists have proposed, that schools should be forbidden for accommodating pupils who, with parental backing, wish to transition sexually. I would argue that schools which wish so to accomodate transitioners should be allowed to do so. But by the same token, parents and children should be allowed to have schools which did not make special provisions for transitioners, were there a demand for them

Current Threats to Parental Rights

However, currently it is not schools like Summerhill which are most in danger, and where parental rights are being overridden. Many schools, state and independent, are currently in thrall to particular ideas about sexuality and race (or colonialism), as was observed at the start of this article. These views, which include the idea that white people are inherently and apparently irredeemably 'privileged' and also a raft of doctrines centering around the notion that gender (or one's sex) is 'fluid' and that one should not be fixed in the gender one is 'assigned' at birth (rather than born with). It seems that in some (many?)

cases, pupils who disagree with the orthodoxy being taught are treated roughly, reprimanded or even ostracized in school, if they have the temerity to express their disagreement (So much for 'critical thinking'!). More likely dissenting pupils will not reveal what they really think. Certainly in many cases they will be being taught, or indoctrinated more accurately, in ways and directions their parents think is wrong, even reprehensible. Worse still, there are cases where children or adolescents who are uncertain about their sexuality are being given advice and support in school, without their parents being consulted or even informed. It is not hard to envisage cases where pupils, possibly encouraged by teachers enthusiastic for the ideas in question, will denounce their parents privately or publicly for having the 'wrong' views, even for 'hate crimes'.

It is not hard to envisage such cases, because this is exactly what happened in the Soviet Union and the Eastern bloc countries under communism, to the extent that in the 1930s Pavel Morozov, a 13 year old 'young pioneer' denounced his parents to the authorities. As a result of this, his father was executed. Pavlik was knifed to death by his relations for his pains, and immediately became a national idol, a martyr to the cause, with an opera and many books produced in his honour. Whether what was celebrated actually happened or not is now somewhat disputed, but what is not disputed is that Morozov was for decades held up as a model for Soviet children to follow. We do not live in the Soviet Union, but there are tendencies within our society which are not completely dissimilar. We can certainly envisage parents being cautious in expressing their real beliefs to 'woke' children, indoctrinated in woke attitudes in school, maybe for fear of unpopularity or worse, for being denounced in school by their children, for example. What is in effect a repudiation of parental rights over what their children are taught in school will, at the very least, be corrosive to family life.

But it may be that schools themselves have little freedom of manoeuvre in this area. An independent school in England has recently lost its head following failure in two mandatory inspections for, in effect, not satisfying the inspectors on its attitude to homosexuality, which they described as a 'particular biblical interpretation'. In the second report the inspectors conceded that the school had actually addressed their concerns from the first inspection. There was now no discrimination against LGBT pupils and various measures had been introduced to cater for their needs, but the school still failed because there were some LGBT pupils who continued to lack self-esteem or confidence. What is striking about this case is that there was no mention in either report of the views of parents, who were not consulted in either inspection. Suppose the parents actually wanted a or the particular 'biblical' view taught? And even if they did not, is the implication that a school with such a 'biblical' view would not be allowed to exist, even if parents wanted such a thing (As has emerged in at least one other case, schools which fail to satisfy inspectors on the regulations governing the inspections can be threatened with losing their right to admit pupils, so one can understand the nervousness of the school in question)? But, providing one does not discriminate against LGBT people, and the school did not, according to the second inspection report, disputed as it might be, it is not (yet) illegal to hold a or the 'biblical' view on such matters. That, though, is the point. The matter is 'disputed', and not just by fundamentalist Christians. It seems to be exactly the type of case where, as Mill puts it, state attempts to bias the conclusions of its citizens are 'evil'. And yet this is just what the state appears to be doing not by legislation, but by a less than transparent inspectoral mechanism deciding on what can or cannot be done regarding a 'disputed' matter in an independent school. Or do we now have to write in an 'independent' school? For it seems that now any school teaching in the 'wrong' way on LGBT etc matters will be failed by inspection, with potentially damaging consequences for its future.

The Morozov case, of a child denouncing its parents, might well seem exaggerated in twenty-first century Britain. But social services already have extensive powers to involve themselves in the doings of families, sometimes appropriate and necessary, unfortunately. But overzealous action by social services and the manipulation of children's testimony is not unknown in this country. Notoriously, in 1991 children in Orkney were removed from their parents and one parent imprisoned over what turned out to be entirely baseless suspicions of satanically inspired child abuse. A particularly troubling aspect of this case was the use the authorities made of statements they elicited from some of the children concerned. One lesson that should be learned from this is surely that extreme care needs to be exercised over the use made of statements made about their parents by children, especially when these statements seem to justify action against the parents, and especially when those statements are elicited by over-enthusiastic officials. Morozov may suggest a general lesson, but not the one the Soviet authorities intended.

More recently, in an attempt to constrain families even more, in 2014 the Scottish Executive proposed a bill in the Scottish parliament to assign a 'guardian' outside the family for every child in the country, from birth until the age of 18. This state guardian would have access to all sorts of information about the children and indeed their families, and have powers to refer cases of concern to a raft of different agencies and authorities. One needs little imagination to conjecture what a guardian might do if 'unacceptable' views on race or gender were found in a family he or she was 'guarding'. The proposal eventually failed for various reasons, mainly to do with practicability, but though there was some opposition to it from bodies concerned with parental rights, it was supported by a number of charities and professional groups, as well as in Holyrood. To readers of Plato, the title 'guardian' has an ominous ring; and the proposal itself is indicative of current attitudes to parental rights among many politicians and officials, who seem to believe that families are problematic in themselves. While in England so far there has been no talk of state guardians poking their noses into the lives of every family, it is ominous that the recent Education bill in the Westminster parliament placed state education more firmly and comprehensively under direct regulation by the Secretary of State for Education than ever before; in that bill the parental right to choose a school with a curriculum they, rather than the Secretary of State, favoured is not even considered. The bill has been dropped for the moment, but its spirit may still be alive in Whitehall, even under a Conservative government.

It is for this reason that we need not only to remember the balance in the Eastern bloc between family and state, but also to see why, here and now, parental rights are important, the ways they are currently under attack, and how best to support and defend them. In this chapter, I have attempted to lay out the reasons for strong family rights particularly in education, as benefiting both members of families and the wider society in which families are allowed to flourish. This may well be timely, given that currently parental rights in education are under threat in a number of areas, either intentionally or simply by neglect and default. (24)

1. Thomas Aquinas, *Summa Theologiae*, IIa-IIae, X, 12. *Rerum Novarum* was issued by Pope Leo XIII in 1891, and sets out the Catholic Church's teaching on social matters.

2. Plutarch, *Greek Lives*, trans. R. Waterfield, Oxford: Oxford University Press, 2008, pp 9-41, esp pp 22-7.

3. Plato, *Republic*, trans. P. Shorey, in *Plato the Collected Dialogues,* Princeton; Princeton University Press, 1978, pp 575-843. The quotations here are from sections 454c to 465e.

4. *Republic,* 556b

5. Aristotle's *Nicomachean Ethics* and *Politics* are quoted in the World's Classics edition, trans and ed. Sir David Ross, (Oxford University Press, 1966) and the Penguin edition, trans. T.A. Sinclair and ed. T.J. Saunders,(London: Penguin Books, 1981), respectively.

6. See my paper 'Morality, Reason and Upbringing' *Ratio*, 33.2, June 2020, pp 106-16, in which I lay out and in the main defend Aristotle's views on the necessity for acquiring virtuous habits when young if one is to reason soundly on morality. A version of this paper forms Ch 4 above.

7. See *N Eth* 1161b18-1162a29 and 11806b 1-10.

8. *Pol*, 1253a20ff

9. *Pol*, 1263b29

10. *Pol*, 1137a11-32

11. See *N Eth*, 1098a16 and 1176a30-1177a10

12. Roger Scruton, *How To Be a Conservative*, London: Bloomsbury, 2014, p 33.

13. Quoted in E. Knight and C. Hall (eds), *Readings in American Educational History*, New York: Appleton, 1951, p 306

14. See, for example, the report *Family Structure Still Matters,* London: Centre for Social Justice, 2020, for a recent survey of this evidence, and copious references to sources.

15. J.S. Mill, *On Liberty and Other Essays,* Oxford: Oxford University Press, 1991. All the quotations from Mill are from pp 116-9 of this edition.

16. Alexander Hamilton, John Jay and James Madison, *The Federalist*, eds G.W. Carey and J. McClellan, Indianapolis: Liberty Fund,

2001. The quotations from Madison are from pages 43 and 271.

17. Thomas Jefferson, *Notes on the State of Virginia, Query 13,* 1784, p 120.

18. A de Tocqueville, trans. G. Lawrence, *Democracy in America,* London: Fontana Press, 1994, Vol 2, Part IV, Ch 6, pp 691-2.

19. John Dewey, *School and Society,* Chicago: Chicago University Press, 1956 edition, p 9.

20, Mill, *op cit,* p 119.

21, William Galston, 'Value Pluralism and Political Liberalism', in *International Meetings in Political Studies (Est. 1993), Vol 1,* Lisboa: Universidade Catolica Editora, 2022, pp 131-41.

22. Galston, *op cit,* p 138

23. Galston, *op cit,* p 139

24. I thank John McIntosh and William Galston for their advice on a number of points in this paper.

Chapter 6

EDUCATIONAL MYTHS

(VYGOTSKY'S CONSTRUCTIVISM, BLOOM'S 'TAXONOMY', HATTIE'S VISIBLE LEARNING, IDENTITY POLITICS, DECOLONISING THE CURRICULUM, CREATIVITY AND INDEPENDENT LEARNING)

Lev Vygotsky and 'Constructivism'

Vygotsky is credited (if that is the right word) with holding that people naturally 'construct or build their own knowledge or meaning, as opposed to having it 'given' or 'delivered' to them'. At least that is what educational theorists take him to have said (1), and this is what generations of trainees in teacher training are told. Few of them seem to see this for the nonsense (literally) that it is. To fill this out slightly, what this constructivism means is that knowledge and indeed the meanings of words and concepts are not things which exist independently of the individual; they are things which arise in each person's individual experience, independently and subjectively. In this view, each person's construction or interpretation is as valid as anyone else's, and in the classroom what we should aim at is to get each pupil to elaborate his or her own 'knowledge' or 'meaning'. The way the world is independently of the pupil or 'knower' plays at best a secondary role in this form of pedagogy.

Back in May 2014, when I was originally working on this note, I learned that Sri Lanka had beaten England in a T20 cricket match. I did not construct this unfortunate fact or build its meaning. Rather against my wishes, it was delivered to me by the BBC, and I just had to make the best of it. More seriously, I didn't build my own 'meaning' regarding the terrible and murderous explosions in Jos (Nigeria), also on May 21st 2014, a place I know from a few decades ago. To the contrary, I have simply tried (and failed) to see any meaning in this act; the knowledge, having been given to me, again by the BBC, is something I am struggling to comprehend, but it is still knowledge, even in the absence of a constructed meaning (in an area where obviously the BBC couldn't see any meaning either, as they quickly dropped all mention of it in their programmes).

To my mind the very phrase 'constructing knowledge' is at best a solecism, a category mistake as used to be said in philosophical circles. Knowledge is a case of (roughly) well grounded true belief, with the emphasis on 'true'. Truth is something independent of us, individually or collectively; it depends on the way the world is, so if we have a mental state (belief), over which we perhaps have some control, we do not have control over what makes a particular belief true (or false). That is not up to us. It is not something we can construct. To speak of knowledge implies that what is known is not believed by a matter of luck, but that in some way we are entitled to have that belief. For example, it is a belief we have some proof or evidence for or is well grounded in some fundamental way, such as the believer being led to believe by being in normal contact with what is believed, or the belief being a key assumption in the believer's regular dealing with the world. And entitlement to believe also depends on things outside of us; whether we are entitled to a particular belief implies that the way we came to acquire that belief in some way latches on to the way the world is, not just that we happen to think it is firmly based. So two of the core aspects of knowledge, truth and entitlement to believe, ought to make us antagonistic to speaking of constructing knowledge. It is an abuse of both thought and language.

All right, it might be said, it is not knowledge that we construct but the beliefs and meanings that go into the making of what we know, into how we come to have the relevant thoughts and commitments. And it is true that in a very broad sense, meaning, human language, and the cognitive frameworks in which our beliefs and thoughts are situated are the results of human activity and culture (Of course, education is part of the way that we induct children into these activities and cultures). But in the way that followers of Vygotsky tend to talk about these things, it appears that children themselves 'construct' their own meanings and beliefs, and do so in an episodic way. So at one moment, I didn't think or believe something. At the next, after a bit of mental constructing, I do!

Except that I don't. This is a complete travesty of the way beliefs are acquired or meanings learned. As the philosopher Gilbert Ryle used to ask people who talked in this sort of way about postulated mental processes and supposed constructions, how many beliefs did you construct since breakfast? Was it hard work? Did you need many tools? The point is that while we have a pretty good idea of how to construct a table, what tools we need, how the plan is to be followed, how long it might take, whether we would need any help, etc., this type of model has no application to the acquisition of a belief. We acquire beliefs, we don't construct them, and we acquire them because of the way aspects of the world appear to us, often without any realisation on our part, or are brought to our attention in some more explicit and focused way (as in the cricket case). And while some beliefs, like the cricket case, are consciously acquired (because someone told us), many are not (like my belief that I am now sitting on a chair, which I certainly had before I wrote this, but was not even conscious of until I thought about it). And, for the most part, we acquire meanings by listening to what others say (especially when we are young), by latching on to the meanings implicit in what they say and the language they use, and then beginning to use words ourselves, in the ways we have heard and understood them being used. If we don't use words in their established usages, we will quickly come to grief; if we are lucky, our mistakes will be corrected, and we will follow the right path in our speech and writing. What we might call our meanings will correspond to the normally accepted ones, and communication will take place with a degree of success which would otherwise escape us. If there is any constructing in any of this, it is not in the least like any constructing we knowingly do, which is another way of saying that it is not a case of constructing at all.

A further, and perhaps deeper point, for anyone who actually thinks about what Vygotsky (as interpreted by Wellington) is saying is that if all people naturally construct their own meanings, then they will all have their own individualistic private meanings. So if I refer to Sri Lanka, I will have the meaning I have constructed, and you yours. We won't mean the same thing by the term 'Sri Lanka' (or anything else), and we will have no means of knowing what others mean by the terms they use, nor they us. Communication between us will quickly become impossible, if it was ever possible under this regime of construction in the first place. For those philosophically inclined, what I have just propounded is a version of Wittgenstein's famous private language argument: meanings are not things each of us 'constructs' in our heads, but elements of systems (of thought and language) in the public world which, in growing up, learning to speak, and being educated, we all learn to conform. Meanings are public, not private, learned and acquired in negotiation with others, not constructed by or for ourselves.

Those who want to get something from Vygotsky and constructivism need to explain how what he says is still valid or valuable in the face of these obvious objections. Unfortunately constructivism and the subjectivism which underlies it, in one form or another, is extremely widespread in the classroom. It rears its head, indeed, every time a well-meaning teacher asks pupils to say how they feel about a text they are reading prior to trying to elucidate the meaning it actually has, or, as one has heard, getting pupils in a maths lesson to 'journalise' their fears about maths, instead of attempting to bend their minds to the logic and structure of the particular problem or theorem before them. The pupils are being told, implicitly at least, that their subjective feelings about what is before them are as valid, or even more valid, than the objective matter that is before them, and about which they are supposed to be learning. (2)

It might be that what constructivists have in mind is the thought, forcefully expressed by the nineteenth century American writer Ralph Waldo Emerson, about our reaction to great writing: 'In every work of genius we recognise our own rejected thoughts; they come back to us with a certain alienated majesty. Great works of art… teach us to abide by our spontaneous impression with good humoured inflexibility… when the whole cry of voices is on the other side…' (3)

You can see what Emerson means – the feeling of recognition when we read or see or hear something that moves us. To be sure, this does occur. It may, though, be an illusion. Proust (say) is not telling us what we already knew, for all the sense of recognition we might feel when reading him about love and jealousy. He is opening us to new ways of looking at the world and relationships, things we didn't know (and perhaps didn't want to know) before we read him. It is the inferior writers who simply reassure us that we were right all the time, and where we find nothing but our own thoughts, rejected or not.

Emerson's attitude is a dangerously reductive, sentimental attitude to art and indeed to the world. This attitude may indeed be prevalent in the educational world, where, perhaps following Vygotsky and his followers, we are constantly told that anything we teach children must be seen to emerge from their own experience, be relevant to them, etc. Great works of art, and culture more generally – what education should be about – do NOT reinforce our own thoughts, whether these are counter-cultural or not. They impress on us things which we had not imagined or thought. They may cause us to reject what we had thought before, because we now see that it is wrong, partial, misconceived, etc. They are objective in the sense that they take us out of our own feelings and conceptions into a wider and truer world, one we neither construct nor recognise from our own previous knowledge. And the same may be true of a real poet or writer, struggling against the grain of the language, and in so doing finding resonances and meanings he had never before imagined. On these points, see Geoffrey Hill's essays on alienated majesty (4) in his *Collected Critical Writings*, Oxford University Press, 2008).

The point I am making here is forcefully expressed by Ruskin, no less, in his praise of the book that has real worth, that in which the author can truly say, 'this is the best of me; for the rest, I ate, and drank, and slept, loved and hated, like another; my life was as the vapour, and is not, but this I saw an knew: this, if anything of mine is worth your memory' (a passage much admired, incidentally, by Proust). If we encounter a book of this sort, our attitude should not be to find our own thoughts expressed in it. In a true book, the author will think differently from us in many respects. 'Very ready we are to say of a book, "How good this is – that's exactly what I think!" But the right feeling is, "How strange that is! I never thought of that before, and yet I see it is true: or if I do not now, I hope I shall, some day."... Go to the author to get at *his* meaning, not to find yours. Judge it afterward, if you think yourself qualified to do so, but ascertain it first.' (5)

We might also consider Karl Barth on the Gospels: 'The Gospel does not expound or recommend itself. It does not negotiate or plead, threaten or make promises. It withdraws itself always when it is not listened to for its own sake.' (6) Yes, better withdrawal than condescending 'accessibility', the now instinctive move of educational élites (i.e. bureaucrats) to spare those they think inferior from difficulty and complexity and (in the true sense) challenge.

I shall have more to say about judging and ascertaining in discussing Bloom's so-called taxonomy in the next section. But it is worth noting here that Ruskin goes on to point out that authors, true authors, often speak in a hidden way, and in parables. There can be a 'cruel reticence' about them, which means we have to work harder to uncover a meaning which cannot be divulged in the common coin of cliché and journalism, or indeed in academic jargon. Talking of which, I have heard educators talking of something they call the zone of proximal development (often capitalised as Zone of Proximal Development, no doubt to make the notion seem more technical and important). The thought, dressed up in important sounding verbiage, seems to be the commonplace that, in teaching, you have to start from where the pupil is, mentally, socially or whatever, and then lead them on beyond that. Maybe; though I think that underestimates the ability of children to imagine themselves into worlds far from their own. However, the point of educating, in the sense of teaching to read, is surely to move the child to a zone of transcendence, out of the unimaginative narrowness in which most of us spend most of our days. But to do that the teacher will have to have knowledge, and knowledge that is worth imparting and which needs to be imparted. Is it too cynical to suggest that for teachers *without* knowledge, getting the pupils to 'construct' (research, actively investigate, etc) their own 'knowledge' is a very good way of letting their own ignorance remain hidden?

Footnote on Vygotsky

One of the things that concerns Vygotsky (and me) is how non-linguistic infants acquire language, more generally how this mewling puking babe can start to enter the human world at all, given that he or she starts with nothing recognisably human in any more than a physical sense. Some say that in this little heap of animality before us there are a host of innate, rationalistic ideas, which allow it to construct hypotheses about the world around it (including the world of adults speaking), and by trying out and testing these hypotheses, the little animal learns to speak, etc. Others, by contrast, say it is all to do with training, that through the classic behaviouristic tale of conditioning through reward, punishment, and reinforcement a babe can move from total inarticulacy to become a fluent speaker of French, Mandarin, or whatever. The latter position was, I think, conclusively demolished by Noam Chomsky in his famous piece on Skinner's behaviourism. (7) But Chomsky's own rationalism (the innate picture) has, in my view, even as amended by Jerry Fodor and others, fared no better. What are these mentalistic concepts and grammatical structures children are born with, and which they use, pre-linguistically, to latch on to actual languages? Where are they? In its mind (but it doesn't yet have a mind in any strong sense)? In its brain (but however much you look into the brain, you will find only neuronal activity; as Leibniz taught long ago, even if you could walk around the brain, you will find no thoughts or concepts)? How do we verify their existence, except as hypothetical postulates, invoked to explain what would otherwise be inexplicable, but with little or no independent verification?

Vygotsky looks far more sympathetic. A child learns language (and doubtless other human skills and abilities) by continuous interaction with adults and others around them. This is not exactly training in the narrow behaviouristic sense, nor does it require postulating a load of innate ideas and invisible mental structures before the poor child can even speak or articulate those ideas, ideas of which, of course, the child is unaware; nor does it have to invoke an unconscious 'mentalese' language of thought, underlying the actual thoughts and language we use and are aware of (Fodor's view). One could possibly put the Vygotskian picture into the language of John McDowell, of a child, in becoming human, acquiring a 'second nature' through acculturation, through being immersed in the history and practices of his or her people. (8) Through this historically mediated acculturation, the child, in McDowell's terms, 'acquires a mind': mind is not something a child is exactly born with, it is something it acquires as it encounters human life and practices. Vygotsky appears to have little truck with any quasi-rationalistic talk of a child grasping meanings through a rationalistic process of discovery and hypothesis testing on its part. Nor, in what I have just represented as Vygotsky's 'sympathetic' account, is there any notion of babies or children 'constructing meanings' for themselves. They come gradually to fall in with the meanings in the language and practices of the adults around them.

Vygotsky is sympathetic, but I am not pretending that he really *explains* anything. He describes (up to a point) what happens. As we might say, babies become children in emerging from the long, inarticulate sleep of infancy into the human world. Children gradually acquire language and a mind through interacting with those around them. But effective use of the simple words and thoughts little children begin with presuppose a grasp of many other thoughts and words before their sense is revealed. If I say that this cup is green, I must have a grasp of it as an object apart from other objects, as this object and not that, of an object of a certain type, with a certain function, of green as a colour, of green as not red, etc. One word, one thought, even the simple ones which we may credit little children with, are always embedded in a net of other thoughts and words. Understanding and working with this network, or a part of it, is what language and thought (as opposed to mere programmed response to stimuli) involve. How does the child enter this system, this sea of meaning? How did our remote ancestors move from the grunting and pointing of primitive reactions, to manipulating a complex system of communication and meaning?

Wittgenstein famously said in answer to these worries, that 'light dawns gradually across the whole'. (9) We cannot learn just one belief or even one word. In acquiring a belief or learning a word we learn a whole system of propositions or language, into which the belief or word fits and has its significance. Yes, but that does not elucidate the mystery of where or how the whole emerged in the first place. For to-day's child, at least, the system exists, all around them, in the discourse and activity and structures of the adults around them; but even here there is still the problem of explaining how the child from outside it comes to grasp what the whole is about and to be immersed it sufficiently to begin using it themselves. How can language be learned *merely* by reacting to stimuli from outside, which is what Skinner held? There must be something already inside us to latch satisfactorily on to those external stimuli, linguistic and sensory, but in such a way as to enable us to apprehend and use words in the way everyone else does, or at least in enough of the way to enable us to speak the public language which exists outside us, which raises once again the conundrum of how language started in the first place. (10)

1. cf J. Wellington, *Secondary Education, the Key Concepts*, London: Routledge, 2006, p 53.

2. On the nature and prevalence of 'constructivist' methods in the classroom, see Peter Boghossian, 'Critical Thinking and Constructivism, Mambo Dog Fish to the Banana Patch', *Journal of Philosophy of Education*, 46.1, Feb 2012, pp 73-84. Boghossian also gives references to constructivist thinkers other than Vygotsky, such as Caputo and van Glasersfeld.

3. Ralph Waldo Emerson, 'Self-Reliance' (1841), in his *Essays and Lectures*, ed. Joel Porte, New York: Viking, 1983, p 259.

4. Geoffrey Hill, *Collected Critical Writings*, ed. Kenneth Haynes, Oxford: Oxford University Press, 2008, pp 493-531.

5. John Ruskin, 'Of Kings Treasuries' in *Sesame and Lilies,* Section 1, in *The Works of John Ruskin*, Vol XVIII, ed. E.T. Cook and Alexander Wedderburn, London: George Allen, 1905, pp 61-3.

6. Karl Barth, *The Epistle to the Romans* (1918), trans. E.C. Hoskyns, London: Oxford University Press, 1933, p 38.

7. Noam Chomsky, 'A Review of B.F. Skinner's Verbal Behavior', in *Language* 35, No 1, 1959, pp 26-58.

8. See John McDowell, *Mind and World*, Cambridge Mass: Harvard University Press, 1994.

9. L. Wittgenstein, *On Certainty*, trans. G.E.M. Anscombe and G.H von Wright, Oxford: Blackwell, 1969, section 141, p 21e.

10. On Vygotsky see David Bakhurst, 'Training, Transformation and Education' in *Mind, Self and Person*, ed. A. O'Hear, Cambridge University Press 2015, pp 301-27. References to Vygotsky and the rest can be found in Bakhurst's article. Chomsky's review of Skinner is 'A Review of B.F. Skinner's *Verbal Behavior*', in *Language*, 35, No 1, 1959, 26-58.

Bloom's so-called 'taxonomy'

I say so-called, and will use inverted commas here, because this
is in no serious sense a taxonomy. All talk of taxonomy here is
pseudo-scientific, an attempt to give a spurious respectability
to a speculation, interesting in its way, but at best suggestive. It
makes it all sound very grand and important, but we shouldn't
be taken in by this. It is not a truth, let alone a scientific truth,
as I hope now to show.

Taxonomies are biological classifications of species. These
classifications are based (in theory) on a) a clear differentiation
of species through defining their essences, and b) underlying the
definition, some sort of chemical structure is assumed, which
causes the species to be what it is, different from other species,
DNA and the like, as we now know, but did not know when
biologists first started classifying species by means of taxonomies. Genetic analyses thus give support of a hard-edged kind
to some of the previously proposed taxonomies, while others
were found to be based on superficial appearances of difference
between groups of creatures or plants that really belonged to
the same species, and yet others show that apparently similar
creatures actually belong to different species.

So taxonomies outline, or attempt to outline, what philosophers call 'natural kinds', different types or essences, occurring
naturally in nature. The notion of a natural kind – and hence
of taxonomy – has been extended outside its original biological
home to physics and chemistry, where it is believed that there
are also distinct and distinguishable types of things occurring
naturally in nature, and which can be analysed in terms of
atomic and subatomic structure.

What the psychologist Bloom is describing as a taxonomy
doesn't even begin to approximate anything biological or scientific, and so should not be called a taxonomy.

First, the categories he mentions (knowledge, understanding, application, analysis, synthesis, evaluation) are not clearly defined in the way required by a scientific taxonomy. A true taxonomy shows clear differences between types of thing, enabling us to mark one type off from another.

Secondly, they are in no sense natural kinds, carving up nature at the joints, to use a phrase dear to philosophers of science (it was originally in Plato). Bloom's categories are vague terms, used to describe various human powers and capacities. They are more or less useful for certain purposes, in certain contexts, but no more than that.

Thirdly, no attempt has been (or could be) made to get to their underlying physical structure or essence (because they have none).

Fourthly, they clearly overlap – how can you actually know anything without a degree of understanding, analysis, and the rest? Or understand without a degree of analysis, etc.? Nothing wrong with this – but it suggests that we are not dealing here with a sequential hierarchy. All the things Bloom mentions are involved to a greater or lesser extent in any intelligent activity. The inference that evaluation is somehow a higher order skill than knowing misconceives the nature of knowing (and indeed of evaluating, which might be quite superficial, failing to come to terms with 'knowledge', 'understanding', etc.; knowing, really knowing something, might in some cases be the hardest, highest thing of all).

There is actually an unfortunate consequence which arises from Bloom putting his aspects of intellectual activity in a sequential hierarchy, with knowing at the bottom, and below understanding, applying, and analysing. It suggests that knowledge is a matter of ingesting some kind of brute datum, which can stand on its own as 'knowledge', no doubt with unfortunate implications of something just being acquired by rote or pure unthinking repetition, an unintelligent collection of Gradgrindian 'facts, facts, facts'. There may be some things which are simply 'known' in this sort of way (telephone numbers, perhaps). But the sort of knowledge at issue in education is always knowledge within a context of understanding and in connection to other things known and understood – or at least it should be. So, if I know the rule for multiplication, really know it, then I will understand its relation to the rule for addition; if I know the dates of the reign of Edward IV, I will understand this as part of a sequence of kings of England and in the light of what it is to be a king, etc. The sort of knowledge we are seeking to produce in the classroom will always be knowledge understood as embedded in a context, and analysable in various ways. And one could say that the more one understands the context and implications of what one knows, the more one actually, really, knows it. The processes Bloom is describing are cyclical, continually turning back on each other and throwing light on each other, not sequential in the sense his hierarchy suggests.

Fifthly, and following on from this, putting evaluation at the top of a cognitive hierarchy may give completely the wrong impression when we are dealing with serious matters. Who am I to 'evaluate' Dante or Homer? Or, indeed, anything which Ruskin would dignify with the name of a book? Or quantum theory and the theory of relativity? Should my attitude not be to forget what I think, set all this chatter aside, and immerse myself in what they have to say, and learn from them, getting behind the author's cruel reticence to immerse myself in the generosity which lies within? Forget alienated majesty, and instead consider this passage from Ruskin (which follows on from what I quoted in the previous section): 'Modern "Education" for the most part signifies giving people the faculty of thinking wrong on every conceivable subject of importance to them... You have... in any serious matters, no right to 'think', but only to try to learn more of the facts' (This is Ruskin, remember, the implacable enemy of utilitarianism and industrialisation, the advocate of truth to nature and of care for one's fellow man, and not Gradgrind, in many ways his economic and social nemesis! But they might strangely have come together on Bloom's 'taxonomy', if by very different routes). To continue with Ruskin: 'You will not be able, I tell you again, for many and many a day to come at the real purposes and teaching of these great men (Ruskin had been referring to Milton, Dante, and Shakespeare); but a very little honest study of them will enable you to perceive that what you took for your own "judgement" was mere chance prejudice, and drifted, helpless, entangled weed of castaway thought... All the true literary work before you, for life, must begin with obedience to that order' – that is, to the order of the teaching of the great men. (1)

So much the worse for Bloom's 'taxonomy', in that it appears to elevate the weed of castaway thought (your own 'judgement') over the hard-won obedience we need in order to read, or indeed to see, or draw or dance. Indeed, slavish adherence to the taxonomy may lead to a situation in which (because of the malign influence of assessment objectives and the like in public exams), a pupil may be given more credit for superficially 'evaluating' some worthless poem or story than for actually getting to grips with the meaning in something full of distance and difficulty, where understanding and appreciating requires real effort, concentration, and intelligence, something like *Paradise Lost*, for example.

It has been pointed out to me that many of the assessment schemes in public exams rely to a greater or lesser extent on Bloom's 'taxonomy', grading according to the hierarchy his 'taxonomy' suggests. As this hierarchy is misconceived for the reasons just mentioned, so much the worse for our teaching – and for our pupils being coached for exams. But the blame is ours for going along with this dogma. You might say that none of this matters very much in practice. After all, if you go through the stages of the 'taxonomy' everything will be there. I'm not so confident, though, and have more than a suspicion that putting evaluating at the top of the hierarchy and knowing at the bottom encourages the widespread fallacy that thinking skills and learning to learn are what is crucial in education, and that these things can be developed and even acquired in the absence of solid and considerable amounts of knowledge.

1. John Ruskin, 'Of King's Treasuries' in *Sesame and Lilies* (1865), in *The Works of John Ruskin*, ed. E.T. Cook and Alexander Wedderburn, Vol XVIII, 1905, pp 76-8. The sentence on modern education is the footnote to p 76.

2. Note that psychologist Benjamin Bloom is not to be confused with the distinguished literary critic Harold Bloom or with the philosopher and friend of Saul Bellow, Allan Bloom. Both these other Blooms have also made significant forays into the domain of education, Harold Bloom, with his stout defence of the Western canon and his 1994 book of that name, Allan Bloom with *The Closing of the American Mind: How Higher Education has Failed Democracy and Impoverished the Souls of To-day's Students* (New York: Simon and Schuster, 1987). Allan Bloom's book appeared in 1987 and was about the situation in US universities at that time. As far as I can see, its diagnosis is just as true in 2023, and applies just as much in Britain. It is stimulating to read, but if you want to find out more about what Allan Bloom thought, you can also look at Saul Bellow's novella *Ravelstein* (New York: Viking Penguin, 2000), which has the additional virtue of being very funny. (Ravelstein=Bloom, A., more or less, and Ravelstein's teacher Felix Davarr looks like the legendary Leo Strauss.)

Hattie and 'Visible Learning'

Because his 'Visible Learning' is being so assiduously promoted, many will have heard of John Hattie, a New Zealander, who has become the educational guru of choice to governments all over the world. And not just governments; his seminars and pronouncements are being used by academy chains and many others keen to raise standards.

In a way you can see why. For although Hattie likes to refer to teachers as change agents (!), some of what he says about teachers (sorry, I mean change agents) being able to counteract the effects of social deprivation and about the change agents actually needing to initiate purposeful activity in classrooms sounds sensible. Certainly it is a good response to those who are constantly telling us that we, as educators, can do little to counteract the effects of bad upbringing and that pupil activity, per se, is always to be preferred to teachers teaching. To those who need it, it might be reassuring to be told by a 'scientist' that teaching actually makes a difference. And, even though to some tastes it might seem overdone, they might also like Hattie's praise of passion in teachers. Nevertheless, he also inveighs against what he refers to as 'the current dominance of monologue' in teaching, which might make some wonder where he has been recently.

Hattie claims to have synthesised some mind-boggling number of studies of an even greater number of lessons, tens of thousands on the one hand, doubtless millions on the other, because he claims to be surveying (from a great height) the activity of 240 million students. It is indeed from a great height: his core data comes from synthesising over 800 'meta'-analyses 'relating to achievement'; so what he is doing is not just analysis, or even analysis of analyses but analysis of analyses of analyses. Somewhere at the bottom of all this analysis there may actually be a real teacher teaching some real children, but very far below the stratospheric regions in which the Hattie machine flies.

The pity is that those in charge of education are so pusillanimous that they apparently think that perfectly obvious truths (teaching can work even with the most deprived; teachers should actually teach) need some sort of vindication from massive exercises in number-crunching, filled out with stacks of meta-analyses. Pseudoscience again, like Bloom, B.

And there is another respect in which Hattie is like Bloom. Those who have been to a 'Visible Learning' seminar will have been given handouts purporting to quantify the effect some 150 separate ingredients of teaching listed by Hattie actually have in the classroom. So, teacher expectations, teacher credibility, formative evaluation, micro-teaching, classroom discussion, teacher clarity, and feedback come out very high (all grist to Ofsted's mill, no doubt, and indeed, up to a point, to mine). Teacher education, out of school curricular experiences, student control over learning, open vs traditional learning spaces, and welfare policies are apparently not much cop, being 134, 138, 144, 145, and 147 respectively in Hattie's league table, over which no doubt many will rejoice (though perhaps out of school curricular experiences may well have an *educational* value, which can't be quantified in one of Hattie's visible learning grids). What they might not be so happy about is that what he calls 'teacher subject matter knowledge' comes in this bottom group, at 136.

How can this be? Anyone minded to take Hattie seriously (even after he has redefined teachers as change agents) should immediately be alarmed. How can teacher subject knowledge not be a, if not the key, factor in teaching, right at the top of any league table? In his book, *Visible Learning: a Synthesis of Over 800 Meta-Analyses Relating to Achievement*, Hattie offers the rather lame explanation for his downgrading of the importance of teacher subject knowledge that 'it is difficult to find evidence that subject matter knowledge is important'. (1) To this one might reply that the centrality of subject matter knowledge to the very concept of teaching is such that it needs no evidence, any more than I need evidence to show that I am here and now writing at my laptop. Moreover, in Hattie's own grid, 'teacher credibility' is no. 4; but, as anyone who has had to flannel in a classroom will know – and we all have from time to time! – nothing undermines teacher credibility quicker than pupils finding holes in one's knowledge. So isn't subject matter knowledge the foundation of teacher credibility – and much else besides?

But maybe this misconception of the nature of teaching indicates that there is more to Hattie's talk of change agency than ugly terminology. Maybe Hattie thinks – as do some operators in the world of education – that teachers do not need to know much, but that armed with teaching techniques (questioning, micro-teaching, 'metacognitive' strategies, etc.) and with materials or resources given to them from on high, which they can then 'deliver', according to recipes prescribed by the companies or groups running their schools, successful learning will result.

Even if this is unduly cynical, one wonders how teachers can have credibility, how they can engage in formative evaluation, how they can micro-teach (whatever that is) or promote class-room discussion, let alone be clear (all high scorers in Hattie's scale) without deep and secure subject knowledge, at whatever level one is teaching.

I am not saying that someone teaching science to seven year olds needs a PhD in astrophysics, but they must know what they are talking about, and rather more than the pupils; nor am I saying that the proverbial PhD in astrophysics would thereby be a good teacher. Hattie indeed makes much of this point in a more recent book *Visible Learning and the Science of How We Learn*. (2) Chapter 2 there is actually called 'Is Knowledge an Obstacle to Teaching?', and in it, he labours the point that sometimes people who know a great deal (especially in maths) are poor at explaining it to those who don't know, and may not understand why beginners are experiencing difficulty (something I myself observed, and long before I read Hattie, with advanced logicians trying, often in a show-offy and arrogant way, to teach logic to first year undergraduates).

All this is true. We want teachers to understand how to deal with pupils at the level they are teaching at, and how to deal with their difficulties and misunderstandings. We don't want teachers to behave like my logician 'friends', forging on, oblivious (culpably oblivious, I'd say) of their students' basic, and often quite understandable difficulties of comprehension, and their consequent failure to grasp the most elementary points. But that does not show that (good) knowledge is not essential; to come close to home, in this country, part of the reason physics has been in decline over recent decades is that too many children have been and are being taught physics in secondary schools by teachers with very low qualifications in physics, a fact to an extent disguised by the lumping together of the sciences in what is called 'double science' at GCSE. And do we really want modern foreign languages taught in primary schools by people who barely scraped GCSE French (if that)? To say, as I am saying, that subject knowledge is necessary for a teacher does not show that it is sufficient, and one would have been foolish ever to claim such a thing. Can Hattie really be guilty here of saying that because subject knowledge on its own is not *sufficient* to make a good teacher, it is not *necessary* either? If he is, he needs a little bit of training in elementary logic himself, specifically, to learn the difference between necessary and sufficient conditions.

There are 4 basic problems with Hattie's methods:

a) the 150 categories Hattie lists are not clearly defined – and if you doubt me, look up *Visible Learning*, where you will find rather vague accounts of what falls under each – so, apart from anything else, how do we know that in the thousands of studies he cites, people are actually meaning the same things by the key terms? But more importantly, the 150 items graded are not all in any sense similar or comparable in the way they influence outcomes, so they cannot legitimately be put on the same scale. And even when they do seem to be in the same line of business, there are some peculiar conclusions, such as 'teacher verbal ability' being ranked 112, whereas 'teacher clarity' comes in at 9. How can a teacher be clear without verbal ability? As with Bloom's 'taxonomy', many of the 150 categories clearly overlap (e.g. teacher questioning, teacher clarity, teacher knowledge, teacher verbal ability), and make no sense in isolation, so their effects cannot be factored out in the way Hattie implies.

b) what is Hattie's criterion of a good lesson, clearly crucial in estimating the contribution of aspects of teaching? He talks in rather general terms about 'achievement' of pupils and about outcomes, but it is unclear whether this is achievement or outcome in individual lessons, achievement over a period of time; and does it just refer to outcomes measurable by test scores or are other outcomes included (Those who think that out of school activities are important – which most teachers and parents do – might want to point out that not everything a school should do is related directly to 'visible' learning)?

Some hint of what Hattie might be about here is given early on in his 2009 book (pp 28ff), where he talks of surface, deep, and constructed understanding. In B. Bloom-like fashion he wants to urge teachers to go beyond both surface and deep understanding to 'constructed' understanding. So what are these things?

Surface understanding is bare knowledge of facts and ideas, deep understanding is integrating at least two separate pieces of knowledge, and constructed understanding is to construct notions and ideas that shape the ways that learners engage in surface and deep learning. Got it? Don't worry if you haven't; I can't really get a handle on these distinctions either, and I would say, as I did with Bloom, that what Hattie is doing here is to point to elements that will all be involved to some degree in any genuine learning whatsoever; that is any learning which both sticks in the learner's mind, and which is more than learning to repeat meaningless sequences of words or numbers.

Hattie's appeal to Karl Popper

The next five paragraphs can be passed over if one's interest is solely in the validity of the visible learning machine, but it may be of more general interest as yet another example of an educationalist attempting to piggy-back on another mode of discourse. By way of giving some backing to his surface, deep, and constructed typology – to his three worlds of learning, as he calls them – Hattie appeals to the authority of the great Viennese philosopher Karl Popper. As no doubt Hattie will know and may be proud of, Popper spent the war years in exile in New Zealand writing *The Open Society and its Enemies*, in which, among other things, he attacked Plato's political philosophy. Long after that, when in London, he devised his theory of the three worlds he thinks we inhabit, in which he is far kinder to Plato. (3)

Popper's first world is the material world as described in physics, chemistry, etc. The second world is the world of subjective experience (our thoughts, feelings, hopes, fears etc.). The third world – and this is the Platonic bit – is the world of the contents of our thoughts and experiences. These thought contents are regarded by Popper as objectively existing systems, with their own logic, coherence and by which we are governed in our subjective thinking. They go to make up what Popper calls World 3.

Popper's basic model here is mathematics. In his view maths is a system that has emerged from human thinking and activity (in World 2), but which, having emerged, then takes on a life of its own in World 3. Mathematics, once set up in World 3, actually goes far beyond anything any of us can understand (and in which there are truths – note, *are* truths, *now* – which may never be discovered by us humans). Popper extends this quasi-Platonic view of maths to other realms which we create by our mental activity, including scientific theories, artistic styles, language itself, and many other things – all human creations initially, but again, once created, have a life and development of their own, controlling us as much as we can control them.

In Popper's view, then, the first world (the world of matter) throws up creatures (us) who can engage in second world activity (our actual thoughts, speech, writing, etc.), which we then use to create third world structures. These World 3 structures, once they get underway with their own logic and development beyond anything we do, come back to influence our thinking etc. (World 2), and thereby have an effect on the first world (World 1) – a delightfully cyclical picture, though one I have criticised, particularly for some of what Popper says about the independent existence of World 3 entities. (4)

But never mind about the validity of Popper's three world hypothesis now. The point is that nothing about it would give any support to Hattie's rather different three worlds, which are all cases of second world activity (thinking, reasoning, etc) about third world contents (ideas, descriptions of facts, theories, etc). And, as far as 'surface, deep, and constructed knowledge' goes, I think that Popper is closer to the truth than Hattie who just seems muddled at this point, in attempting to separate out things that can't really be separated. In a good lesson there will be elements

of surface, deep, and structured knowledge; but, given that anything we learn will in some way or other connect to other things
we know, and also have its influence on whatever we will learn
in the future, there probably will be in 99% of bad lessons too.

End of Popperian digression

To resume on Hattie, our third objection (c) to his methodology is that teaching is a far more holistic and even individual
activity than Hattie's approach would have it. It is not something from which, in abstraction from particular contexts and
situations (and even particular teachers), we can easily pull
strands of effectiveness on which to base universal generalisations, supposedly applying to all teachers, all pupils and in
all contexts. On Hattie's passion for generalising, it is worth
mentioning that Nancy Cartwright, the distinguished philosopher of science, has over the last few years been conducting
a campaign against the misuse of 'evidence-based' policies,
which is not uncommon in the case of governmental policies
based on 'research' and randomised trials. (5) Her point is
that the attempt to generalise from studies conducted in one
set of circumstances may involve ignoring crucial differences
between different contexts, particularly pertinent in the case
of generalising about human activity. These differences of
context will invalidate generalisations which discount them
precisely because they will ignore crucial social and personal
factors which make all the difference in human activity. Be
suspicious, she seems to be telling us, of tracts which begin in
an unqualified way by saying that 'studies show' (show what?),
and which go on to say 'it works' (but what is the 'it'? the thing
the 'study' claims to have isolated, or the whole activity in all
its humanly rich multifariousness, its motley, as Wittgenstein
would have it?) Believing as I do that teaching is a human

activity, where the most important variables are the pupils, the ethos of the school and the personality of the teacher, all this is highly congenial to me, and a good corrective to the attempt on Hattie's part to elide the all-important differences between the millions of 'studies' he claims to be synthesising?

Finally, our fourth criticism of Hattie (d), we can question the assumption underlying his work that what is important in education can be quantified. Even if we could be sure that in his analyses he is always talking about the same thing (points a and c above), much of what we want from education is not in any strict sense quantifiable. For example, how do you quantify depth of understanding, grasp of principles underlying something like multiplication or love of learning or sensitivity to nuance – all very much the sort of thing we want from a humane education, yet all strikingly absent from Hattie's data?

To conclude this examination of Hattie, I have heard a defence of his view of knowledge along the lines that all he is saying is that there is no correlation between a teacher's level of degree (PhD, Masters, first, second, or third class, etc) and their effectiveness as a teacher. This is not actually what he says, as far as I can see, but even if it were, it would be a weak defence. What is at issue here is *knowledge*, not class or level of degree, which, as we all know, may have little bearing on the actual knowledge a teacher may have, or on the relevance of what he or she knows to what they are teaching. I know a maths teacher whose degree is in a modern oriental language, but she is an excellent teacher of maths (and now the Head of the Maths Department in a prestigious academic school). Not coincidentally, she knows a great deal of maths, about which she is passionate, and she wouldn't have been appointed in the first place, let alone promoted, had the school not been confident of this. But the school had the wit and confidence to understand that knowledge is what we are talking about here, rather than academic qualifications, and knowledge and passion for maths is what she has in abundance. (6)

1. John Hattie, *Visible Learning: A Synthesis of Over 800 Meta-Analyses Relating to Achievement*, Abingdon: Routledge, 2009, p 127.

2. John Hattie and Gregory Yates, *Visible Learning and the Science of How We Learn*, Abingdon: Routledge, 2014.

3. Karl Popper, *The Open Society and Its Enemies*, Fifth Edition, 1966, 2 Vols, London: Routledge and Kegan Paul, 1966. Popper's Three World theory can be found in his *Objective Knowledge*, Second Edition, Oxford: Clarendon Press, 1979, pp 106-90.

4. Anthony O'Hear, *Karl Popper*, London: Routledge and Kegan Paul, 1980, pp 181-200.

5. See Nancy Cartwright and Jeremy Hardie, *Evidence-Based Policy: A Practical Guide to Doing it Better,* Oxford: Oxford University Press, 2012.

6. In 2014 the Sutton Trust published its own research on teaching effectiveness, based on work done at Durham University (*What Makes Teaching Great*, by Rob Coe, Cesare Aloisi, Lee Elliott Major and Steve Higgins, London: Sutton Trust, 2014). According to this, teacher subject knowledge comes out *top* in importance. Coe and his colleagues and Hattie can't both be right, which I think suggests, at the very least, that one should treat the results of educational 'research' with caution. Having said that, Coe and his colleagues do seem eminently sensible in what they say. They also point out that lavish and indiscriminate praise, allowing learners to discover key ideas for themselves, bending to pupils' preferred 'learning styles' and active learning (rather than listening 'passively') are not effective strategies for successful teaching.

On the last point (in favour of 'active' learning), they say that 'this claim is commonly presented in the form of a 'learning pyramid' which shows precise percentages of material that will be retained when different levels of activity are employed. These percentages have no empirical basis and are pure fiction.' I have to confess that I do not know what a 'learning pyramid' is, and I don't know how far I trust the methodology is which is being employed in the Sutton Trust work – it may like Hattie be a case of 'studies showing', in abstraction from variations in context, but I warm to the straightforward, even iconoclastic, spirit of the Durham researchers.

Group-Think and Identity Politics

'The emancipation of the individual was indeed the great spiritual revolution which led to the breakdown of tribalism and to the rise of democracy… This individualism, united with altruism, has become the basis of our western civilization. It is the central doctrine of Christianity ('love your neighbour', say the Scriptures, not 'love your tribe'); and it is the core of all ethical doctrines which have grown from our civilization and stimulated it.' (K.R. Popper, *The Open Society and its Enemies*, 5th edition, Routledge: London, 1966, Vol 1, 101-2.)

Having mentioned Karl Popper in connection with John Hattie, I will now recall my favourite Popper anecdote. In 1974-5 Portugal, having emerged from half a century of authoritarian dictatorship, only narrowly survived two serious attempts by communist revolutionaries to impose something even worse. The leader of the new and genuinely democratic country was Mario Soares, a prominent socialist politician who had returned in 1974 after years of exile in Rome and Paris; during his time of exile he had become a student and admirer of Popper's *The Open Society and its Enemies*. Later on, and having been Prime Minister and then President, as a mark of respect to the book's author, Soares invited Popper to visit Portugal. In the course of this visit, Popper was taken to the National Palace at Sintra, one of the gems of Portuguese history and architecture, but when he arrived there he was told by its custodians that he would have to go round as a member of a group. Popper went mad, and jumping on a table, announced 'I vill not be in a collectif.' Eventually the bureaucratic jobsworths were convinced that this guest of Mario Soares himself, a leading opponent of tyrannies and dictatorships everywhere, and a man of immense culture and sensitivity to boot, should be allowed the freedom to go round the old palace at his own pace and in his own time.

Unfortunately collectivist thinking has not ended with the demise of Portugal's Estado Novo and of the far worse Eastern bloc against which Popper wrote and campaigned so effectively for so long. Collectivism is treating individuals as members of groups, rather than as individuals. It is the basis of most modern tyrannies, where individuals are seen first and foremost in terms of a larger group to which they are held to belong.

But collectivism is not to be found only in obvious and explicit tyrannies; its style is well entrenched close to home. For Ofsted currently demands that pupils in schools being inspected are categorised and their achievements calculated according to a bewildering number of groups, racial, ethnic, and even sexual, to which they are supposed to belong. Not only do schools have to put their pupils in these groups for the statistics Ofsted requires; they are also expected to be able to account for differences in performance between the various groups, and Ofsted will come down hard on the school for differences its inspectors discern.

My own initial reaction to this is to say that my paternal ancestry is predominantly Irish and Catholic, as part of the fallout from the Great Irish Famine of the 1840s; but it is also English through my mother, Scottish (my Glaswegian father was part Scottish and captained Scottish universities at football), Dutch (my mother was a Gompertz), Jewish (I believe), and doubtless much else, if I were to go into it. So what am I, here and now, with my mongrel blood and heritage? Which group(s) should I be in (On the complexity of identity in the modern world, and the near impossibility of establishing just what group(s) any given individual should place him or herself in, Amin Maalouf's *In the Name of Identity: Violence and the Need to Belong*, is interesting on the complexity of each person's identity, at least until the rather lame conclusion. Rather more vigorous on the whole topic of ethnic categorisation is Ayaan Hirsi Ali: see her *Infidel: My Life*, but that is presumably not on Ofsted's reading list)? (1) And, even assuming that I am able to pin myself as this or that (English? Hardly, except by assimilation; British? Not sure what that means post-devolution; Irish?) What do I want to be? In a modern liberal democracy, I am not stuck with that, nor should I feel myself constrained by it (and, rightly, we feel outraged when we hear that even in Britain to-day some women (usually) are locked into an oppressive identity they would rather escape from, but whose very existence leads the police and other agencies to treat their protestations of violence with kid gloves). I feel like shouting out (like the Prisoner, in the famous 60s television series) 'I am not a number, I am a free man!', and I always refuse to fill in the surveys on these matters which come from just about every agency that sends one a form these days, including, it has to be said, from the Government's own Cabinet Office. But my own impatience aside, what sort of attitude should we encourage in our pupils? Isn't the education we want to give partly about allowing people to emerge from their initial definition or categorisation into a broader and less restrictive sense of self?

Surely most of our pupils think of themselves first and foremost as individuals; they want to be treated as such, and judged on their own merits and achievements. Certainly that has been the attitude I have found in pupils I have talked to from places such as Iraq, Afghanistan, Sudan, and Somalia, who have not wanted to be seen in those terms, or indeed to be given any concessions because of their often terrifying origins, which they instinctively (and correctly) would see as patronising. And even if it weren't, in a genuinely 'diverse' society, shouldn't we want people to think of themselves as individual members of that society, free to make their own way and life within it, rather than being pigeon-holed and corralled willy-nilly into 'groups', over which they have no choice. Further, as teachers, does it help us to think of the pupil before us as coming from this or that group, with whatever (stereotypical) profile and set of expectations that doubtless engenders, rather than the individual actually before us, probably with a pretty mixed background like me, and certainly with his or her own individual character, ability, motivation, and potential? And there is also the point that once having been corralled into groups (whether they like it or not) individual people will find themselves being spoken on behalf of by 'leaders', often self-appointed and always self-interested, who may in no real sense represent either the opinions of the individuals they are speaking for, or for their true interests.

I have taken some of these points up with Ofsted officials, and they inevitably say that the Equality Act 2010, and the ensuing so-called Public Sector Equality duty, require them to collect statistics about race and what are called in that act 'protected' characteristics (age, race, religion, sexuality, disability and much else besides). There is also usually bluster about legal advice on the interpretation of the Act. Well, I have read the Act, and in particular section 149, which is the key section in this regard. What this actually says is that there should not be discrimination against people on any of these grounds, and that equality between persons with protected characteristics and others without them should be advanced, with which it is hard to quarrel. I do not see that it requires public bodies to collect and obsess over statistics on possibly spurious and permeable identities, and if Ofsted's lawyers say that it does, I have spoken to barristers in the field who take a different view. (It is worth remembering that you can, of course, usually find the legal opinion you are looking for, particularly on ill-drafted and recent legislation, which is neither clear in itself, nor has been subjected to testing in the courts).

Still, all this is not the main point, which is not the interpretation of a far from perfect piece of legislation. The key point is the extent to which we should categorise and think of people, including our pupils, as individuals first and foremost, or in terms of group identities. At the very least, emphasising group identities would seem to militate against the social cohesion we all desire, and which is sadly lacking in many areas, possibly because of two or three decades of group think. However, at a more fundamental level, the moral premise on which liberal society is founded is a belief in the value of individual freedom and responsibility, the idea that whatever my origin I can (and should) pursue my journey through life according to my choices and my sense of myself. And that is why Karl Popper (a German speaking, Viennese Jew from London, where he received a British knighthood, but via Christchurch, New Zealand) got so angry in Sintra, because he felt that the attitude he encountered there – that one could do something only as a member of a state-sanctioned group – went against everything he thought Mario Soares should have learned from his teaching.

Maybe Popper went over the top on that occasion, but one has to admire his instinct and his passion. We should fight group-think wherever we find it, but nowhere more than in education, which should surely be all about liberating the individual from the group. The next time an Ofsted official starts talking to you about Raiseonline (the database they hold about groups, and which is simply and lamentably a new manifestation of tribal-ism at the very heart of our society), politely suggest that they might read *The Open Society and its Enemies*.

1.   Amin Maalouf, *In the Name of Identity: Violence and the Need to Belong*, London: Penguin, 2003; Ayaan Hirsi Ali, *Infidel*, London: Simon and Schuster, 2008.

Decolonising the Curriculum

By 2023 groupthink has become even more insidious and entrenched than it was when I originally wrote the previous section. Black Lives Matter and 'Critical Race Theory' are indeed predicated on what is now referred to as identity politics, though without considering the complexity of most people's identity, to which I have just referred in mentioning Maalouf. That this should happen, alongside the apparently unquestionable implication that to be white is to be privileged and to be black a victim, automatically and by definition, it seems, shows how far we have departed from Popper's optimistic analysis of enlightenment individualism, an optimism also enshrined in Martin Luther King's famous hope that we might be approaching a time when colour and race had become unimportant. It also emphasises, against 'critical' race 'theory' the need for some genuinely critical thinking, and perhaps for some genuine theory, as opposed to ideological dogmatism.

Maybe, though, it is not surprising that in a field as intellectually weak as 'education' that this newest form of ideological dogmatism should have taken root in so many of our educational institutions and practices; not surprising, but nonetheless deeply regrettable, not least for many of the alleged victims, who often do suffer from genuine deprivation and are cut off from the wider society, but who, it seems, are now destined to be siloed within what leaders of opinion and their teachers deem to be their identities, thus making any effective entry into the wider society that much more difficult than it already is. I should say at the outset that I am by no means opposed to broadening the curriculum to include coverage of histories and cultures other than the British and the European. What I am against, strongly against, is the attempt to disparage the British and European in a mood of aggressive and ignorant resentment which inevitably colours talk of decolonising in educational circles.

A striking, but by no means atypical example of the ideology which is to be found all over the contemporary educational world, from universities and their administrators right down to the training of primary school teachers can be found in the following official description of a compulsory module in the University of Suffolk's BA in Childhood: Primary Education with QTS:

Drawing from postcolonial, subaltern, decolonial, post-qualitative and posthuman critiques, this module aims to explore the Southern 'turn' in domains of knowledge – hierarchies, 'production', erasures and circulation – resulting in the delegitimization of knowledge from the 'rich peripheral countries' to build an understanding of the impact of knowledge as capital. Engaging with this upsurge of interest in decolonisation within professional and academic environments will not only extend the University's currency but importantly enrich students' understanding of the current demand to decolonise educational and practice settings, and why acknowledging other knowledges and decolonisation matters, towards enabling a critical approach to future thinking and practice. In doing so, the module will interrogate what place curriculum and policies have within these calls for decolonising education and practice in the UK.

As style in these things is as significant as substance, we can note first of all the pompous and pretentious jargon, no doubt derived from the francophone writing of Foucault, Althusser, Derrida, Badiou and the like. Then there is the dogmatic and hectoring tone, brooking no dissent from the activist programme of decolonisation indicated. Clearly the 'critical approach' mentioned towards the end will not make room for a criticism of the whole 'postcolonial, subaltern, decolonial', etc critiques, which are not, of course, critiques at all. Just as 'Critical Race Theory' from which much of this thinking derives is not critical, nor indeed theory in any scientifically or philosophically recognisable sense, the critical approach of the module will allow no result other than signing up to the activist programme envisaged. It is, in fact, an application of Marx's adage to the effect that the philosophy of the past has sought to understand the world, not to change it, whereas the new philosophy (i.e. Marxism) aspires to change it, and to change it in the light of what it, and it alone, knows to be true. All criticism, then, is simply a factitious attempt to stand in the way of what is known (by its adherents) to be true, and to obstruct the programme of reform and revolution. In the case of the decolonising limb of what should be seen as a mutation of the original economic Marxism, the programme which must not be criticised or impeded is that of 'delegitimizing' what has hitherto counted as knowledge. But this so-called 'knowledge' is nothing but the preserve of the 'rich peripheral countries' (i.e. Europe and the US, mainly). We must expose this knowledge for what it is, knowledge as racism and capitalism's capital, delegitimize it, and recognise instead the 'knowledges' from other parts of the world.

Do they really mean this? Will they have us refuse (delegitimize) antibiotics on the grounds that they derive from the rich peripheral corner of the world (the European archipelago, if you like)? When one has meningitis, does decolonising mean we should turn to the traditional healers I observed in Nigeria a few years ago and their remedies? I imagine that I will be castigated for even asking this question, even though I freely acknowledge that traditional healers and their remedies may have healing virtues unsuspected in the average UK medical degree, but not, I will insist, the virtue of curing meningitis.

In a way, though, we are skirmishing around the edges here. What is really at issue is what is meant by knowledge, and the misuse of that term in the description of the Suffolk module. We have already touched on this in our section on constructing one's own knowledge, but the point is worth returning to here.

We can begin by noting that the Suffolk modulists constantly talk of knowledges, plural, as if in different societies knowledge is different. It is not. As Aristotle taught long ago, to say of what is that it is, is to say the true, while to say that it is not, is to say something false. Conversely, to say of what is not that it is is to say the false, and to say of what is not that it is not is to say the true. And this is true in every society, whether peripheral or Southern. Knowing is to say or think what is true, and with some good reason or prompting; knowledge, in other words, is well-grounded true belief. (Well-grounded, because just believing something true will not count as knowledge if I have no grounds for the belief, and think it for no reason at all or for some inadequate reason that doesn't really support the belief).

Although there are some philosophical complications which we need not go into here, that is basically all it is. Knowledge is well-grounded true belief. It is as simple as that. It doesn't matter where it is or when, or who says it or believes it, or indeed who denies it. If we or anyone is fortunate enough to have a well-grounded true belief, then they have knowledge. Knowledge is when a belief (whoever's belief) is both true and well founded. Knowledge is when belief reflects the way the world is, and this is the same whether one is a peripheral European or a colonised Southerner. There are not knowledges; there is just knowledge, and knowledge in this sense is pretty well distributed around the world (human survival depends on it).

It is particularly important to realise this point about the universality and impartiality of knowledge when we consider scientific knowledge. For scientific knowledge is specifically and expressly universal about the way the physical world is independent of human concerns and wishes, and prescinding from what we or anyone might think. It is penicillin that works, not magic or prayer or hope or some ineffective treatment, however scientifically investigated. If the investigations do not lead to something that works or a theory that can be substantiated through observation and experiment, then in the practice of science it will be dropped, and will not be taken to be knowledge, however interesting or plausible.

When astronomers back in the early nineteenth century noticed that the planet Uranus was not following the orbit around the Sun they calculated it should be following according to their Newtonian principles, they postulated that it was being pulled away from what they thought was its true course by another planet outside its orbit, which was pulling Uranus out of what they thought it should be doing. Thus they were led to discover Neptune, in what was clearly a triumph for the critical method – taking a criticism of one's treasured theory seriously, not explaining it away, but using its apparent falsification to make an epoch-making new discovery.

It was then noticed that Mercury also deviated from the Newtonian norm. So, it was reasoned that this must be because of Vulcan, a small planet between Mercury and the Sun, that had somehow proved very hard to observe. It proved hard to observe not because of its small size or its proximity to the Sun, as might have seemed to be the case, but because of the more radical factor, that it did not exist. Mercury does not follow the course Newtonian calculations predict because those calculations were based on principles (theories) that were not true, not because of any interference from the non-existent Vulcan. Mercury eventually proved to be one of the test cases which led to the adoption of Einsteinian Relativity over Newton's laws.

One lesson that this little story might give us is that, for all its prodigious successes, Newtonian physics is not true, or at least not wholly true. It does not exactly reflect the way the world is, and so cannot be thought of as knowledge simpliciter, Western or otherwise, even though a lot of knowledge of a very precise sort is encapsulated within its theories and is yielded in its detailed predictions and calculations. But rather than emphasising the uncertainty of scientific theories here, what I want to point to is the way the Uranus-Mercury story transcends regional and national boundaries. The predictions made by Newtonian theory are held to apply everywhere and at all times. They can be observed anywhere by anyone with the appropriate instruments. Verifications and falsifications of the theory can be made anywhere by anyone. And the language of science itself is international, transcending linguistic boundaries, which is why scientific conferences will be much the same whether they are in London, Paris, Copenhagen, New York, Moscow, or Beijing, and scientists the world over will understand and take account of their findings. Even though it could be argued that the scientific method has its origins in ancient Greece and then in post-medieval Europe, the scientific method is essentially a critical method, subjecting theories and guesses (for that is what theories are) to testing of a rigorous and impartial nature. The scientific critical method is not, like an artistic style or a natural language, tied down to any place or culture or biased in any national or ethnic direction. It is open and available to anyone who looks into its theories and procedures. That is why philosophers of science, such as Karl Popper, have often insisted that the provenance of scientific ideas, where they come from, who devised them, and so on, is unimportant. What is important is the extent to which they survive testing, and that is due to the way the world is, rather than the culture, nationality, or language of the scientists concerned. We should not speak of Western science, as if there might be another sort of science. It may be our good fortune that the scientific method historically originated and was originally practiced in the West, though this is no longer the case. It is now practiced all over the world, presumably because all over the world people can see its virtue in uncovering truth about the physical world, which is all to the good. And, wherever it is practiced, the discipline of science and the key to its success is the way it depends on factors of an impartial and universal kind, factors which apply everywhere and impersonally.

So talk of 'decolonising' science is fundamentally misguided, suggesting as it does that there is another sort of science, an un- or decolonized science, which ought to be studied and taught. Of course one can and probably should criticise some of the uses to which scientific theories and methods are put, and there could well be cultural biases here that need to be pointed out, perhaps from the perspective of people in the 'South' who may be adversely affected by scientific developments elsewhere. But what should be resisted is the suggestion that science itself is uniquely or narrowly the preserve of the 'rich peripheral coun- tries'. And for analogous reasons, much the same can be said of mathematics. Once mathematical reasoning and principles emerged (from Babylon? Ancient Greece? Medieval Arabs?), we enter, as the mathematician Cantor held, a realm of undreamed of paradises of quantitative existence, formulated in its own universal, abstract and trans-cultural language.

Talk of decolonising science and mathematics can appeal only to people who understand nothing of the methods involved in each, methods which essentially focus on the world or on number in a way that specifically transcends any narrow or culturally specific boundaries, and takes us away from where the theories may have originated (Quantum Theory is as valid in Kilgali or Barbados or Chingford as in Copenhagen). What, though, of subjects which are culturally specific, such as literature, history, and the arts? Is there a case for 'decolonising' curricula here? Clearly humanities curricula have always been permeable and subject to changing emphases and fashions. They are not tied down to hard external realities like the sciences, or to the unavoidable conclusions of abstract calculation like mathematics. I myself follow Charlotte Mason in hoping to see our young people learning something in school about China and India and their cultures and histories, though I can also see huge timetable pressures in all subjects. However, I also believe that if there is to be any hope of transcending class, ethnic, and other divisions in our society, at the core of the curriculum should be study of British history, treated in a narrative way and as something belonging to all of us, and of the literature and arts of this country and of Europe, which have made our culture what it is, a heritage to be understood and cherished.

The decolonisers do not like any such suggestion because, as they rightly point out, there are stains on the history of this country, but so there are on the history of any country. Historical stains are by no means unique to this country. In every history there are tales of murder, plunder, and rapine, and I mean every, including those 'erased' histories which the decolonisers want to have studied in British schools. Every present possession of land and territory of which we know the history can be traced back to some or several earlier invasions, conquests, thefts, and other acts of violence. It would be a pretty poor narrative history of Britain which did not deal with the Roman conquest, the Anglo-Saxon and Viking invasions and the Norman conquest, to say nothing of later depredations, such as the Wars of the Roses, Tudor and Jacobean religious persecutions, the colonising of Ireland and, of course, the conquest of many other parts of the world, including the slave trade. Maybe a century ago there were books for children which managed to gloss over or even omit the terrible events which coloured our past, but any such papering would be inconceivable in 2023. But that does not mean that more admirable trends and moments in our history – of which there are many – should not also be given due prominence, especially those relevant to our life to-day, conditioned as it is by the rule of law and a long tradition of peaceful governance and expectations of justice and fairness. It is hard to know if this is what the decolonisers want, but if it is, and they want to present British history as lacking a centuries-long growth of a sense of justice and peaceable existence, then they will be making it far harder for the children they educate to expect and demand equitable treatment from the authorities, whom they will increasingly come to see as their enemies, incapable of understanding and sometimes at least ready to deal with cases of injustice and oppression. And without wishing to harp on these points here, no one should forget that the anti-slavery movement itself and subsequently a lot of the drive to grant independence to the former colonies of the British Empire came from movements within this country, within Britain itself, movements which saw imperial conquest, possession, and rule as inconsistent with the development of democratic norms and processes which was simultaneously going on here. Many of the leaders of the independence movements in their own countries had been educated in their anti-colonial feelings by teachers in the British-run schools to which they went, and even in some notable cases, in universities in Britain. One can, though, concede to the decolonisers that room might reasonably be made in history syllabuses for giving greater attention to aspects of non-British and non-European history – provided that it did not displace British history, fairly and objectively taught from the core of the school curriculum, because it is through understanding the history of one's own country that a sense of unity and community might be fostered.

On what literature and art should be taught, and how calls to decolonise in these areas should be addressed, one or two obvious points should be made. Again there is a question of who and where we are, the art and literature which, over the centuries, have become essential reference points here and now, and often for good reason. The works which ought to be at the core of any relevant curriculum should be ones which have stood the test of time, as memorably expressed by David Hume in his essay 'Of the Standard of Taste' of 1757: 'The same Homer, who pleased at Athens and Rome two thousand years ago, is still admired in Paris and London. All the changes of climate, government, religion and language, have not been able to obscure his glory. Authority or prejudice may give a temporary vogue to a bad poet or orator; but his reputation will never be durable or general. When his works are examined by posterity or foreigners, the enchantment is dissipated, and his faults appear in their real colours. On the contrary, a real genius, the longer his works endure, and the more wide they are spread, the more sincere is the admiration which he meets with.'

In a way Hume says all that needs to be said. True artistic quality is long-lasting; it can be perceived in quite different times and places; it is in this sense universal, which certainly seems to be the case with writers such as Homer, Virgil, Dante, Shakespeare, Milton, Dickens and others it would be easy to point to, and similar figures from music, painting and the other arts. Not to give young people at least a passing acquaintance in their education with some of these figures will not only deprive them of irreplaceable enjoyment and appreciation. It will also deprive them of a heritage they should be entitled to, and they will most likely be deprived of it if they come from backgrounds where these things are not appreciated and taken for granted.

The decolonisers may complain that there are unacceptable attitudes to be found in some of the figures that would feature in a rounded education in the humanities. It may be so, but teaching and studying the works does not mean that a teacher or a pupil is expected to endorse everything that is to be found in them. Critical study is not a passive genuflection to what one before one. Nor, even in the tiny list I have given, are the writers all English. I included Homer, Virgil and Dante so as to hint at the universality of the great writers, to suggest that they are culturally diverse, and as such give us some measure by which to understand and judge our own time and culture. What the Suffolk modulists call other knowledges are at the heart of any reasonably extensive list of great writers and artists who can be seen as having created the best that has been thought and known. (True even of the English writers: who to-day thinks or feels even a tiny proportion of what Milton believed so passionately?). They are, of course, all dead, but that is of necessity. It is only the dead whom we know to have stood the test of time in the way Hume describes. But as having survived the test of time, they are also the ones who to a large degree have formed the sensibility of our culture, to the extent of providing a touchstone by which to examine the works of our own time. We may indeed agree with the decolonisers that there is room for other voices, for new voices, for so far unheard voices; all entirely reasonable, providing they are voices worth hearing and not just purveyors of vulgarity or agit-prop, and providing also that they do not deprive young people of hearing and seeing at least some of the best that has been thought and known.

Nor in thinking about decolonising should we overlook the way that in the past it has been scholars from this country and Europe who over a few centuries have opened up for people in Europe some of the riches of the cultures of India, the Middle East and the Far East. Of course some of this went along with often objectionable colonial activity, but that should not detract from the devotion and objectivity which many European scholars and translators showed to the cultures they were bringing to the West. Far from denigrating or dismissing these cultures, they found in them poetry, art, and ideas which had eluded their compatriots in the West. Indeed it seems to be a signal, almost unique facet of Western learning to have been interested in non-Western achievements in literature in the arts, appreciative and admiring it as touching on values and styles not recognised or appreciated in the West. The shame is that this genuinely scholarly activity, often engaged in purely for its own sake, should so often be characterised nowadays as cultural appropriation or orientalism in the main by people who know nothing or little of its history. (1) But rather than dwelling on this, we should rather be grateful for the way that cultures other than those of the West have been opened up for us in the West to our immeasurable benefit, which is why I would like attention to be given in schools to some of these other great civilisations in a spirit of mutual recognition, as opposed to the confrontational stance of the decolonisers, and in part to remove the stigma of confrontation which so often attends cultural interchange in the 2020s.

1. See Robert Irwin's *For the Lust of Knowing: the Orientalists and their Enemies*, London: Allen Lane, 2006, a detailed and scholarly account of Western study and translation of Middle and Near Eastern cultures and languages since the 16th century, which shows how the scholars involved were, with one or two exceptions, in no sense racist or dismissive of the cultures they spent their lives in studying, but did so in the conviction that what they were working on had an incalculable value for its own sake.

All Children Are Naturally Creative

It might be nice if they were, though it might lead to what Nietzsche called a pandemonium of free spirits, a veritable cacophony of creativity, rather like being bombarded by the outputs of a thousand social media sites at once and without intermission or pause.

It is true that everyone can talk and everyone can, after a manner, sing and put paint on paper. No doubt, as Dewey famously said, even very young children can play around with coins and find that putting five cents together with another five makes ten. But does this mean that the child is a discoverer, as Dewey claimed? If a young child fills a space with brightly coloured paint is he or she being creative?

We need here to make a couple of distinctions. Our little discoverer and creator is certainly doing something new in the sense that (probably) they have not done that thing before. In this sense, subjectively, they might be said to be a discoverer, a creator. But in a more objective sense they have not discovered anything which is not already known, nor have they created anything that would truly be said to enlarge human experience in any significant way, which is what we might call objective creativity.

Once the distinction is made between objective and subjective in the realm of discovery and creativity, what we need to ask is whether or to what extent we should encourage subjective discovery and creativity. In most areas, there is certainly a role for even young children doing things for themselves and also for trying things out. We do not want to programme them to reproduce things robotically, for that would produce neither understanding nor flexibility, seen as the ability to apply what has been taught in new circumstances. But in areas of significant human achievement – music, painting, maths, the sciences – this personal doing and trying should be part of a disciplined initiation into what has gone before. Otherwise the efforts produced by subjective discovery and creativity are going to be woefully inadequate, something I believe young children can recognise for themselves. If they are, let us say, trying to draw a face, they know well enough when what they are doing is no good. It is almost cruel to deny a child who wants to be an artist the tools they need really to express what they want to show, simply on the grounds that it would inhibit creativity. In fact initiation into what has emerged through centuries of human effort and discovery is what makes real creativity possible. And once we start looking at things in that way, few people every generation are really creative, really discoverers, adding anything really new to the sum of human experience.

In a way all this is almost too obvious to need underlining. To think about music, for example, while some of us might enjoy listening to Hummel, say, or John Field – for a time anyway, for their works are not negligible – no one has any difficulty in saying that, compared to their contemporaries Beethoven and Chopin, they were not really creative. It is Beethoven and Chopin with whom we want to live, and to return to again and again, who were the truly creative ones. Similarly no one considering the visual arts seems to have any difficulty saying that salon painters like Bouguereau and Makart and Lord Leighton were doing little more than reproducing tired old formulae when Monet and Manet and Renoir were opening new windows in the world of art. Of course, the salon painters may have been doing a worthwhile job, up to a point, and perhaps we unfairly disparage them – they were, after all, highly skilled and talented – but in the great scheme of things they were lacking in genuine creativity.

The picture of culture which underlies what I am arguing here goes something like this. There exist forms of knowledge and experience in human history, which have developed over the ages. We would like young people to be introduced to these forms, so that their own talents and desires can be channelled into these forms, and so they can actually say something in them. Of course, after they have been so channelled, they may well want to break out, to say something new, to do something personal (though we should be cautious about simplistically identifying the personal with the genuinely new and even less with the really worthwhile). But to get to the point of saying something new, they have to know how to do what is done, what has been discovered, and build on that acquired expertise – dwarves standing on the shoulders of giants, as Newton described his own relationship to his scientific predecessors. Though we have to recognise that the dwarf, because of his higher position can actually see more than the giant, I think that we also have to recognise that very few of the dwarves, even as they do enjoyable and worthwhile work, are in any deep sense creative or really, objectively speaking, discoverers of real importance.

It would follow from what I have so far said that in education, that there is a role for what I have called subjective discovery and creativity, in order to prevent robotic teaching and learning. We want pupils to practice and develop the knowledge and skills they have learned, and to put something of themselves into this activity. But in order that this putting something of themselves into whatever it is that they are working at, if it is not to be blind and awkward fumbling in the dark, their own activity needs to be within a context of learning and instruction in which they are taught what human beings have discovered and created, and how, within the limits of their age and capabilities, to work within this context.

Indeed, I would offer a further thought at this point. Much or even most of what people these days call 'creative' (as in the 'creative' professions, in student art portfolios, in commercial art galleries, in most popular music, etc.) is nothing much to write home about. Even when there is something genuinely new, as opposed to merely yet another twist on a tired cliché, what we usually have is just a mutation at most, and more often a dilution or a distortion. Most 'creative' people, even ones we admire, are more often re-assemblers, inverters and extenders of what has already been done, though not necessarily the worse for that.

Worse than those working within a tradition are those who are motivated by an obsession with themselves, who are incapable or unwilling to learn or accept what tradition teaches, who enclose themselves – and us – in a personal idiom legible for no longer than its inventor's existence. Too many artists to-day are what have been described (by Lincoln Kirstein) as rebellious solipsists, unreckoning challengers of tradition, narcissistic aesthetes, blocking our vision to anything beyond them, rather than showing us a reality beyond. (1) They obsessively prefer 'personal difference in self-serving isolation' proclaiming 'the triumph of the self.' (1) In slightly less vehement terms T.S. Eliot said much the same thing of the poet (the real poet, that is): 'What happens is a continual surrender of himself as he is at the moment to something which is more valuable. The progress of an artist is a continual self-sacrifice, a continual extinction of personality.' (2) And remember that in his later years, Bach – the supreme example of an artist whose mundane personality was burnt away by the refining fire of true creativity – was criticised for being insufficiently creative, too tradition-bound!

Probably, Dewey's more extreme rhetoric aside, when it comes to maths and science many, if not most, teachers and education-alists would agree with the general line I am developing here. But when it comes to the arts and humanities, in the twenty first century there is a very different attitude abroad. In a fascinat-ing interview with my late friend Peter Fuller, the distinguished painter and influential art educator Victor Pasmore said this: 'You see modern art is straight out of the romantic movement; whether it is Picasso or Matisse or a constructivist like Gabo, or an abstract expressionist, like Jackson Pollock. But it isn't Turner's romanticism, or Shelley's romanticism; it is what Jean-Jacques Rousseau writes about in *Émile*, where he describes the teaching of children, based on organic development from within. The classical romantics, Turner and so forth, moved into an area of cosmic consciousness; but they still looked at nature from the outside. But the romanticism which Rousseau was talking about in the eighteenth century was nature *inside*; and it's nature *inside* which for me is modern romanticism.'

Pasmore then goes on to describe his own artistic career, a series of false starts and stops, and starts again, ending up in a particularly subtle, if not diffuse form of abstract painting. His art history, as laid out in the previous paragraph is no doubt somewhat tendentious, but it leads him to the significant conclusion that because of the discontinuities and ruptures in art in the twentieth century, art schools no longer have anything to teach. As a matter of empirical fact, this is largely true: they don't teach any more. They don't teach partly because of the fragmentation of the visual arts in recent times, so no one knows what to teach, but more, I think, because of an uncritical and well-nigh wholesale acceptance of what Pasmore describes as the new romanticism, just what Kirstein and Eliot were deprecating. If what is vital is the Rousseauan nature *inside* what is the need for teaching? Even more, if what we are interested in is bringing out what is already inside us, isn't teaching of some external technique or practice likely only to adulterate the pure, organic stuff inside (which is what Rousseau himself believed, for young children at least)?

It is interesting how what Pasmore is saying about Rousseauan attitudes to teaching and to the child can help to explain the mess that the art world is currently in. In that world now anyone, with no talent or technique whatever, *can* be recognised as creative (and such people are routinely so recognised). Of course, not all talentless people who try their hand at the arts are so recognised, but we all know the names of the ones who have been, because they are publicly lauded celebrities, akin to pop stars. Why the ones who are recognised have been recognised and rewarded would demand a sociological investigation of the art world and art schools which I am not in a positon to offer. But the question which a belief in the innate power of childhood creativity raises clearly has ramifications far beyond the school-room.

As well as his own art, Pasmore was famous for his work on the new town of Peterlee in County Durham. Pasmore designed the layout of the town, as a form of abstract art. In its centre is a concrete pavilion, its roof cantilevered out over a lake. No one really knew what this pavilion was for and after a while, predictably enough, it became a centre for vandalism and anti-social behaviour, its walls covered with obscene and pornographic graffiti. Amid the ensuing controversy, some years after his pavilion had been constructed, Pasmore revisited it: 'When I got there, I couldn't see any graffiti on the outside; but upstairs it had become like a modern child art class, where the children could do what they liked... I was delighted with the decoration of the interior and I had myself photographed in front of the graffiti. I told them this was exactly the sort of thing I had been trying to do myself. The children had done what I couldn't do; they had humanised the place and made it a social centre. I said the adults had been too late; they didn't know what to do with the place. But the children had the imagination to make use of it. I was given a good lunch and all that sort of business; but I have never been back since.'

Those who live in Peterlee, many of whom see the pavilion as an eyesore, don't of course have the luxury of never going back, nor, because of some Rousseauan romanticism should we have art (or any) classes in which the children can do what they like. We might also note Pasmore's identification of children doing what they liked with what, in his own art, had been trying to do himself. But this confusion over creativity on the part of a major figure in the art world may lead people to think that Rousseauan classes, in which inner childhood creativity is allowed to flourish unchecked and undirected, are some sort of ideal. The Apollo Pavilion, by the way, survived local attempts to have it pulled down, and is now a Grade II listed building. (3)

Of course, Pasmore is not the only artistic eminence to roman-
ticise the child. Joseph Beuys, the egregiously charlatanic figure
so beloved by the avant-garde of the sixties and subsequent
generations of the art world, was not just an indefatigable
fantasist (and no, he had not, as he claimed, been wrapped in
fat-impregnated fur by Crimean Tatars after having been shot
down in the Second World War as a Luftwaffe pilot). In his
favoured oracular mode he was fond of pontificating to the
effect that 'every human being is an artist... the essence of man
is captured in the description 'artist''. To this a short answer
would be that in that case some men (and women) are more
artists than others, and it is the more artists who interest the rest
of us. So let us just distinguish the more artists from the rest of
us (i.e. learn to distinguish those who can draw, paint, write, etc.
in interesting and even novel ways from those of us who only
dream). Unfortunately, because of the influence of the likes of
Beuys and Andy Warhol it is now the case that anyone can be
acclaimed as an artist, including many who cannot draw, paint,
write, etc.: skill is no longer required, though attendance at an
'art' school and a good publicist and sharp elbows might be.

On this last point, it is interesting to read what (Sir) Michael
Craig-Martin RA, the presiding genius at Goldsmith's College
for many years, and patron of the so-called Young British Artists
(Damien Hirst, Gary Hume, Sarah Lucas, etc) had to say about
art education in *The Royal Academy of Arts Magazine* in 2019.
(4) According to Sir Michael, in what he calls 'normal' academic
subjects, 'the subject exists in its own right... it is indifferent to
whether one studies or not'. The student 'must approach the subject
submissively, start on a general agreed basis, and gradually build a
more and more complex network of understanding', a pretty sensible recipe, one would have thought, for gaining true understanding
and eventually creative freedom in what one is studying. However,
none of this applies in art, apparently. 'Art is not in the academic

sense at all'. One learns about art 'through the direct experience of making it oneself.' Like Pasmore Craig-Martin believes that in art and art education 'there are no obvious or agreed basics', which after decades of teachers like Pasmore and Craig-Martin might well be true, empirically, in to-day's art schools. In art education 'it is the individual who plays the central role, who accesses and animates the subject', and art, 'far from being indifferent', like those pesky academic subjects, 'responds accordingly'.

In one sense, of course, Craig-Martin is setting up a false dichotomy. Art education is, or should be about, making things oneself. Nor is it about robotically copying what one has been taught or what has gone before. But without mastering what has gone before, or at least the best of it, one's creativity is severely limited and one's limitations will be sorely exposed (the 'young' British artists). One wonders what any of the great artists of the past would have made of that, as they began their creative apprenticeships, let alone those to whom they went for instruction and training. Of course, they all departed in one way or another from their masters, but only once they had learned their techne, their art.

And as for non-submission and self-centering, there is surely a sense in which the really creative among us do submit to a reality outside them, and seek to lose the dross of their personality in doing so, a point beautifully captured by Ruskin in his account of his revelatory drawing of a tree as a young man in Fontainebleau. He had been in a depressed and nervous state, finding satisfaction in nothing, when, lying on his back, he began to draw a small aspen tree against the sky:

> Languidly, but not idly, I began to draw it; and as I drew, the languor passed away: the beautiful lines insisted on being traced, – without weariness. More and more beautiful they became, as each rose out of the rest, and took its place in the air. With wonder increasing every instant, I saw that they 'composed' themselves,

by finer laws than any known of men. At last, the tree was there, and everything that I had thought about trees, nowhere.' (5)

We find accounts of this sort from many of the great artists, and not just from those of the past. David Hockney makes very similar points about the role of looking and drawing, and seeing what is there for the first time, and precisely by the mastery of skill and forgetfulness of self. To artists of the past, from Leonardo and Michelangelo right up to the major figures of the twentieth century before Duchamp and Warhol, and even beyond, as we see with Hockney, it would have been regarded as a deception all round, had someone suggested that you could be truly creative without a disciplined grounding in the art, one often lasting a decade or more of dedicated study, both of art and nature, and practice in what one is doing. As teachers, let us not connive in this deception. Let us give to those who have talent and who have motivation to develop it the means to do so.

1. Lincoln Kirstein, 'A Ballet Master's Belief' in *Portrait of Mr B*, A Ballet Society Book, New York: The Viking Press, 1984, p 21. (Mr B is the choreographer George Balanchine.)
2. T.S. Eliot, 'Tradition and the Individual Talent' in *Selected Prose of T.S. Eliot,* ed Frank Kermode, London: Faber and Faber, 1975, p 40.
3. Victor Pasmore, 'The Case of Modern Art', *Modern Painters*, Vol I, No 4, Winter 1988-9, pp 22-31.
4. Michael Craig-Martin, *The Royal Academy of Arts Magazine*, No 142, Spring 2019, p 25.
5. John Ruskin, *Praeterita* (1885-9), Bk 2, Ch 4, in The Complete Works of John Ruskin, Vol XXXV, edited by E.T. Cook and Alexander Wedderburn, London: George Allen, 1908, p 314.

Independent Learning

This is a phrase which is often said and often heard, and usually passes approvingly, without comment. In one sense it seems perfectly reasonable. After all, don't we want pupils (and adults) who can study on their own without teachers standing over them all the time, who can sometimes at least work things out for themselves, and who ultimately have the ability and desire to pursue studies of one sort or another on their own and off their own bat? We also want pupils who take some responsibility for their work, who are conscientious about their work and who see themselves as accountable for their own successes or failures.

Unfortunately in educational circles 'independent learning' has another set of connotations. It refers to a desire educators and teachers of a certain mentality have to want pupils, even very young pupils, continually finding things out for themselves, forever actively 'researching' as would be said, with the teacher (in the phraseology of John Dewey) as little more than the leader of pupil activities, with his or her 'suggestion' not 'a mould for a cast-iron result', but 'merely a starting-point to be developed into a plan through contributions from the experience of all engaged in the learning process'. (1) We have already covered some of the ground here is discussing the 'creativity' of pupils and we have already referred to Dewey's opinion that the young child who 'discovers' that five plus five makes ten is a 'discoverer'. Only, one has to say, in a rather restricted sense.

But what is at issue here is not simply a quibble about the meaning of 'discover'. The more fundamental point is how we should conceive the relationship between the teacher and the pupil. Pace Dewey and those who want independent learning in his sense, the teacher has whatever authority they have because they know more than the pupil. The teacher's role is to pass on to the pupil bodies of worthwhile knowledge and experience, gathered over the course of human history from the earliest times to the present day. It is not just a question of efficiency, clarity, and accuracy in the passing on that the teacher should be charged with doing this, though that is certainly part of it, but the teacher also has a vital role to play in the formation of human community: being a member of a living community means that one's elders should pass on what they and their ancestors have discovered and created to the young, to those as yet ignorant of their heritage. And this is what the teacher is doing, or should be doing, as a living link in this great chain of human culture. To say that some of the things a good teacher will be passing on do not amount to 'cast-iron results' is, to say the least, disingenuous on Dewey's part.

The *Oresteia* of Aeschylus, the poetry of Virgil, the Divine Comedy, the tragedies of Shakespeare – we can debate and discuss and learn from all these things until the end of human time, but there is plenty here 'cast-iron' to start off with, the texts for a start, and what we know of what they say and how they have been interpreted; as there is in the physics of Newton, the biology of Darwin and Mendel, the chemistry of Lavoisier, the biochemistry of Crick and Watson – and yes, I know that none of these has the last word, but plenty of the bases on which these giants raised their superstructures remain; plenty of their observations, and plenty of the conclusions they drew, remain fundamental in their respective sciences, and it is hard to see how they will not so long as these sciences are studied. And all this is to say nothing of mathematics, from Euclid to Cantor, Hilbert, Gödel and beyond.

Expecting the young to 'research' these things for themselves as 'independent learners', with teachers not teaching, guiding, directing, cajoling, and encouraging their pupils is not just wasteful of time and effort, it also strikes at the very notion of human community, at the bonds which link us to the past, and our children to their elders.

This, of course, may have been part of Dewey's point as a committed advocate of modernity, quite happy to speak of much of the learning of the past as dead knowledge, and to disparage what he calls technical abilities in algebra, Latin, and botany, as 'not the kind of intelligence which directs ability to useful ends'. (2) He is anxious to see education as a preparation for children to live in democratic communities solving to-day's problems scientifically through continuous participatory discussion. And Dewey was an enthusiastic advocate of applying Darwinian thinking in all spheres, the social and political as much as in the biological. The idea of continuous evolution, whereby old species and old ideas die out once their utility had evaporated was for Dewey 'the greatest dissolvent in contemporary thought of old questions'. In the twentieth (and *a fortiori* the twenty-first century) politics and the education for that politics must be directed to what he called the 'intelligent administration of existent conditions', and in the process old myths and old certainties must be thrown out, particularly the idea that time-less essences of things had been or could be discovered. Much of what children had been taught in the traditional grammar school of the past was, in Dewey's view, 'static', 'cold-storage', 'miscellaneous junk'. This lumber would be of no use to to-day's mini-researchers, boldly and busily working on to-day's pressing political and social problems, untroubled by knowledge of or sensitivity to the past, with their teachers seeing themselves as no more than the leaders of group activities, what might to-day be called coordinators or facilitators.

I am not saying that all of to-day's advocates of 'independent learning' for children as young as six (I have seen them!) subscribe to the whole Deweyesque package. Many of them will, in all probability, never have heard of Dewey. But whenever one begins to hear of the point of education being to produce pupils who are learning how to learn (as opposed to learning the old subjects and disciplines) or that we need to produce a generation of independent learners equipped to deal with the problems of the twenty-first century (and hence can omit consideration of what has been learned in times earlier than now), and who therefore need not to be told things by their teachers (which would only be old stuff, of no relevance to the future or even to the present), but to 'research' for themselves (even children of six), the spirit of Dewey is hovering.

And it is the spirit of Dewey which inspires much of the talk of 'independent learning' and licences the child centred methods and 'research' I am deploring. You may have noticed that there is no mention of 'independent' learners or learning in the current teacher standards. There is no mention of these things because I fought (and had to fight) to keep them out, and I did so for the reasons I have touched on here. Conversations with various people since the standards came out in 2012 suggest to me that this omission has not generally been noticed, because many speak of the standards as if independent learning *is* there. What is there is the requirement that teachers 'encourage pupils to take a responsible and conscientious attitude to their own work and study', which is a statement of the innocuous sense of independent learning, with which we began. But there is no implication in the standards that dependent learning, in the sense of learning in which pupils depend on their teachers for knowledge, guidance, and advice, is inferior to pupils independently 'researching' on their own.

Nevertheless there are still those who act as if independent learning in the objectionable sense is still in the standards, from which I conclude that it would be unwise to expect people in education to see what they don't want to see, or even to read carefully! But it gratifies me to see in reading Ofsted's latest descriptors for grading teachers there is no mention of independent learning there either. I'd be interested to know if all the inspectors currently inspecting have noticed this.

What might be more important in this context is that all involved in education should look at a fairly recent article entitled 'Why Minimal Guidance During Instruction Does Not Work: an Analysis if the Failure of Constructivist, Discovery, Problem-Based, Experiential and Inquiry-Based Teaching.' It is by Paul A. Kirschner, John Sweller and Richard E. Clark and was published in *Educational Psychologist*, 41(2), 2006, 75-86. The article claims to be reporting on 50 years of research and was published more than a decade ago, you will notice. Apart from developing some of the points I have made here, and backing up what is said by research, the authors point out that in scientific work beginners cannot work like researchers (formulating hypotheses, testing them, etc.) until they have mastered the elementary knowledge on which researchers develop their hypotheses. In other words, a pre-scientific child cannot 'research' the topic he or she is 'investigating' – they are not yet the dwarves standing on the shoulders of giants that Newton likened himself to. To stand on the giant's shoulders you have a) to know a lot and b) to have been inducted by guidance and instruction into the ethos and practice of science the science in question, and also to gain a sense of what might or might not be a good hunch (hypothesis) to follow or test. Someone without prior knowledge and guidance cannot effectively be an independent learner, in other words.

This strikes me as a strong point and also true, and in different ways it would apply to any developed field of inquiry or art, be it history, literature, music, or the visual arts. So why, after fifty years plus a decade or more, is the opposite to it so fiercely promulgated in educational circles? Kirschner and his co-authors say that what they are attacking is an ideology, a religion I would say: a set of dogmatically held beliefs about the nature of children (as mini-researchers etc.) and about knowledge. As if to underline this last point, within one year another article appeared, replying to Kirschner and his colleagues. (4) The article in question, peer-reviewed and in the same prestigious journal as Kirschner et al, actually begins with the solecistic assertion 'All learning begins with knowledge construction in one form or other'. In the light of our earlier comments on Vygotsky this alone might throw into question the value of educational 'research' as well as the reliability of peer review.

1.   John Dewey, *Experience and Education* (1938), New York: Collier Books, 1963, p 72.

2.   John Dewey, *Democracy and Education* (1916), New York: Free Press, 1966, p 39.

3.   Paul A. Kirschner, John Sweller and Richard E. Clark, 'Why Minimal Guidance During Instruction Does Not Work: An Analysis of the Failure Of Constructivist, Discovery, Problem-Based, Experiential and Enquiry-Based Teaching', *Educational Psychologist*, 41 (2), 2006, pp 75-86.

4.   Cindy E. Hmelo-Silver, Ravit Golan Duncan and Clark A. Chinn, 'Scaffolding and Achievement in Problem-Based and Inquiry Learning: A Response to Kirschner, Sweller and Clark (2006)', *Educational Psychologist*, (42.2), 2007, pp 99-107.

Chapter 7

'D'OÙ PARLES-TU?' REFLECTIONS ON POWER, TRUTH AND THE OPEN SOCIETY

'That's not the way the world works anymore. We're an empire now, and when we act, we create our own reality. And while you (journalists) are studying that reality... we'll act again, creating other new realities... you, all of you, will be left to just study what we do.' Thus an advisor to George W. Bush, castigating the journalist Ron Suskind for attempting to report on what he took to be a discernible reality, out there and open to objective scrutiny, but, as he has just been told, the world is not like that any more. (1)

It would be hard to find a more succinct statement of what has come to be known as a post-truth position in a post-truth world. Crudely expressed as it is, what it amounts to is the claim that there is no truth or reality out there. Truth and reality (or, better, 'truth' and 'reality') are things we, that is, those in power, construct, and what the Bush advisor is saying is that the rest of us just have to march to their tune. Which simply invites the rejoinder from those who don't like this, all right, then, we will 'construct' our reality, and use what power we have to confront and contest yours.

The example I have just quoted from is from a right-wing source, but the attitude to truth is by no means confined to the political right. If anything, attitudes of this sort are more deeply embedded in left-wing thinking, where the implications of such views are more fully argued and elaborated. For many

so-called post-modernist thinkers, particularly when dealing
with matters of history, morality, and politics, not only is there
no such thing as the truth, but any view that is expressed is to
be seen as no more than the vehicle of some interest, class, race,
gender or whatever. The question of the source of an opinion
or a 'fact' – d'où parles-tu? – becomes far more important than
its truth or validity, because there is no such thing as truth or
validity. Truth and validity are simply words we use to enhance
the standing of what we construct.

It cannot be too strongly emphasized or too often repeated
that, philosophically speaking, talk of 'constructing' truth and
knowledge is not just linguistically barbaric; it is nonsensical.
You can actually know only what is true, and what is true is true
because it actually is the case, independently of what anyone
thinks or believes. Beliefs and thoughts are, in a certain sense,
constructed, psychological entities in our minds underpinning
our actions. With luck and experience and work, and also
thanks to our biology and upbringing, many of our beliefs and
thoughts are true, and amount to knowledge in the sense that
we have good grounds for holding these truths.

No doubt we, or our forebears, have produced social norms,
like those of politeness, institutions such as money, artistic traditions in painting, music and the like, and theories in science. We
could, at a pinch, talk of 'construction' in these contexts, though
bearing in mind that much of what emerges in human culture
is unplanned, and only loosely tied to deliberate decisions. But
we do not construct knowledge or truth, ours or anyone else's.

Some of what we think we know, though, we do not know, as,
for example, Newton did not know that space and time were
absolute, although he had plenty of reasons for thinking thus,
reasons which were elaborated in the theory he 'constructed'.
For 200 years or so nearly all good scientists followed him in
this erroneous belief ('Newton's Theory'), which should make

us cautious in claiming to know. Knowledge transcends what we construct – it is not in our gift. None of which stops those in charge of educating our children from asserting that children (and adults) 'construct or build their own knowledge… (rather than having it) 'given' or 'delivered' to them', to quote from one of the most widely used texts in teacher training, as we have already seen when considering Educational Myths. (2) This way of thinking, often ascribed to Vygotsky, is taken as gospel in great swathes of teacher training. The rot in this area starts early.

Nor is there anything new in this rot, in undermining (or deconstructing) foundational concepts that are normally and properly taken to refer to reality in a substantial way. In Book One of Plato's *Republic* the sophist Thrasymachus famously announced that morality and right are nothing other than the advantage of the stronger, or what serves that advantage. (3) We might say in reply that in any particular society what are *called* morality and right may reflect the status quo and the interests of the rich and powerful, but that there is nevertheless an absolute standard (true justice, true morality) against which particular acts and institutions and societies are to be judged, as indeed Plato judged his own society when he advocated female equality among the rulers, but that would not move Thrasymachus. He knew what Thucydides knew, that, particularly in times of struggle and strife key words – those like 'justice', 'right' and 'truth', which refer to basic values – are slippery. The way people use them changes; there are Orwellian shifts in their meaning.

Writing of the civil war in Corcyra (Corfu) in 427BC, Thucydides says this: 'To fit in with the change of events, words, too, had to change their normal meanings. What used to be described as a thoughtless act of aggression was now regarded as the courage one would expect in a party member. To think of the future and wait was merely another way of saying one was a coward. Any idea of moderation was just an attempt to disguise one's unmanly character. Ability to understand a question from all sides meant one was wholly unfitted for action... If an opponent made a reasonable speech, the party in power, so far from giving it a generous reception, took every precaution to see that it had no practical effect.' (4)

And he adds that 'love of power, operating through greed, and through personal ambition, was the cause of all these evils', which indeed it was and still is to-day, when we see similar linguistic deformations. Power and self-interest, or the interest of one's party, distort what is said and even the use and meaning of words. But what if there is no truth or justice, absolutely speaking, but only what particular people *call* truth or justice, to further their own ends or causes? Then there is nothing left in discussing an opinion or 'fact', but to ask where it comes from, whose interest it is serving.

This is precisely what, over two millennia after Thucydides, we find in Nietzsche: what we call 'truth' 'is a mobile army of metaphors, metonyms, anthropomorphisms, in short a sum of human relations which have been enhanced, transposed and embellished poetically and rhetorically... truths are illusions about which one has forgotten that this is what they are; metaphors which are worn out and without sensuous power...', a famous passage from an early work (5), and, though contested as representing Nietzsche's settled view, it is highly popular in post-modernist circles to-day. In a way more striking, this time from *The Genealogy of Morals*, at the end of his career, we have this: 'Pale atheists, anti-Christians, immoralists, nihilists; these sceptics (that is people who might have expected support from Nietzsche)... cannot see... (that) this ideal is precisely *their* ideal, too...' and he goes on to say that they are 'far from being free spirits: *for they still have faith in truth.*' Contrasting present-day pale atheists with the medieval Assassins, Nietzsche concludes that for them freedom of spirit means that 'nothing is true, everything is permitted… in that way the faith in truth was *abrogated*'; so, we too must call into question the value of truth.(6)

In other words, if truth is an illusion, then all we can do is to ask where an opinion is coming from: 'd'où parles-tu?', not 'is what you say true?'. Of course, there is in Nietzsche the same elision between what people say is true, and what is actually true, which we saw in Thrasymachus on justice. Nor does Nietzsche appear to ask himself what credence we should give to his views. If there is no truth, they are not true. Why, then, should we accept them, coming from *that* somewhat self-dramatising source?

It is just this aspect of Nietzsche's thinking, along with its inherent confusions, that has been gaily adopted by postmodernists, such as Foucault, Derrida, Baudrillard, and Lyotard, who argue that in the face of the Nietzschean undermining of what they call the 'narratives of legitimation' of Enlightenment thinking (no truth in other words), we are obliged to adopt a stance of opposition to everything which appears to them to be a product of the power structures and institutions which those narratives upheld, Western culture, in other words. What, though, of the self-refuting nature of their own position? In Roger Scruton's words, 'the advocate of deconstruction cheerfully accepts the disproof of his own philosophy; for what matters to him is not the truth of an utterance, but the interest that is being advanced through it. Your criticism shows you to be a denizen of the 'traditional criticism', a parasitical resident in the house of Western culture… to think that you can get rid of deconstruction by disproving it, is to fail to recognize that proof itself has been deconstructed. Proof is what Others do; and it's Them that we're against.' (7)

Scruton is here expressing somewhat polemically what Richard Rorty argued perfectly in more measured tones in the opening pages of *Contingency, Irony and Solidarity*. (8) Arguments about fundamental concepts like truth and reality are bound to be inconclusive and question-begging, he says, because either side in such an argument will simply be using his or her own incommensurable concepts. 'Interesting philosophy is (usually)... a contest between an entrenched vocabulary which has become a nuisance and a half-formed new vocabulary which vague promises great things'. So, in what he is about to write in his book, he says, 'I am not going to offer arguments against the vocabulary I want to replace'. He is also going to drop any notion of fitting the world (in discussing knowledge claims) or of intrinsic nature (in analysing political aims or the morality of desires), and simply seek a set of increasingly useful metaphors. But useful in whose interest, one might ask? And can it be true, as Rorty suggests elsewhere, (9) that there is no such thing as an intrinsically evil desire, and, agreeing with President Bush's advisor, that we make truths?

We are back to Thrasymachus and Thucydides with a vengeance. No truth, no natural goodness, no valid arguments, no firm vocabulary or concepts in which to discuss such things, but only contests between rival interests and power groups, each sheltering behind their own redescriptions and shifting linguistic forms. In such a context, as Rorty has correctly told us, argument is futile. We are each going to mean different things by our words, depending on where we stand, and what the words describe are simply our own constructions, with no objective validity. Moreover, each person's words are only a way of asserting his or her own power, or that of their group. In these circumstances, argument counts for nothing. What counts is what is hiding behind the words, the interest that is being promoted in each case. And allowing someone a voice is allowing their interest some weight, which is something that is not necessarily desirable. As long ago as

1974, Sartre wrote that in all the conflicts of our time, 'class, national, racial... are particular effects of the oppression of the under-privileged... the true intellectual finds himself, as a man conscious of his own oppression, on the side of the oppressed.' (10)

We can speculate as to why the true intellectual finds himself on the side of the oppressed (Heidegger and Nietzsche, two of the precursors of to-day's postmodernism certainly didn't), and also as to just how oppressed Sartre was, but what we are now in a position to understand is why for many of to-day's intellectuals what matters is not the quality of an argument (for arguments have none), but, as would be said, where they are coming from, and why, consequently, some should not be heard – if they are promoting the interests of the oppressors, or those who are perceived to be oppressors.

We need at this point to go back to the beginning. The whole postmodernist position, like that of Thrasymachus, rests on a failure to distinguish between what is true and what is believed to be true, and also on a failure to acknowledge that its inherent nihilism and consequent repudiation of argument and validity undermines its own acceptability. Far from speaking truth to power, postmodernists misrepresent any attempt to search for truth as simply a mask for the exercise of power: and where, as all too often, they deny others the chance to speak, censoring what they want to say, their own position stands revealed as simply an exercise of power. They would return us to the situation of the Corcyreans in 427BC, the outcome of which I need not spell out.

If, on the other hand and unlike the Corcyreans, we are prepared to accept the possibility of reasonable speech and to recognize it when it occurs, which is surely a fundamental aspect of an open society, we should also recognize that good ideas (and indeed truths) can come from any source. Let us begin by underlining the distinction between what is true and what is believed by us or others to be true. Bearing in mind the fate of Newtonian physics and admitting that even the best of what we believe may not in fact be true, should (in Karl Popper's words) lead not just to a humility on our own part, but also to the view that 'everybody with whom we communicate (is) a potential source of argument and of reasonableness'. (11)

It is important to emphasise here that Popper thinks that everyone involved in or affected by a social or political issue should be included in the conversation. There is a tendency in such matters to attend only to the articulate, the so-called 'educated', and to the political and administrative mandarins. But, Popper insists, if we really want to know what the effects and indeed the value of an institution or a policy are, we should also listen to those who are at the bottom of the heap, so to speak. For it is they who are most likely to be adversely affected, even if they may on one scale of evaluation be marginalized, or even, on another, regarded as 'deplorables'. I admire Popper's humanity here, and, pragmatically speaking, we now know all too clearly just what eventually happens when deplorables are ignored.

Refusing to respect reason and 'the other fellow's point of view... (will) produce an attitude which considers the person of the thinker instead of his thought. It must produce the belief that 'we think with our blood', or 'with our national heritage', or 'with our class.'' Considering the thought rather than who has the thought will, by contrast, establish what Popper calls 'the rational unity of mankind.' The contrary will, as Popper emphasises, lead to splitting mankind into friends and foes, with all the potential for censorship, repression and worse, characteristic of closed societies. (12)

What Popper calls rationalism – basically admitting one's own fallibility, combined with a readiness to allow anyone who is not intolerant their right to be heard and to defend their arguments – depends, as he also says, on the existence of 'social institutions to protect freedom of criticism, freedom of thought, and thus the freedom of men.' (*ibid*, p 238) Foremost among such institutions will be universities, which is why intolerance there is no small matter. It is something which is serious for the society in which they exist (as was shown all too vividly in post-1933 Germany).

We live in paradoxical times. The internet and social media allow anyone to express and publish a view on anything. In many ways this is a good thing. But this freedom also generates great swathes of hostile and cruel messaging, which make individuals afraid to express themselves. Universities should be places where individuals should be able to express their opinions, discuss and disagree, without fear of censorship, mob hostility, or loss of job. To the extent that they allow censorship of views some find objectionable and tolerate violence in their suppression, as seems to be the case in 2023, they are no better than Corcyreans described by Thucydides. In considering this dismal scene we should not overlook the way in which postmodernist thinking in the academy has contributed to it. (13)

1. Quoted in A. Jones, *Losing the News*, New York: Oxford University Press, 2019, pp 219-20.
2. See above, p xx; the authority in question is J. Wellington, *Secondary Education: the Key Concepts*, London: Routledge, 2006, p 53.
3. Plato, *The Republic*, trans. R. Waterfield, Oxford: Oxford University Press, 1993, 338c and ff.
4. Thucydides, *History of the Peloponnesian War*, transl Rex Warner, London: Penguin Books. 1954, Bk 3, Section 82.

5. F. Nietzsche, *Truth and Lying in an Extra-Moral Sense*, 1873, trans. W. Kaufmann, in *The Portable Nietzsche*, New York: Viking Press, 1976, pp 46-7.

6. F. Nietzsche, *The Genealogy of Morals*, 1884, (3.24), trans. W. Kaufmann, in *The Basic Writings of Nietzsche*, New York: The Modern Library, 1968, pp 585-6.

7. Roger Scruton, *Modern Philosophy: An Introduction and Survey*, London: Sinclair-Stevenson, 1994, p 479.

8. Richard Rorty, *Contingency, Irony and Solidarity*, Cambridge: Cambridge University Press, 1989.

9. Richard Rorty, *An Ethics for To-day: Finding Common Ground Between Philosophy and Religion*, New York: Columbia University Press, 2010, p 15.

10. J-P. Sartre, *Between Existentialism and Marxism*, trans. J. Matthews, London: Verso, 1974, p 254.

11. K.R. Popper, *The Open Society and Its Enemies*, Vol 2, fifth edition, London: Routledge and Kegan Paul, 1966, p 225.

12. Popper, *op cit*, pp 235-6.

13. Paper given at The McDonald Centre for Theology, Ethics and Public Life Conference on Academic Freedom Under Threat,, Oxford, May 2019, published in Standpoint, Aug/Sept 2020, pp 29-31.

Chapter 8

MY TRUTH

'Well, that's my truth' or 'That's my truth, and you are ignoring it'. Concessive or aggressive, we hear a lot these days about 'my' truth. As an old-fashioned (and elderly male) philosopher, my instinctive reaction is to bridle, and to huff. 'Your truth', 'my truth' – it's all nonsense. There is just truth, not yours or mine; if something is true, then it is true, objectively, true for everyone, independently of what anyone thinks. End of story! Though even that is a bit off; truth isn't 'for' anyone, not even for 'everyone'. As Aristotle taught us long ago, to say that something is true means that that is just how it is – and how it is, whether anyone recognizes it or not.

But I now think that there is something over-hasty and perhaps a little unkind about my Aristotelian dismissal of 'my' truth. For it is true that many people's views on important and sensitive topics are often overlooked, or contemptuously dismissed, particularly by experts, or those whom fashion regards as such. And what, as a philosopher, I should remember is not just Aristotle's pristine view of truth (with which, in essence I agree), but also an old philosophical chestnut, the so-called paradox of G.E. Moore, dating from 1942. Moore pointed out that there is something peculiar, even obtuse, about saying that something *is* true, and then immediately adding 'but I don't believe it'. In other words, it is inconsistent to drive a wedge between what I believe and what I think is true. Belief aims at truth, and so does asserting something to be the case.

So, if I say that something is so, or that I believe it, I am also saying that it is true.

So what I believe *is* 'my' truth, then? Not quite so simple. My belief, my statement, *aims* at truth, and in asserting something I *am* implying that it is the case. Unfortunately, though, truth is not so easily attained, and this is partly why it is so misleading to talk of 'my truth'. We all, each one of us, know that we can be wrong, and wrong even on things we believe most strongly. I was sure that the train left at 6.00 pm, and being of a somewhat dogmatic disposition, told everyone that. Unfortunately it left at 5.55 pm. I missed the train, and was left looking unreliable and foolish to boot. My belief was simply not true, even though my telling people that it was 6.00 pm implied that I thought that that was true. Indeed, if my hearers had not thought that I believed that it was true that the train was leaving at 6.00 pm, they would not have taken any notice of what I was saying. So it is not just that belief aims at truth. Everyday communication depends on the assumption that people are generally intending to say what is true. One result of this little vignette is that people will now be less ready to accept my blustering and self-assurance as a guide to what actually is.

May we though, after all, still speak of what I say and believe as being 'my' truth? In a number of ways this would be highly misleading. As we saw in the case of the train, 'my' truth was not true; and neither was Jones's, who thought the train was leaving at 6.05. There was only one belief that was actually true, and that was the belief that it was leaving at 5.55 pm. And maybe no one had *the* truth. Maybe everyone was wrong in this or in some other case. But each one of us thought that what he or she believed was the truth. This is where I have some sympathy for some of those who speak about 'my' truth, for it is often the case that their beliefs and feelings – which they strongly believe to be true – are dismissed or trampled on. And these are often cases where, in distinction to train times, people have invested a lot of emotion and even felt a lot of pain. Worse, they may be dismissed or trampled on by people whose own beliefs are not actually true, but who simply have the power or authority to shut others out of the conversation.

But this does not justify sloppy talk about 'my' truth. Although my beliefs aim at truth, there is a distinction between the belief and its target, even where the target is hit. The belief is one thing and its being true is another, even when it is true. I may be fortunate enough to have a true belief, but while the belief is mine, the truth is not mine. A statement or belief that is true is true independently of anyone's believing it. Its truth is due to the way the world is, not due to its being believed by someone truth. The belief is mine, something that I think and hold to, but truth is not something that can belong to anyone in that way. Truth is impersonal in a way beliefs and opinions are not, that against which people's beliefs and opinions are judged.

Apart from glossing over this crucial logical point, talking of 'my' truth actually makes things more difficult for those who feel their views are being crowded out. Instead of seeing ourselves as believers as aiming at something which transcends particular beliefs, and to which all particular beliefs are aiming, talk of 'my' truth or 'your' truth or 'their' truth will have the effect of enclosing people in their own beliefs or thought worlds. This bad effect of this way of talking would quickly become apparent if we are talking about trains and other narrowly factual matters, and so the 'my truth' attitude does not get much of a hold in these areas. Where it does hold sway to a much greater extent is where talk of life experience and of interpretations of history and political and social attitudes are concerned. Some might feel that the notion of truth is more difficult to apply in these areas, which are in various ways value-laden, but actually the same principles apply as in discussions of train times and the like.

After all, these are the very areas in which talk of 'my' truth is rampant, so people do make claims to truth very strongly in them. Moreover – and here I agree with part of what underlies the 'my' truth talk – it surely just is the case that slavery is wrong, that torture is wrong, that child abuse is wrong. There just are truths and falsehoods here; some things simply are the case, and to argue the opposite (as unfortunately Aristotle did on slavery) is mistaken, and possibly a reflection of self-interest or some moral failing as well. Even if you are squeamish about using the term 'truth' here, someone who asserts that their experience has been that of a victim, or that the historical fact of colonialism demands reparation now, is certainly saying that these things are the case, and demanding that such and such be done.

As such, these assertions and demands are not being presented purely as matters of opinion or taste. They are being presented as objective, as how things are or should be, independently of any individual prejudice or factional perspective (which is presumably why there is talk of 'educating yourself' here). So, from a logical point of view, the assertions and demands in question are being treated in the same way as ordinary truth claims, with the same force and implication – that what they say is so, independently of what any individual or any group might think or want.

In these contested cases we could think of what different people might call their 'truths' as perspectives on something that is or is not the case beyond the particular perspective, that is objectively so or not, in the same way as the train actually left at 5.55 pm and not at 6.00 pm, whatever anyone thought or believed. In the case of attitudinal perspectives we could also recognise that some might have more validity than someone's mistaken belief in a train time, and some more validity than others. Aristotle, as already mentioned, believed that slavery was not wrong, but rather that, as he put it, some men are by nature slaves. Did he actually talk to any slaves about this? Did he attempt to see things from their point of view? From their perspective? And if he did, did he simply dismiss what the slave said with haughty contempt? Equally Darwin, in commenting that the Tierra del Fuegians he met in his famous voyage were more distant from civilized men than were wild from domesticated animals, signally failed to make any serious effort to understand them and their way of life.

In cases of this sort a recognition of the incomplete or partial validity of different perspectives, including above all one's own, is almost a precondition for the adoption of a more correct, more inclusive, more objective view. But it is just this movement to a more correct view which is precluded by talk of 'my' truth, implying as it does that there is no truth beyond which particular groups might believe as 'their' truth. But this position, as we have learned from G.E. Moore, misunderstands the nature of belief as aiming at truth. It also undermines successful communication, which depends on the presupposition that what one asserts is to be understood as true, as reliable, independently of what I or anyone else thinks. Of course, it might be wrong or even a lie, but one's listener is being offered it as describing what is actually the case, and will normally understand it as such (which is why lies can have devastating effects). Hardly surprising, then, that when 'my' truth has become all the rage, and one overlooks the impersonal universality of truth, people are increasingly enclosed mentally in their own prejudices and thought bubbles.

An example of this phenomenon comes from J.R. Moehringer, the actual writer of André Agassi's spirited *Open* (a revealing account of some of the problems, psychological and physical, of the life of a top tennis player), and also of Prince Harry's *Spare*. He took to twitter seemingly to defend *Spare* against accusations that claims in it are not actually true. He quoted Mary Kerr (author of a book called *The Art of Memoir*), who apparently said, 'The line between memory and fact is blurry, between interpretation and fact. There are inadvertent mistakes of those kind out of the wazoo.' Moehringer meanwhile pointed to several passages from *Spare* where the Prince says that his words in the book are how *he* remembers the situation he is describing. One such passage said that 'whatever the cause, my memory is my memory. It does what it does, gathers and curates, as it sees fit, and there's just as much truth in what I remember and how I remember it as there is in so-called objective facts.' (1)

Recollections may indeed vary, as Prince Harry's grandmother famously put it, and as Harry seems to allow in the passage just quoted, there is often an unintentional element of distortion even in memories which seem to the subject to be completely clear and accurate. There is a well known police training video in which an armed police officer says adamantly and sincerely that he fired two shots at a suspect, when the film clearly shows him firing five. If we are honest, we will all recognise occasions in our own lives where our own clear and subjectively certain memory turns out to be clearly and equally certainly wrong, and we are shown this beyond any shadow of doubt. But this all too human predicament does nothing to obliterate the crucial distinction between memory and fact, crucial because so much of our lives, from court cases to promise keeping to personal relationships and even to sporting matters depend on it. And we hardly need to speak here of the harm and destruction to lives wreaked by what psychologists refer to as false memory syndrome, where disturbed people, often under pressure from therapists and counsellors, 'remember' being sexually abused by family members, teachers, carers and the like, abuse that is later shown never to have occurred.

Similar examples of eroding the distinction between one's no doubt strongly held feelings and the truth might be some cases where people of one sex feel that they are really of the other sex (and I mean sex, so as not to complicate matters with the slippery and ambiguous notion of gender). Or we can think of the notorious case of Rachel Dolezal, of Eastern European extraction, claiming to be of black and North American descent, rising to be head of her local branch of the US National Association for the Advancement of Colored People: her 'essential essence' (or perhaps her 'truth') was that she was black. And many of her supporters (and she did have some!) seemed happy to go along with this, saying that how she perceived herself internally was what mattered, was the authentic person. Textbook cases, indeed, but in all this farrago of words meaning what I feel them to mean, we are clearly in danger of losing the ability to communicate with each other. For at the most basic level, that ability depends on us all using words in more or less the same way, and on an understanding that the words we use, when we are speaking descriptively, refer to a world we all inhabit and are made true or false by the way things in that world are. And I mean 'are', and not 'seem to me to be'.

We should recognize that we all have perspectives on various political, ethical, social, and religious matters, and perhaps deep feelings about them – to that extent we can have sympathy with Prince Harry and Rachel Dolezal – but we should also recognise that in holding and entertaining these perspectives we are treating them as true. Hence, misleadingly, 'my' truth; misleading because other people will have differing perspectives, which doubtless they also think of as being true. In most, if not all of these cases, none of the differing perspectives are completely true. Even as they aim at the truth, as an ideal, they fall short of that ideal. Indeed, recognizing that some view I have on a contested issue is my perspective (rather than my 'truth') amounts to a recognition that it is or may be partial. Other people's differing perspectives may (will almost certainly) contain some of the truth.

Thus, I am opposed to socialism as a political creed, but I recognize that there are important truths underlying socialism, truths to do with poverty and power, and that my own political position will have to have some means of addressing these issues. At the very least, we should recognize that no influential ideology would ever have caught on and become influential if it did not contain some truth or truths. It may also be that there are ideals and perspectives which may not be realizable, such as equality, or which may not be jointly realizable, such as equality and liberty, and which may in that way also fall short of the truth.

We inhabit a world of differing perspectives on important human questions, all of which implicitly aim at a truth which is independent of them. Further the world in which we live may be such that the ambitions of our perspective may actually be impossible. Realising these things should make us open to discussing and comparing our perspective ('my truth') with that of others. We should be open to engage with others and their perspectives, and ready to modify our own in the light of such engagement. Lenin believed, or said he believed, that truth is what serves the revolution. Unlike Lenin, I do not believe that truth is whatever serves my vision of conservatism; I believe that there may be political and ethical truths which are hidden or distorted in my political philosophy. And again unlike Lenin, I believe that progress will be made in this area only by discussion with those who may have part of the truth which my own view overlooks.

Unfortunately, as things are in 2023, it seems that just as there is more and more communication in the world, more and more noise, there is less and less actual discussion and dialogue, particularly on controversial and contentious matters. I suspect that this paradox has arisen partly because much of the communication in question is not face to face. It is done through the internet or on electronic devices, where we do not come into real human contact with our interlocutors, or with those who hold perspectives different from our own. And we may not want to anyway. We may want only to see our own prejudices being confirmed from a host of like-minded communicators. So, many of us manage to live hearing (or rather seeing) no opinions but our own, which are magnified and endlessly repeated in the so-called social media, without any attempt at qualification or examination in the light of opposing views. AI and the internet actually contribute to this sorry state of affairs by filtering to people only those views and opinions with which they already agree, thus making it far less likely than it should be that they will ever have to deal with objections and differences from their original position, far less likely to advance to what might be less prejudiced and closer to the actual truth.

If we actually met people who disagreed with us, we would have to realise that what they thought were not the vapourings of disembodied aliens, but opinions, often deeply and sometimes reasonably held, of real human beings. And seeing our interlocutors as human beings, rather than as, to us, simply the invisible sources of disagreeable messages on screen, would also make it more difficult to insult and belittle them and their ideas. Not impossible, but more difficult, and a step towards realizing that our own perspective may not be the whole truth. Other, not entirely unreasonable people hold other views.

So, genuine dialogue with others should be the result of realising both that 'my' truth is not 'the' truth, and, more fundamentally, that truth, *the* truth, is something independent of any particular perspective, or, indeed, of all of them. The philosopher C.S. Peirce once suggested that *the* truth is that fated to be agreed by all honest and genuine enquirers. To my mind this is too simplistic, unless, like Peirce himself, you believe that honest and genuine enquiry is guided by a divine hand. Contra Peirce, the idea that honest and genuine enquiry in any area, even that of science, is ultimately going to converge on a single, agreed view has little support from history. The history of ideas and even of science is much more a history of divergence and upheaval, of ideas and theories always being overthrown and supplanted sooner or later, or at least modified out of recognition. But even if some impressive convergence did come about in a given area, it would not follow that what was converged on was true. Thus, in the history of science, Newtonian physics commanded almost unanimous support from leading scientists (honest and genuine enquirers, all) for two centuries. But it is – and was – false. As Karl Popper used to say, even in science, we can't know, we can only guess. Historically, convergence does not guarantee truth. And even if a convergent view were true, its truth would come not from human agreement, but from its correspondence with the way things are. Logically, *pace* Peirce, convergence of opinion and truth are different things.

So, to sum up, 'my truth' is not the same as truth, even if (some of what) I believe is true. 'My truth' is an oblique way of referring to my beliefs, which then have to be compared to the reality from which they are separate, and by which they are judged. 'Our truth', our beliefs, in other words, is not the same as the truth with which they are to be compared, even if what 'we' believe is true, and even if the 'we' who believe were the whole of humanity. However, the situation in which we find ourselves is not one in which in many important areas the whole of humanity is all converging on a single set of beliefs, even though as beliefs, all these different positions aim at truth (the truth), and may capture some of that truth.

Truth, then, is what belief aims at – there is, logically, a distinction between the two. Recognising this crucial distinction should induce in all of us a certain humility regarding our own perspectives and beliefs. Even as we fight shy of the horrible locution 'my truth', all too often all of us tend to treat what we believe and what we take as expertise, as the truth. We may then find that some of those who feel that their voices are not being sufficiently attended to, begin talking about 'my truth'. We then criticize them for this logical ineptitude, not realizing that our own quite proper rejection of talk of 'my' truth carries with it an obligation. The obligation is to accept that the fashions and claims to expertise embedded in our own perspective may themselves hinder progress even in the growth of knowledge, let alone in human affairs more generally. The irony is that it is precisely the insistence on 'my truth' by those who see themselves as under-privileged that will make it easier for those in established and fashionable positions to dig in where they are, avoiding the obligation to talk to the opponents who have themselves repudiated dialogue.

1.   Reported by Jennifer Newton on line in *The Mirror*, 12/01/2023.

Epilogue

EARLY DAYS OF THE DEPARTMENT OF EDUCATION AT THE UNIVERSITY OF BUCKINGHAM: A PERSONAL VIEW

In the year 2000 Chris Woodhead stepped down as Her Majesty's Chief Inspector of Schools. In the next year Terence Kealey became the Vice-Chancellor of the University of Buckingham, and I resigned as Professor of Philosophy at the University of Bradford. It was the congruence of these three unconnected events which led in 2002 to the formation of the School of Education at the University of Buckingham, which within a decade and a half became the largest provider of teacher training in the country.

For a number of years I had been friends with both Chris and Terence, in Chris's case a very close friend. Terence I had met in the mid-1980s in conservative think-tank circles, when he, a Cambridge bio-chemist, had become a leading advocate of independent education for all, and also the author of a striking essay arguing against the state funding of science It was called 'Science Fiction', and was published by the Centre for Policy Studies in 1989, at a time when there were noisy campaigns to 'save' British science, or at least its funding by central government. This did not endear him to the scientific establishment. I was also beginning to publish somewhat polemical articles in national newspapers on education and other topics.

Chris and I originally met in 1989, when we were both on the government's advisory body on teacher training (the Council for the Accreditation of Teacher Education). Chris was the representative of the National Curriculum Council, where he was deputy chief executive, and I was there as the author of a pamphlet called 'Who Teaches the Teachers' (Social Affairs Unit, 1988), which questioned the desirability of university based teacher training as opposed to a school centred approach. The pamphlet attracted the attention of Kenneth Clarke, then Secretary of State for Education, who, provocatively it seemed to some, and egged on by Tessa Keswick, his special advisor, put me on CATE, as the body was known.

Chris and I found that we agreed on teacher training and on many other things to do with education and culture more generally. I also worked with him on SCAA, the School Curriculum and Assessment Authority, he as its first chief executive and I as a board member (1993-7). He became Chief Inspector and head of Ofsted in 1994. We kept in close touch, and I also had a period as a board member of the Teacher Training Agency, the successor body to CATE, though, with the change of government, this and my membership of SCAA came to an end in 1997. Chris, meanwhile soldiered on at Ofsted in characteristically forthright style, advocating high standards in schools, criticizing poor and mediocre schools and teachers, and encouraging strong and traditional teaching and subject knowledge in both teachers and pupils. At the same time he cast doubt on the value of a strictly academic education for all and on the value of child-centred education for any. He was implacably opposed to what even at that early date he termed the blob, the educational establishment dominant in educational bureaucracies, including the civil service and local authorities, in university departments of education and in the higher echelons of the teaching profession. Needless to say this provoked much hostility and several campaigns against him, and he resigned in 2000.

It was in the autumn of 2001 that I saw that Terence had been appointed Vice-Chancellor of Buckingham. I contacted him to see if I might do something there once I had left Bradford. I also said to him that it was quite normal for Chief Inspectors of Schools to be given Chairs of Education on their retirement, but oddly no such offer had come Chris's way, though he did have a column in the *Sunday Times*. Terence was intrigued, and I set up a meeting for the three of us, which took place in l'Estaminet, a restaurant in Covent Garden favoured by Chris. Terence then set about establishing an education department at Buckingham, with professorial posts for Chris and me (though not wanting to exceed my professional competence I insisted on being Professor of Philosophy, rather than of Education). Perhaps more important, Terence got funding for each of us for four years, from the foundations run by Stanley Kalms and Guy Weston, to enable us to set the department up.

Having been appointed to start a department of education, we then had to find something to do. We were already thinking along the lines of a genuinely independent course of school-based teacher training. This would be in contrast to the traditional university based courses, which had in addition to conform to the governement's criteria for qualifiying as a teacher. These were encapsulated in a document of 94 pages, consisting of 33 standards, many sub-standardds and a welter of what was some-what disingenuously called 'guidance', all of which government accredited courses and teachers had to satisfy. Luckily for us, Geoff Lucas, who had worked for Chris at SCAA, was then secretary of HMC, the professional body for Heads of independent schools. Working through Geoff we had a meeting with the HMC sub-committee concerned with teacher training and development. We found that that committee was very much of our way of thinking, very opposed to the bureaucratic methods of the government's system and even more to its apparent hostility to what it saw as élitism, that is, traditional rigour in teaching, assessment, and subject content. At that time practically all teacher training was based in university departments of education with school placements for teaching practice as a rather secondary aspect. We were proposing a genuinely independent and employment based course. Schools which wanted to participate would send new teachers they had appointed to work in their schools for a year within a framework set by Buckingham rather than by the blob. Employment in a good school was to be a prerequisite, which underlined the sense in which the course would involve genuine partnerships with schools. This course would be tailored to the needs specifically of individual independent schools and should be trialled as soon as possible.

It quickly emerged that institutionally at Buckingham the best way of doing this was to set up a postgraduate certificate in education. Our PGCE, as it inevitably became, was to be based on the assumption that what was needed in a teacher was, first, good subject knowledge at whatever level was appropriate. Secondly, subject knowledge, while necessary, was not sufficient; teachers must be able to practice the craft of the classroom. And thirdly, teachers must have good moral standing and be able to relate positively to the young people they would be teaching.

Putting the subject knowledge requirement first was designed to counter the widely held belief that teachers were primarily facilitators rather than teachers. It also gave the lie to the sentimentalism that teachers teach children not subjects. Of course they teach children, but their authority and their role stem from their expertise in some worthwhile field of activity, their subject in other words; teachers are primarily teachers, not social workers or childminders, even though there may be some overlap in these areas.

But teaching is not simply a matter of the teacher having learning or expertise. A teacher must also be able to transmit what they know to the young people to be taught, and ideally to enthuse them with what they know and value. Hence, the second requirement, the craft of the classroom. In our view this is largely a practical matter, one which requires the ability to put a subject over and to interact with pupils in classrooms individually and collectively. Hence craft. One could know all there is to know theoretically about managing behaviour or about child psychology or the psychology of learning and still be a poor teacher. All too often university courses in education were dominated by academically abstract lectures and seminars, often of questionable validity and usually promoting a child-centred and ideologically skewed view of education.

Even if the prescriptions one found in fashionable books were sensible, which is occasionally the case, their sense usually arises from the fact that they are basically common sense, dressed up in jargon. But to be told that one should, let us say, cultivate a 'growth mindset' (i.e seek to transcend one's perceived limitations, accept failure and move on from it, take criticism positively, etc.) does not actually tell one how to behave in an actual and unique (always unique) situation. Then the whole trick is to know how to apply the nostrums in practice, here and now, when actually faced with difficulty, and often with little time to think. By definition this transition from theory to action, from the words on the page to the life before one, cannot be in the book, at which point the difficulties begin and may be insoluble even to someone who has worked long and diligently at the theory, and has read everything that there is to read about resilience, well-being or behaviour management, for example. If the knowledge in the theories is useful at all to a teacher (and my feeling is that all too often even an apparently sensible theory is just a matter of words, words, words), its usefulness must manifest itself in practice. In the view of Chris and me, which has its roots in Aristotle and was embodied in our PGCE, the

best way of acquiring a practice, here the practice of teaching, is
to practice it, under the guidance of an experienced practitioner.

So, while, as will become clear, we did plan some residential
meetings in the university for our trainees, the bulk of their
training would consist in actually teaching under the guidance of
mentors in their schools, and of tutors sent from Buckingham.
A further advantage of firmly practical training in the school
where the trainee is teaching is that it can be adapted to the level
and age at which the trainee is teaching, and also to the style
of teaching in the school and fitted to the trainee's personality.
Not every successful teacher teaches in the same way; while
some very basic principles of teaching are universal, different
schools, different pupils, and different teachers will work well
in different ways, according to the circumstances of the school,
the nature of the subject, and the pupils involved, to say nothing
of what the individual teacher and their personality can bring
to the work. Nor in any case does anyone have a monopoly of
wisdom in what makes good teaching (or anything else come to
that), not even the Secretary of State for Education. If different
methods work in different schools for different pupils and at
different stages, who has any justification for insisting that all
work to the same pattern?

The third desideratum, moral probity and the ability to relate
in proper ways to children and young people, is not something
that can be described or assessed in abstract or ticked off against
a list of bullet points. But it is something that will make itself
apparent as the trainee works in a school and in classrooms over
the year of the PGCE. The trainee actually being a full member
of a school community, and not parachuted in from an academic
base for a few weeks on a school 'placement', was thus a crucial
aspect of our thinking in devising the Buckingham PGCE. The
trainee's mentor and other senior staff in the school would be
well placed to comment on the indefinable contribution a trainee

makes to the school community in the broadest sense, because the trainee is already part of that community and, unlike those on university organized placements, taking part in every aspect of the life of that community, such as dealing with other staff and parents and taking part in extracurricular activities.

With our background thinking of teacher training in mind, I can now describe the course programme as we set it up. The course's duration would be a full school year, from September of one year, when the autumn term begins, to June or July of the next year, the end of the summer term. Before the September starting point the school which wished to place a teacher on the course would apply to Buckingham on behalf of the trainee, and agree to the various course requirements, including providing a mentor (often the relevant head of department or other senior teacher), allowing for weekly meetings between mentor and trainee and agreeing to release the trainee for the Buckingham residentials. The school would also agree to pay the university the fee for the course (even if this was sometimes in part recouped from the teacher's salary). At Buckingham we would scrutinise the application and, among other things, assure ourselves that the trainee had a decent degree and relevant subject knowledge and that the school was of sufficient quality to carry out the training programme. It is worth noting two caveats here: while normally the trainee's degree would be in the subject(s) they are teaching, we were prepared to be flexible on the actual degree if we were satisfied that the trainee had the knowledge and competence for the subject being taught, even if it wasn't on the face of their degree; and while a weekly mentor-trainee meeting would be the norm, some of our trainees were already teachers with several years' experience, in which case some flexibility would be allowed on this.

Each term a tutor from Buckingham would visit the school, primarily to observe lessons and assess the trainee, but also, and importantly, to check that the trainee was being mentored properly, with regular observations of their own lessons, constructive meetings with the mentor, and the opportunity to observe other lessons to widen experience. The school mentor and the Buckingham tutor would write a report each term on the trainee against a set of eleven simple standards, the final one being a joint report by both, leading to a judgement on the trainee's quality, originally simply whether they met the standards or not. These standards – a few sentences each – covered such key classroom matters as expectations in teaching, subject knowledge, lesson planning and delivery, assessment, behaviour management, and pupil progress, and also one relating to the trainee's collegiality and overall contribution to the life of the school. During the year, the trainee would keep a folder in which evidence would be filed. This evidence would include such things as lesson observations, lesson plans, their own assessments of pupils, details of dealings with pupils and parents and of other activities in and for the school, and so on. This folder would be looked at regularly by both mentor and tutor.

There were, as already said, three residential meetings of three days each at Buckingham, one each term. At them there were lectures and discussions of the aims of education as mediated through important thinkers such as Plato, St Augustine, Locke, Rousseau, Dewey, Newman, Arnold, and their more modern followers and critics. There were sessions on the political and historical context of education, and on practical matters, such as the nature of the school, behaviour management, lesson planning and delivery, special needs, and English as a foreign language, as well as separate meetings on specific subjects. Speakers at these meetings, apart from Chris and me, included figures of the calibre of Eric Anderson, Martin Stephen, Nick Gibb, Peter Norris (head of music at the Menuhin School), John Venning (head of English at St Paul's), and John McIntosh (head of the

London Oratory School). Backing up the residential sessions, each term trainees would write an essay, of university standard and suitably academic, the first on the aims of education, the second on teaching their own subject, and the third a reflection on how the trainee had developed professionally over the year of training. To be awarded the PGCE – which most were – trainees had to fulfil the teaching standards and get at least a pass in each of these essays.

The Independent PGCE course was planned and ratified by the Buckingham senate in the first half of 2002, in what in retrospect was an amazingly smooth and stress-free process (At that time Buckingham was not hamstrung by the requirements of the misleadingly entitled Quality Assurance Agency, another instance of the blob being given massive power and influence by central government). We advertised the course in the early summer, and 13 trainees started the course in September 2002. Of these all but one were from senior schools, and four were from Stowe, Buckingham's local public school, with which the university has a good relationship. We had not originally thought to include teachers from primary and prep schools, but our thirteenth – a music teacher and baroque violinist from a prep in Norfolk – convinced us that we should do this.

At the start of the course we had a meeting for the school mentors at Buckingham, at which I, as the somewhat bashful Head of Department, tried to explain what was needed for trainees to do the course and meet the standards. As some of the mentors were senior teachers with far more knowledge of what went on in schools than I had, this could be awkward for me. Exactly how many lesson plans did trainees need to produce each term? Should every aspect of a lesson be reported on in a lesson observation? Did all lessons have to conform to the then fashionable famous or notorious tripartite structure, with an exciting starter of dubious relevance to main content? My personal feeling, strongly felt, if not explicitly expressed, was that you are professionals, you should know what to do on such matters, how much is required, how to balance the thing against the trainee's personal experience, ability, and need; I certainly tried to suggest that there were no fixed rules on any of this, and that within broad limits what should be done would depend on the circumstances. What is enough for one trainee might not be enough for another, some trainees might need more attention in certain areas than others, teachers who were already quite experienced should be treated differently from absolute beginners (and there were always a few of them to balance those in their first year), and so on. What might have seemed vagueness on my part (and sometimes actually was vagueness) didn't always go down well, but we all learned by experience in what was a new venture. After a while I got better at handling these meetings, or more confident anyway – and the mentors on the whole were supportive and sometimes gave helpful suggestions and advice, which led to finessing the programme. After all, the course was (and is) a partnership between the university and the participating schools.

Chris and I did some of the tutoring on behalf of the university, but other tutors were found for specific subjects we were not so confident in, such as art, music, maths, and the sciences. In the early days of the course John McIntosh was particularly helpful, not only tutoring maths himself, but also lending us two of his senior science teachers to work for us. For the second year of the PGCE we got a request from King's School in Madrid to take on a couple of trainees, and after some heart-searching and financial research, we agreed to take them on in the same way as home trainees. This aspect of the course has grown over the years, as has the Independent course itself. For some schools and some trainees its very independence (from government regulation and from Ofsted inspection), combined with necessary rigour and a university qualification, has been part of its attraction. In a way this is hardly surprising, as very few teachers in independent schools ever go on to teach in state schools, so for them there seems little point in having the government's qualified teacher status (QTS), which is valuable mainly or even entirely because it allows its holder to teach in maintained (state) schools. What is and was even more surprising is that many heads of independent schools do not see things in that way, which may make some wonder how they see their independence.

In 2003, in our second year of existence, and after the completion of our first course, we were invited to Dublin, where the HMC conference was taking place that year, to publicise the course. A group of 30 or 40 heads came to hear what I had to say, and the response to the programme and its rationale was very positive, except for one thing. Many of those there said that they would be keen to send teachers of theirs on the course, but they would not, because it did not give QTS. This was rather different from what we had heard from the earlier sub-committee, and caused Chris, Terence and me some soul-searching. However, we did not want to appear inflexible, so we eventually decided (by two votes to one) to seek QTS.

This is not the place to go into the details of the process, save to say that it took the best part of 18 months, and a great deal of time and effort on our part. Interestingly at the first meeting organized by the Training and Development Agency for schools (the TDA, the successor body to the TTA) for 'potential new providers', as we were called, there were around 50 institutions represented. I think that no more than half a dozen were in the end successful, and, if this is so, it is hardly surprising. The process was bureaucratic, prescriptive, and inflexible, seemingly (to me anyway) almost designed to put people off, if not by intention, then certainly in practice. It involved endless meetings both with TDA officials and with Ofsted inspectors. One lot was monitoring and the other supporting (or was it guiding?). I can't remember which was which, maybe because there seemed little difference between the two. Different people came to different meetings, and were not always in agreement with each other. Sometimes the people who turned up showed little awareness of what had been said earlier or even of the documents we had tabled. We made some progress over the months, but still did not satisfy the TDA, and a crunch meeting was called at their headquarters in mid-2004. What apparently was missing from our course, which focused on subject knowledge and the craft of the classroom, seen in largely practical terms, was something the TDA official called 'pedagogical knowledge'. To Chris's horror (he could be diplomatic at times) I insisted that, while I understood subject knowledge and the practice of pedagogy, I had not the faintest idea of what he meant by pedagogical knowledge as a discrete category of what was apparently a body of propositional knowledge, somehow distinct from the other two. His answer I found unhelpful – he had clearly not understood Aristotle on practical wisdom or Gilbert Ryle on knowing how, and TDA HQ was hardly the place to enlighten him. The situation was, I think, finally resolved only by Terence having a word with someone close to government. (Not all New Labour grandees were enamoured of the blob). Anyway, be that as it may, we were finally accredited to award QTS at Buckingham University, and our first QTS trainees were admitted in 2005.

So now we were running two somewhat separate PGCE courses, one with QTS and the other without. The QTS course differed from the Independent one in two important respects. The standards QTS trainees were being assessed against were the 33 government ones and not our simple 11, and the QTS also involved trainees having a placement in a second school, which had to be a maintained one. As regards the QTS standards, for the first mentor meeting I arranged a two day meeting in a decent local hotel, as I thought it would take us a long time to cover everything. In fact the meeting was very positive, and we had very little more to say by the end of the second morning. We broke up early to give our attention to a more important matter (the final Ashes test of 2005).

The second school placement I have come to think is actually a good aspect of the QTS programme. Initially I worried that it might be hard to find schools willing to let teachers from independent schools into their schools, but in practice this did not prove much of a problem. Enough schools on both sides of the divide seemed keen to cross the boundary, and without any financial reward. Many of the maintained school teachers involved were very helpful to our trainees, and some clearly liked having our trainees, keen and highly qualified as they often were, around their departments, especially if they themselves were working in minority subjects, such as classics. And even if the experience was tough, our trainees certainly benefited from it professionally and personally. (Perhaps this is the point at which I should stress that over the years I gained immense respect for most of our trainees. They were usually extremely well qualified, some with doctorates in their subject, and almost without exception hard-working, dedicated, conscientious, willing to learn, and highly idealistic).

A further complication brought about by the QTS course was the spectre of Ofsted lurking in the background, because courses awarding QTS were and are subject to Ofsted inspections. During my time running the department, until 2010, we had two inspections, the first in the second year of our existence. For this we were ranked 'satisfactory', that is we were judged to have met the governmental requirements, or more precisely, as it was pedantically put, we had not been found to have broken any (there is nothing like the bureaucratic caution so ingrained in the mentality of the blob). We would keep our accreditation, but 'satisfactory' is a bare minimum (and now is not even that, having been changed to 'requires improvement'). This 'satisfactory' grading annoyed Chris and me, because the reason we were not ranked good was because our trainees had apparently not shown enough progress during their PGCE year. We felt that this was unfair and, even if it were not, that Ofsted, despite their normal obsession with 'evidence', did not have the evidence they would have needed to make this judgement, as they had not seen the trainees at the start of the course. We appealed, and some small revisions were made to the report, though not the overall grading. Still, we were satisfactory and could go on. None of the schools who used us subsequently – and their numbers grew fast on the QTS course – seemed in the least bit worried about Ofsted's 'satisfactory'. The second inspection in which I was involved was in 2009, and we were ranked 'good'. We had a sympathetic lead inspector, who said that he knew that we were a different type of course from the norm, but that he was interested in what we were doing, and would judge us on what he saw, which I think he did.

Before concluding this survey of the early years of the Buckingham department of education, it should be stressed that a guiding principle of both PGCEs was that, the essays aside, the trainees would not be made to do much more than they would be doing as a matter of course in the early years of their career. The point of the course was to ensure and assess their competence in what they were called on to do, and not to produce otiose commentaries and reflections on what they were doing and massive files of dubious relevance and value (which in all probability no one would look at in more than a cursory way). In many cases they would have had mentors in place in their schools even if they had not been on the course, and almost always they would have been observed and guided by senior teachers. In a way what we were doing was to make more systematic what was already good practice in good schools, and certifying what was done. We wanted to avoid all unnecessary bureaucracy and the irrelevant collection of pointless 'evidence' with which many teachers in training (and their mentors) were and are burdened. We also wanted the course to mesh seamlessly with the work being done in the school where the trainee was being employed.

One further very important point should be made. For the Independent PGCE we could take anyone we wanted on the course, with no restrictions on numbers. Most QTS courses at the time were state funded, and the Department for Education would centrally allot to teacher training institutions the numbers of trainees they were allowed overall, and also the numbers they were allowed in specific subjects, according to some mysterious process of 'manpower' planning in the DfE. We, as a non-state-funded institution, were under no such restriction, and could take as many trainees as we liked, in whatever subjects. The schools in which the trainees worked paid the university, not the state. This independence would have been lost had we started taking state money for the training, so I always refused any money for that from central government. Freedom or death was (and is) my view, and I made sure that this freedom was not compromised when the government, through the TDA, and despite my protests, insisted on paying us a small fee for assessing our trainees for QTS.

So, by 2005 we had two PGCE courses running in parallel. They shared the residential meetings, and many of our tutors worked on both. Numbers on both grew slowly but steadily, more on the QTS course than on the Independent. The latter benefited from Chris's chairmanship of Cognita, a company which owned a number of schools. Groups of trainees came regularly from Cognita schools, and also from our international reach, which included countries as far away as China, Thailand, and Russia, as well as places closer to our European home.

In the summer of 2010 I took a term away from Buckingham – my first since 2002. It was as a research fellow at Bowling Green State University, in rural Ohio, where I wrote an article on education and began what eventually became a book on religion and philosophy (*Transcendence, Creation and Incarnation*, Routledge, 2020). The article ('Liberal Education: Where Could and Should It Be?') drew on my experiences and teaching at Buckingham and part of it was published under the title 'Education and the Modern State' in the journal *Social Philosophy and Policy*, 29.1, Winter 2012, pp 322-35, and it is in the current volume in a slightly updated form.

However, when I was in the States, I stepped down as head of the education department. I was replaced by Peter Ireland, who had recently established the M.A. in Educational Leadership in the department. Other new appointments were made, and new chapters in the department's development began. Over the subsequent decade new courses were added to the menu, and changes were made to the PGCEs, though without changing their basic structure. And the department, from its small and uncertain beginnings, became the largest provider of teacher training in the country.

Before concluding this account of the early history of the department, a footnote should be added, because it brings one aspect of the early history to a surprising and satisfactory conclusion. In 2011 Nick Gibb, who was now minister for schools (or was it Michael Gove, then the Secretary of State for Education?), asked John McIntosh and me to serve on a large committee to re-write the teacher standards. We also went on the much smaller drafting sub-committee, where, it is fair to say, we played a significant role. After several months of meetings and intensive work, we produced a short and succinct document – one and a half pages – containing 8 straightforward and well-focused standards, to replace the earlier 94 pages and 33 standards. Surprisingly enough the 8 new government standards, which emerged after months of sometimes fractious controversy, argument, and drafting can easily be seen as a slight re-packaging of the 11 Buckingham standards Chris and I had drafted one afternoon in a couple of hours after lunch back in 2002. John and I also insisted in the preamble to the new standards that the 8 standards were not to be subdivided into sub-standards and judged in an atomistic, bullet-point way (Needless to say, despite our heart-felt caveat, this is precisely how many trainers and government agencies themselves are now treating our 8 simple standards; but this is not the place for further comment on the cast of mind which is unable to operate in any other way).

For those interested in the history of this, more important perhaps than what is in the new QTS standards is what is not in them. Thus, for example, there is no mention of 'independent learning', which in educational circles is often code for child-centred learning, nor is there anything about teachers facilitating or talk of pupils 'constructing their own knowledge' (a dreadful and philosophically illiterate solecism). In our standards, teachers teach, pupils learn, and subject knowledge is seen as central.

One further point about the new standards is also worth mentioning. We were required to include a statement about 'fundamental British values' in a section on the general responsibilities of teachers. What was handed down to us from the then current 'Prevent' agenda said that we were supposed to have mutual respect and tolerance of different faiths and beliefs. I jibbed at this: there were beliefs and faiths that should not be tolerated, let alone respected, so I inserted the words 'those of' between 'different' and 'faiths', a small but I thought significant difference, which is now in the standards, but has not generally been noticed or recognized. It should be, and so should my redrafting of the DfE regulations for teacher training, which I did at the behest of Nick Gibb in 2012. Anyone who wants to know what these actually mean is free to consult me at any time!

To end this coda on the new standards, because they were pretty much a re-drafting of the original Buckingham standards, the governmental 8 are now what is required in the Independent PGCE. QTS and Independence are here, at least, aligned, with slight movement from the one side and a considerable shift from the other.

Acknowledgements

Some material in this book has been published in earlier versions as detailed below. It is reproduced here with permission from the publishers and copyright holders concerned, to whom we express our thanks.

Ch 1. Partly published as 'Education and the Modern State', Social Philosophy and Policy, Vol 29, no 1, Winter 2012, pp 322-335; published by Cambridge University Press.

Ch 2. Published as 'Classics and Not Hog-Wash', in Western Civilization and the Academy, edited by Bradley C.S. Watson, Lanham MD: Lexington Books, 2015, pp 97-110.

Ch 3. Published as ''Philosophy and Educational Policy' in Philosophy and Public Affairs, edited by John Haldane, Royal Institute of Philosophy Supplement 45, 2000, pp 135-56.

Ch 4. Partly published as 'Morality, Reason and Upbringing', Ratio, Vol 33.2, June 2020, copyright John Wiley and Sons Ltd., pp 106-16.

Ch 5. Published on line as 'Family and State in Education: 'What Role for Parents' Rights?' by Civitas, November 2022.

Ch 7. Published in Standpoint, Aug/Sept 2020, pp 29-31.

Ch 9. Published in Buckingham Journal of Education, Vol 3, 2022, pp 93-104

Index

Aeschylus 85, 234
Agassi, André 254
Alighieri, Dante 8, 62, 83, 162, 193, 194, 221, 222
Althusser, Louis 116, 213
American Association for the Advancement of Science 68
Anakreon 63
Anderson, Eric 267
Antigone 41, 52, 92
Aquinas, Thomas 13, 42, 57, 154, 167
Aristotle 13, 22, 24, 25, 26, 38, 41, 51, 52, 79, 80, 107, 122, 126, 127, 131, 132, 133, 134, 135, 139, 140, 142, 144, 145, 146, 147, 157, 158, 159, 160, 161, 162, 215, 249, 252, 253, 264, 271
Arnold, Matthew 9, 23, 28, 31, 33, 37, 56, 83, 84, 85, 92, 267
Art of Memoir, The 254
Arts Council 75, 76
Association of Christian Classical Schools 57, 58, 61
Augustine, St 13, 127, 267

Bach, Johann Sebastian 227
Bacon, Francis 25, 26, 27
Badiou, Alain 213
Barth, Karl 186
Baudrillard, Jean 243
BBC 84, 125, 181
Beatles, the 84
Beethoven, Ludwig van 84, 225
Bentham, Jeremy 27, 75, 82
Beuys, Joseph 230
Bloom, Allan 12
Bloom, Benjamin 12, 186, 191, 192, 193, 194, 197, 200, 201
Borgia, Cesare 141
Bouguereau, William-Adolphe 225
Bradley, F.H. 83
Brookings Institution 171
Brubacher, John 118
Buonarroti, Michelangelo 232
Burke, Edmund 3, 7, 163
Burt, Cyril 118
Bush, George W. 239, 244

Callicles 137
Camões, Luis de 8
Cantor, Georg 218, 234
Cantos 67
Cartwright, Nancy 203
Castro, Fidel 58

CATE 261
Catullus 63
Charlemagne 74
Charterhouse 26
Chaucer, Geoffrey 8
Chesterton, G.K. 136
Chomsky, Noam 187
Chopin, Frédéric 225
Christodoulou, Daisy 12
Churchill, Winston 88
Cicero 26, 38, 139
Cimabue 57
Clare, John 14
Clarke, Kenneth 14, 261
Clark, Kenneth 76
Clark, Richard E. 237
Clinton, Bill 171
Clive of India 87
Cognita 274
Colet, John 42, 43, 44
Confessions 115
Contingency, Irony and Solidarity 244
Core Knowledge 67, 68, 86, 90, 117
Craig-Martin, Michael 230, 231
Crick, Francis 234
Curry, Oliver Scott 128

Daily Telegraph, The 14
Darwin, Charles 3, 27, 234, 253
Da Vinci, Leonardo 232
Declaration of Independence 164
Democracy and Education 104, 112
Democracy in America 167
Department for Education 29, 31, 54, 260, 274, 277
Derrida, Jacques 213, 243
Dewey, John, 11, 13, 27, 28, 29, 31, 33, 39, 95, 98, 103, 104, 105, 106, 107, 108, 109, 110, 111, 112, 113, 115, 116, 117, 118, 119, 168, 224, 227, 233, 234, 235, 236, 267
Diamond, Cora 123
Dickens, Charles 221
Divine Comedy 57, 83, 234
Dolezal, Rachel 255
Duchamp, Marcel 232
Duke of Sussex, Prince Harry 254, 255
Dulwich College 75, 76

Educational Psychologist 237
Education, Society and Human Nature 14
Edward IV 193
Eliot, T.S. 5, 6, 8, 12, 24, 38, 106, 227, 228
Emerson, Ralph Waldo 184, 185

Émile 23, 55, 98, 99, 100, 116, 227
Eminent Victorians 127
Emin, Tracey 75
English National Curriculum 34, 36
Erasmus 42
Euclid 234
Euthyphro 125, 126
Evans, Richard 87, 88
Ewan, Ruth 125, 133
Experience and Education 103

Federalist Papers, The 166
Field, John 225
Fodor, Jerry 187, 188
Foucault, Michel 116, 213, 243
Fröbel, Friedrich 101, 102
Fuller, Peter 227

Gabo, Naum 227
Galilei, Galileo 26
Galston, William 171, 172, 173
Genealogy of Morals, The 242
Genet, Jean 135
Gibb, Nick 267, 275, 277
Gilbert and George 75
Giotto 57
Gödel, Kurt 234
Goethe, Johann Wolfgang von 8, 83
Gordon, Charles George 127
Gorgias 137
Gove, Michael 86, 88, 275
Guardian, The 96

Hare, R.M. 123, 129, 130, 141
Hattie, John 180, 196, 197, 198, 199, 200, 201, 202, 203, 204, 207
Hay Literary Festival 87
Heidegger, Martin 245
Hilbert, David 234
Hill, Geoffrey 185
Hirsch, E.D. 67, 68, 70, 72, 86, 90
Hirsi Ali, Ayaan 208
Hirst, Damien 230
History of the Problems of Education, A 118
Hitchens, Christopher 127
Hitler, Adolf 141
HMC 262, 270
Hockney, David 232
Hoggart, Richard 84
Holt, John 19, 20, 22, 55
Homer 7, 8, 9, 62, 83, 85, 140, 193, 221, 222
*Home Schooling: Political, Historical and Pedagogical Perspective*s 54
Horace 62
How Children Fail 19
HSDA 59

Hume, David 7, 8, 61, 128, 139, 140, 143, 221, 222
Hume, Gary 230
Hummel, Johann Nepomuk 225

Idea of a University, The 38, 82
IES 55
Iliad, The 8, 85, 139, 142
Independent Association of Preparatory Schools 46
Independent, The 89
Infidel: My Life 208
In the Name of Identity: Violence and the Need to Belong 208
Ireland, Peter 275
'Is it Good to Co-operate? Testing the Theory of Morality as Cooperation in 60 Societies' 128

Johnson, Samuel 88
Joyce, James 8

Kalms, Stanley 262
Kant, Immanuel 82, 128
Kealey, Terence 260, 262, 271
Kepler, Johannes 26
Kerr, Mary 254
Keswick, Tessa 261
Keynes, John Maynard 76
Kierkegaard, Søren 106
Kilpatrick, W.H. 113
King Edward VI School 97
King, Martin Luther 212
King's School, Madrid 269
Kirschner, Paul A. 237, 238
Kirstein, Lincoln 227, 228
Kohlberg, Lawrence 102, 103, 122

Lammas School 125
Lamarck, Jean-Baptiste 3
Lavoisier, Antoine 234
Lawrence, D.H. 77, 78
Leavis, F.R. 12, 61
Leibniz, Gottfried Wilhelm 187
Leighton, Frederic 225
Lenin, Vladimir 256, 257
Lewis, C.S. 12, 38
Locke, John 13, 26, 27, 267
Logos School 58
London Oratory 44, 268
Lost Tools of Learning, The 56, 57
Lucan 62
Lucas, Geoff 262
Lucas, Sarah 230
Lycurgus 155
Lyotard, Jean-François 243

Maalouf, Amin 208, 212
Macbeth 11
Madison, James 166, 171
Makart, Hans 225
Manet, Édouard 225
Marx, Karl 21, 214
Maslow, Abraham 111, 112, 115
Mason, Charlotte 219
Matisse, Henri 227
McDowell, John 188
McIntosh, John 267, 269, 275, 276
Meistersinger von Nürnberg, Die 5
Melian Dialogue 41
Mendel, Gregor 234
Microsoft 58
Mill, J.S. 13, 27, 33, 34, 35, 47, 74, 75, 82, 92, 164, 165, 166, 167, 170, 171, 172, 175
Milton, John 8, 83, 194, 221, 222
Mochringer, J.R. 254
Monet, Claude 225
Montaigne, Michel de 140
Montessori, Maria 102, 103
Moore, G.E. 249, 253
Moral Thinking 141
More, Thomas 42
Morozov, Pavel 174, 176
Mother Teresa 127
Mullins, Daniel Austin 128
Murdoch, Iris 12, 129, 131
Murray, Charles 12
Musgrove, Frank 45

NAACP 255
Nagel, Thomas 129, 130
National Curriculum Council 261
National Research Council 68
National Science Teachers' Association 68
Neill, A.S. 19, 22
Newman, Cardinal 23, 26, 33, 38, 56, 60, 61, 62, 82, 92, 267
New St Andrew's College 58
Newton, Isaac 5, 24, 78, 216, 226, 234, 237, 240
Nicomachean Ethics 133, 146, 157, 158, 159
Nietzsche, Friedrich 127, 136, 140, 141, 224, 242, 243, 245
Nightingale, Florence 127, 131
Norris, Peter 267
Nozick, Robert 141

Oakeshott, Michael 12, 25, 123, 145
Obama, Barack 67
Odyssey, The 8, 24
OECD 90
Ofsted 97, 197, 208, 210, 211, 236, 261, 269, 271, 272, 273

On Liberty 33, 47, 74, 164, 165
Open 254
Open Society and its Enemies, The 201, 207, 211
Oresteia, The 85, 234
Orwell, George 88, 139, 156
Ovid 8, 62

Paradise Lost 194
Parvus, Johannes 5, 24
Pascal, Blaise 106
Pasmore, Victor 227, 228, 229, 230, 231
Patrick Henry College 58, 59, 62
Peirce, C.S. 258
Pericles 133
Pestalozzi, Johann Heinrich 101, 102
Petrarch, Francis 138, 139
Philosophiae Naturalis Principia Mathematica 5
Piaget, Jean 102, 103
Picasso, Pablo 227
Pilkington, Edward 96, 97
Pitman, Mary Anne 54
Plato 7, 13, 20, 22, 37, 38, 39, 51, 52, 63, 125, 126, 136, 139, 144, 146, 155, 156, 157, 159, 161, 164, 166, 177, 192, 201, 241, 267
Plutarch 155
Politics 51, 158, 159
Pollock, Jackson 227
Popper, Karl 108, 201, 202, 207, 208, 211, 212, 217, 246, 258
Pound, Ezra 8, 67, 73
Propertius 63
Proust, Marcel 20, 83, 184, 185
Purgatorio 162
Pushkin, Alexander 83
Putnam, Hilary 141

Qualifications and Curriculum Development Authority 72
Quality Assurance Agency 268

Racine, Jean 83
Rainbow, The 77
Rand, Ayn 41, 140
Recovering the Lost Tools of Learning 58
Rembrandt 36, 84
Renoir, Pierre-Auguste 225
Republic, The 52, 136, 139, 155, 157, 241
Rerum Novarum 154
Roehampton Institute 96, 97
Rogers, Carl 111, 112, 113, 115
Rorty, Richard 129, 130, 243, 244
Rose, Jonathan 84
Rousseau, Jean-Jacques 11, 13, 21, 23, 25, 55, 89, 95, 98, 99, 100, 101, 103, 106, 108, 110,

111, 113, 114, 115, 116, 117, 118, 227, 228, 267
Royal Academy of Arts Magazine, The 230
Royal Statistical Society 131
Rush, Benjamin 32, 164, 166
Ruskin, John 38, 39, 77, 92, 139, 185, 186, 193, 194, 231
Ryle, Gilbert 123, 182, 271

Sartre, Jean-Paul 245
Sayers, Dorothy L. 38, 56, 57, 62
SCAA 261, 262
School and Society, The 103, 119
School and the Social Order 45
Scottish Executive 71, 80, 82, 97, 176
Scotus, Duns 57
Scruton, Roger 162, 243
Seven Myths About Education 12
Shakespeare, William 8, 11, 83, 84, 194, 221, 234
Shelley, Percy Bysshe 78, 227
Singer, Peter 132
Skinner, B.F. 187, 189
Smith, M. Lynne 54
Soares, Mario 207, 211
Social Affairs Unit 261
Social Philosophy and Policy 275
Socrates 27, 51, 75, 82, 125, 126, 135, 136, 137, 139, 166
Some Thoughts on Education 26
Sophocles 41, 52
Spare 254
Stephen, Martin 42, 43, 267
St Louis 74
St Paul's School 42, 43, 44, 267
Strachey, Lytton 127, 131
Strauss, Leo 12
Summerhill 19, 173
Sunday Times, The 262
Suskind, Ron 239
Sweller, John 237

Tawney, R.H. 38
Teach Your Own: A Hopeful Path For Education 55
Tempest, The 124
Tennyson, Alfred 8
'The Future of England' 77
The Home School Legal Defense Association 55
The School of Freedom 42
Thrasymachus 135, 136, 137, 139, 241, 243, 244, 245

Thucydides 41, 241, 242, 244, 247
Times, The 89
Tocqueville, Alexis de 74, 167
Tooley, James 48
'Tradition and the Individual Talent' 6
Training and Development Agency 270, 271, 274
Transcendence, Creation and Incarnation 275
Troilus and Cressida 11
Truffaut, François 21
Turner, J.M.W 227

UNESCO 72
United Nations 152, 153
University of Bradford 260
University of Buckingham 13, 260, 262, 263, 265, 266, 267, 268, 271, 273, 275, 276, 277
University of Cambridge 75, 76, 87, 89
University of Jos 14
University of London 89
University of Oxford 89, 128, 185
Utilitarianism 27

'Value Pluralism and Political Liberalism' 171
van Galen, Jane 54
Venning, John 267
Virgil 8, 62, 83, 221, 222, 234
Visible Learning and the Science of How We Learn 199
Visible Learning: a Synthesis of Over 800 Meta-Analyses Relating to Achievement 197, 200
Vygotsky, Lev 180, 182, 183, 184, 185, 187, 188, 238, 241

Wagner, Richard 5
Warhol, Andy 230, 232
Watson, James D. 234
Wedgwood, Josiah 132
Weil, Simone 39, 91, 139, 140, 141, 142, 144
Welch, Graham 96, 97
Wellington, J. 183
Welsh Assembly 72, 74, 79
Weston, Guy 262
Wheaton College 59
Whitehouse, Harvey 128
Wilson, Douglas 58
Wittgenstein, Ludwig 140, 183, 189, 203
Woodhead, Chris 260, 261, 262, 264, 267, 269, 270, 271, 273, 274, 276

Yeats, W.B. 8